Temperature Rising

Temperature Rising

Iran's Revolutionary Guards and Wars in the Middle East

Nader Uskowi

ROWMAN & LITTLEFIELD
Lanham • Boulder • New York • London

Published by Rowman & Littlefield
An imprint of The Rowman & Littlefield Publishing Group, Inc.
4501 Forbes Boulevard, Suite 200, Lanham, Maryland 20706
www.rowman.com

Unit A, Whitacre Mews, 26-34 Stannary Street, London SE11 4AB

British Library Cataloguing in Publication Information Available

Library of Congress Cataloging-in-Publication Data

Name: Uskowi, Nader, 1948–, author.
Title: Temperature rising : Iran's revolutionary guards and wars in the Middle East / Nader Uskowi.
Description: Lanham, Maryland : Rowman & Littlefield, 2019. | Includes bibliographical references and index.
Identifiers: LCCN 2018031357 (print) | LCCN 2018032265 (ebook) | ISBN 9781538121740 (electronic) | ISBN 9781538121726 | ISBN 9781538121726 (cloth : alk. paper) | ISBN 9781538121733 (pbk. : alk. paper)
Subjects: LCSH: Sipāh-i Pāsdārān-i Inqilāb-i Islāmī (Iran) | Islamic fundamentalism—Iran. | State-sponsored terrorism—Iran. | Terrorists—Training of—Iran. | Paramilitary forces—Iran. | Military training camps—Iran. | Shī'ah—Iran. | Islam and politics—Iran.
Classification: LCC UA853.I7 (ebook) | LCC UA853.I7 U84 2019 (print) | DDC 355.3/1—dc23
LC record available at https://lccn.loc.gov/2018031357

∞ ™ The paper used in this publication meets the minimum requirements of American National Standard for Information Sciences Permanence of Paper for Printed Library Materials, ANSI/NISO Z39.48-1992.

Printed in the United States of America

In memory of my father, Major General Nasser Uskowi
(Iranian Imperial Army)

*A soldier and a military historian who taught me that
military strategy is key to national statecraft*

To my wife, Parvaneh, and our son, Omid

Whose unending love, support, and inspiration kept me going

Contents

List of Figures ix

Acknowledgments xi

Introduction: The Revolution Is Not About Iran— It's About the Whole Region xiii

1 Iran at War: The Push for Primacy in the Middle East 1

2 The Shia Liberation Army 17

3 The Years of Revolution and War 33

4 Gateways to Afghanistan and Iraq 49

5 Uprisings, Civil Wars, and Insurgencies 63

6 Land Corridor to Syria 77

7 The Iraqi Campaign 97

8 Sanaa Calling 115

9 Unfinished Business in Afghanistan 129

10 Resourcing the Quds Force Regional Campaigns: Military and Financial Support Network 139

11 Long Road, Uncertain Future 161

Conclusion 177

Notes 183

Selected Bibliography 195

Index 199

Contents

About the Author   207

List of Figures

On the western front, the Quds Force has built a land corridor 2
linking Iran through Iraq to Syria and Lebanon and building
permanent bases not far from the Israeli northern front lines. On the
southern front, the Quds Force is pressuring Saudi Arabia and the
United Arab Emirates through its Zaydi-Shia Houthi proxies in
Yemen. To the east, the Quds Force wages covert operations to
empower the Taliban in their fight against the U.S. and its allies.
Iran is a country at war. *Courtesy of the University of Texas
Libraries, University of Texas at Austin.*

The Quds Force successfully led the war against the Sunni 78
opposition to the Assad regime. Now it has changed its strategy and
is directing its forces to counter the Israelis at their northern fronts,
raising the specter of direct military conflict with Israel. A new
Great Game has engulfed Syria: Russians and Iranians in the
western region, from Aleppo to Damascus and points south, to
secure the Alawi Shia–dominated region of Syria; the Turks
countering the Kurdish influence in the north; Israel and Jordan
preventing cross-border attacks by the Iranian and Shia militia
forces; and the Americans and their Kurdish allies in the Sunni
heartland in the east, from Raqqa to the Iraqi border, countering
Iranian-led forces. *Courtesy of the University of Texas Libraries,
University of Texas at Austin.*

Iran and Iraq share a long border: 906 miles. After the 2003 U.S. 98
invasion of Iraq and the collapse of Saddam's regime, the Quds
Force and Iraqi militant groups in exile in Iran crossed the border
into a chaotic Iraq and have since then established their influence

over the Iraqi state. Today a land corridor connects Iran through
Iraq to Syria and Lebanon and the Israeli northern fronts. The light-
shaded areas are Iraqi Kurdistan in the north and the Sunni-
dominated region in the east. The dark-shaded area in the south
toward Baghdad is the country's Shia-stan. If Iraq fractures, those
areas would likely become three autonomous or independent rump
states. *Courtesy of the University of Texas Libraries, University of
Texas at Austin.*

Four Yemeni cities tell the story of the conflict. Saada (or Sa'a) is in   116
northwest Yemen. The town and its surrounding region, bordering
Saudi Arabia, are the ancestral home and the power base of the
Zaydi-Shia Houthis. Sanaa is Yemen's capital. In 2014, the Houthis
stormed the city and captured it, kick-starting the current Yemeni
conflict. The Saudi-Emirati coalition then intervened militarily to
push the Houthis back to Saada. Hudaydah is Yemen's major Red
Sea port. A Saudi-Emirati–led coalition was recapturing the town
from the Houthis in 2018 and cut the strategic Sanaa-Hudaydah line
of communication. Finally, Aden is a port city on the Gulf of Aden.
The south Yemenis, backed by the coalition, recaptured the town
from the Houthis and are positioned to declare independence,
reestablishing the state of South Yemen with Aden as its capital.
*Courtesy of the University of Texas Libraries, University of Texas at
Austin.*

The Quds Force conducts covert operations along the long Iran-   130
Afghanistan border, from Herat to Farah to Zaranj, to maintain its
arc of influence in western Afghanistan. It can deploy thousands of
Afghan Shia militias, mainly from the Hazarajat region in the north,
all fighting under its command, in Syria and into western
Afghanistan. The Quds Force is aiding the Taliban in their fight
against the Americans in the south and the east to raise the cost of
the presence of U.S. forces in Afghanistan. *Courtesy of the
University of Texas Libraries, University of Texas at Austin.*

Acknowledgments

This book is a collective effort by those who directly assisted me and those whose work, past and current, has informed and guided me throughout the process of researching and writing it. I am indebted to so many people, but for brevity's sake I can thank only a few.

For four years I worked as senior policy adviser to the United States Central Command, the branch of our military whose area of responsibility includes the Middle East. The opportunity was priceless for understanding the military landscape in the region.

The Washington Institute for Near East Policy generously supported me with a fellowship to write this book. For the fifteen months that it took to complete the research and the writing, the institute was my home, for which I am forever grateful. The institute's director, Rob Satloff, and research director, Patrick Clawson, did not hesitate to help me in any way they could.

I am in great debt to many research assistants at the institute. Erika Naegeli played a key role, conducting research, becoming my in-house copy editor, and helping me define the scope of the book. I began the project with the assistance of Emily Burlinghaus and later Varun Chandokhar. During the last phase of the project, Hannah Kazis-Taylor, a rising senior at Yale, interned for me diligently.

The institute's senior fellows were always a source of inspiration and intellectual stimulation. I am in debt to them all, particularly to Hanin Ghaddar for her invaluable help on Hezbollah; to Bilal Wahab for his great assistance in navigating the complex Kurdish political landscape; and to my other esteemed colleagues—Dennis Ross, David Makovsky, Patrick Clawson, Matt Levitt, Mike Eisenstadt, and Mehdi Khalaji—for their informed comments on various topics covered in the book. And to Soner Cagaptay, who guided and inspired me the most, I am in so much debt.

Ilan Berman of the American Foreign Policy Council was a constant source of support. The American Foreign Policy Council became a home away from home. Jay Solomon, with whom I share a passion for change in Iran, was a great friend and advocate. I knew him as a great journalist during my Pentagon days, and we worked together at the Washington Institute as visiting fellows.

I am grateful to Jon Sisk at Rowman & Littlefield, my publisher, for believing in my work, and to Kate Powers, an editor at Rowman & Littlefield, who guided me through the publishing process.

I dedicate this book first to the memory of my father, Nasser Uskowi, a major general in the Iranian Imperial Army, who was and remains my hero. He was truly a soldier and a scholar, who wrote many books and taught me to appreciate military strategy as a vital component of foreign policy.

My son, Omid, was my counselor. His advice and guidance and his unending love sustained me throughout the process. My wife and love of my life, Parvaneh (Patti), endured me and kept encouraging me during the long months of research and writing, and without her support and encouragement this project could not have been finished. This book is dedicated to them as well.

Introduction

*The Revolution Is Not About Iran —
It's About the Whole Region*

I was in Paris in November 1978 when I received a message that Ayatollah Khomeini would like to see me. I drove to Neauphle-le-Château, a suburb west of Paris where the ayatollah had taken up residence. The reception chamber was covered with carpets and lined with leaning cushions. The future supreme leader of the Islamic Republic was sitting cross-legged on the carpet and leaning on a large cushion, wearing the black turban denoting descendants of the Prophet and a brown cloak. I sat down, cross-legged, directly in front of him. After exchanging greetings, he wasted no time asking me what my future plans were. I told him I intended to go back to Iran. He stared at me from under his heavy dark eyebrows and said, "No, you shouldn't go back to Iran." I stared back in disbelief. "The revolution is not about Iran, it's about the whole region," he said. "We have many revolutionaries in Iran, but we need people like you to drive the revolution abroad."

At the time, I didn't pay much attention to the ayatollah's advice, and I boarded a plane to Tehran the following month. When I shared the story with my colleagues at the Confederation of Iranian Students, the response was almost uniform. The ayatollah did not want secular opposition to the shah to be a force inside the country, challenging the Islamist movement. But as the years passed, I became convinced that Khomeini was expressing his true beliefs on that day. In his eyes, the revolution was not just about Iran. The whole region was on his mind.

Equally surprising were the views among Khomeini's senior advisers. They were planning to establish a "people's army" inside Iran to stage a protracted armed struggle against the shah. Led by Ebrahim Yazdi, later foreign minister of the Islamic Republic, they did not believe that the shah's government could be toppled peacefully and were sending their cadres to training camps in Lebanon run by Mustafa Chamran, the future defense minister, to learn the ways of armed uprising.

Unknown to the ayatollah's men that day in Neauphle-le-Château, the Iranian monarchy was actually collapsing in on itself. Within two months, the shah would leave Iran to seek treatment for lymphatic cancer, and Khomeini would return in triumph after fourteen years in exile. But the idea of establishing a popular army lived on. Days after the victory of the Islamic Revolution, Khomeini ordered the establishment of the Islamic Revolutionary Guard Corps (IRGC), the people's army.

In an interview, Mohsen Sazegara, a member of the original IRGC Command Council, confirmed to me that the IRGC was what they had envisioned as the people's army. But instead of leading an armed uprising against the shah, the IRGC was tasked with defending the revolution. Sazegara recalled how Khomeini and his circle of senior advisers expected and feared an imminent U.S.–led military coup by the remnants of the shah's army against the new regime.[1]

As the IRGC became the guardian of the Islamic Revolution, its political directorate began organizing an extraterritorial branch, the predecessor of today's Quds Force. Its mission was to guide revolution in the region, as Khomeini had wanted all along.

THE SHIA LIBERATION ARMY

There are nearly 200,000 Shia youths mobilized, trained, and armed by the Quds Force across the Middle East. Hezbollah, Iraqi militia groups, Afghan militants, and the Yemeni Houthis form the nucleus of the Quds Force–led militia forces. As insurrections and civil wars engulfed the Middle East in the wake of the Arab Spring, the Quds Force and its highly trained Shia militias were positioned to take full advantage of the breakdown of political order. This book will examine how that force was organized and how it has evolved during the four decades of the Islamic Republic. Today the Shia militias form a united front—the so-called Shia Liberation Army (SLA)—to safeguard Shia interests and impose their own brand of militant Islamist ideology on the region.

THREE FRONTS

I was in my office at the Pentagon in summer 2014 when the news came that the Islamic State (ISIS or Daesh) had overrun Jalula, an Iraqi city only nineteen miles from the Iranian border. At the time, I was serving as senior policy adviser to the United States Central Command (CENTCOM), the branch of the U.S. military whose area of responsibility includes the Middle East. Daesh could soon advance toward Khanaqin, a city on the border with Iran. The Iranian regular army, Artesh, had deployed an armored division near the border, and after Jalula was overtaken, it sent an armor column over the border into Iraq to stop Daesh's advance. The Quds Force also redeployed the Iraqi Shia militias under its command from the battlefields in Syria back to Iraq to defend Baghdad and the Shia-majority south. Iran was now at war with Daesh.

Three years earlier, Iran had begun its military involvement in the Syrian conflict. By the time Daesh started its advance across Iraq, the Quds Force and its SLA were fighting the Syrian opposition at several battlefields inside the country. Now they had to fight in Iraq against Daesh. Before long, their partners in Yemen captured Sanaa, and the Quds Force opened a third front to support the Houthis and their gains in Yemen. Iran was now at war on three fronts, and the Quds Force and its SLA were put to the test. The book will explore how the Quds Force and its Shia militias answered the challenge.

THE LONG WAR

For the past four decades, Afghanistan has been the setting of war and revolution. The IRGC and the Quds Force have been an integral part of that violent landscape, from fighting the Soviets and the socialist government in the early days of the Islamic Republic to fighting alongside the Americans to oust the Taliban government, and now working with the Taliban to bleed the Americans out of Afghanistan. All along, the Iranians have used Afghan Shia militants to fight their fights, from the Iran-Iraq War to the Syrian conflict. This has added to the shared history of the two nations, enabling the Quds Force to establish a strong influence in the country, especially in western Afghanistan. During my travels to the region, from Herat to Farah to Nimruz, I could witness the extent of Iran's influence. In the chapter on Afghanistan, we will look at the Quds Force's mainly covert operations in the country and examine the challenges it faces.

A COMPLEX POLITICAL SYSTEM

Throughout the last four decades, the Islamic Republic has grown into a complex political system with two parallel headquarters. The government, headquartered in the presidential palace, is in charge of running the day-to-day affairs of the country, overseeing a huge bureaucracy. The Office of the Supreme Leader, also headquartered in Tehran, controls all revolutionary organs, including the IRGC and its nuclear and ballistic missile programs, and the Quds Force as the command center of the Shia militancy in the region. The system resembles that of the former Soviet Union, with its government running the day-to-day affairs of the country and a second head office in Moscow, that of the Communist International Movement led by the Communist Party. The two systems feed off each other but can also compete with each other, especially regarding resource allocation. The book will describe the history and the current operations of the Quds Force within the context of this dual system of the Islamic Republic.

FINANCING THE REVOLUTION

The Quds Force's projects in the region are to a large extent funded by a business empire run by the IRGC and the Office of the Supreme Leader. They control a dozen megafoundations, which in turn control more than five hundred business enterprises, together accounting for nearly half of the Iranian economy. Understanding this network is key to understanding how the Quds Force funds its current operations through the regional branches of those foundations and will maintain a continued presence in the region for years and decades to come.

MILITARY SUPPORT NETWORK

The Quds Force is a military command that draws its ground forces from SLA units. It also draws specialized units, like armor, artillery, rockets and ballistic missiles, unmanned aerial vehicles (UAVs), and special forces, from the wider IRGC and occasionally from Iran's regular military, Artesh. These units are deployed to specific battlefields on temporary duty under the operational command of the Quds Force. The Quds Force organization also provides intelligence, logistics, and training support. The model provides it with the flexibility of combining irregular forces, the proxies, with regular forces, from the IRGC or Artesh, to wage hybrid warfare against opposing forces. This book looks at these Quds Force–led forces as a hybrid expeditionary force with all the potential and challenges that such a model brings to the table.

The book will also examine the ways in which the Quds Force provides advanced arms and associated training to its major Shia militia partners, focusing on ballistic and cruise missiles supplied to Hezbollah and the Houthis. As much as such advanced weapons strengthen the militias' capabilities, they also create serious issues for the Quds Force and the Islamic Republic. The rockets and missiles used by Hezbollah against the Israelis, the ballistic missiles fired by the Houthis against targets in the Saudi capital, and the cruise missiles hitting Saudi and Emirati vessels off the coast of Yemen each could incite a direct military conflict between Iran and various foreign militaries that could spiral into a major regional conflict.

THE WAY AHEAD

The founders of the Islamic Republic intended to create a revolutionary movement that would encompass not only Iran but the entire region. Four decades after the revolution, the Quds Force has come to embody that doctrine. By establishing a land corridor connecting Tehran to Lebanon and the Israeli northern front, through Iraq and Syria, the Quds Force is succeeding in creating a Shia arc of influence across the Middle East. This book will consider how the Quds Force could maintain and expand its operations and influence in the region. In thinking about the way ahead for the Quds Force, we will see how Ayatollah Khomeini's revolutionary project is fraught with danger as it could drag Iran into a major military conflict with regional and global powers.

Chapter One

Iran at War

The Push for Primacy in the Middle East

Iran is a country at war: in Syria, Iraq, and Yemen, and with covert operations in Afghanistan. On Iran's western front, Iranian-led forces maintain a land corridor connecting Iran, through Iraq, to Syria, Lebanon, and the Israeli northern front on the Golan Heights. On the southern front, Iranian-backed insurgents operate on Saudi Arabia's borders and have the ability to interfere with the free flow of commerce at Bab el-Mandeb, one of the most precarious chokepoints in the world. On the eastern front, Iran has for four decades been involved in operations in war-torn Afghanistan. Through multifaceted military engagements, Iran is carving out a role for itself as a dominant regional power.

The founding supreme leader of the Islamic Republic, Ayatollah Ruhollah Khomeini, believed that the Islamic Revolution involved not only Iran but the whole region. He envisioned a revived Islamic state governed according to his militant interpretation of Shia Islam that would transport the revolution across the region. One of the first institutions he set up after the victory of the revolution was the IRGC, whose members were to serve as the guardians of Shia Islam. Four decades later, an IRGC official continues to describe the organization's mission in identical terms.

> The Islamic Revolution does not have any borders. . . . The Islamic Revolution Guard Corps does not have the word "Iran" in its title. This means that it seeks to defend the Islamic revolution and its achievements without regard to particular borders.[1]

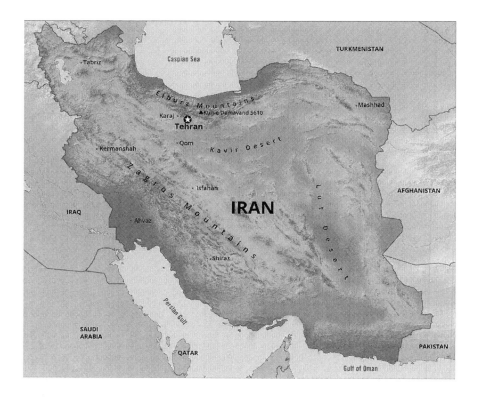

The Quds Force is involved in conflicts on three fronts.

A complex political system of parallel institutions similar to that of the former Soviet Union emerged in post-revolution Iran. The Soviet government ran the country's internal affairs—but at the same time, the Kremlin also served as headquarters for the worldwide militant Socialist movement. Likewise, the government of the Islamic Republic runs the country's day-to-day affairs, and the Office of the Supreme Leader is the vanguard of the revolution.

The Quds Force, IRGC's expeditionary force whose commander reports directly to the supreme leader, is the headquarters of a growing Shia militancy across the Middle East. It was given a broad and continuing mission to provide command-and-control of all militant Shia organizations and groups affiliated with the Islamic Republic operating outside Iranian borders. Forty years after the revolution, the Quds Force has recruited, trained, and armed nearly 200,000 young Shia militants across the Middle East[2] and organized them into its ground forces, popularly known as the Shia militias (and recently as the SLA).[3]

A NEW IRANIAN MILITARY STRATEGY
FOR A VOLATILE AND TURBULENT REGION

The situation in the twenty-first-century Middle East is highly unstable. Nearly a decade after the 2011 Arab Awakening, failed political transitions, power vacuums, and broken social contracts fuel continued unrest. Endemic state corruption, weak economic growth, poverty, and unemployment exacerbate discontent. These issues have created an environment conducive to radical ideologies and extremist organizations; insurgencies, civil wars, and terrorist campaigns have engulfed the region. Sectarianism has risen to unprecedented levels, and Shia and Sunni actors are vying for power and influence across the region. This turmoil has shaken the Shia-Alawi government in Damascus and the Shia-led government in Baghdad, nearly unseating both.

Witnessing the near demise of two of its closest allies, the Islamic Republic went on the offensive against militant Sunni organizations and powerhouses in order to establish a Shia arc of influence across the region.

The militant Shias formed a united bloc led by Iran's Quds Force, which already had years of experience in support of sectarian-political organizations in the Middle East. Its proxies and partners included Twelver-Shia Hezbollah; Twelver-Shia Iraqi militant groups; Zaydi-Shia Yemeni Houthis; and Afghan, Pakistani, and Bahraini Shia militants. While no equivalent to the Quds Force existed among the more disparate Sunni actors, the Sunni powerhouse of Saudi Arabia led efforts to counter Shia Iran's ambitions and operations in the region. As these powers clashed, conflict deepened across sectarian lines, especially in Iraq, Syria, Yemen, and Afghanistan.

Reacting to the changing situation in the volatile and turbulent post–Arab Awakening Middle East, the Iranian military shifted from a long-standing strategy of deterrence to one emphasizing preemptive action.

The Quds Force became the expeditionary army of this new offensive strategy, and it was designated the lead agency for military operations in the region. Shia militias acted as its principal ground force, a key component for countering Sunni militants. The Quds Force commanders stood up infantry and mechanized brigades and battalions that were composed of militant Shia youths from across the Middle East who were trained in military camps inside Iran. On the battlefield, the Shia infantry was augmented by armor, artillery, and special forces elements deployed on temporary duty from the IRGC and Artesh. The IRGC also provided theater ballistic missile support and a fleet of UAVs.

The IRGC ballistic missile force, the largest in the Middle East, provided both offensive and deterrent capabilities. It opened the option of retaliation against foreign militaries operating in the same battlespaces as the Quds Force, and a major attack on Quds Force–led forces could be answered by missile attacks. The ballistic missiles were also used in attacks by the Quds Force or its proxies against Saudi and Israeli targets. Likewise, IRGC anti-ship cruise missiles (ASCMs) were used on the sea against Saudi and Emirati vessels off the Yemeni coast.

Currently, this mix of asymmetric and symmetric military capabilities, Iran's hybrid way of war, is used in offensive operations in the near abroad. The same forces could serve to deter foreign interventions against Iran that might threaten the existence of the Islamic Republic.

THE WESTERN FRONT

The Land Corridor

The recent establishment of a land corridor connecting Iran through Iraq to Syria, Lebanon, and Israeli fronts is the latest effort in Iran's long-term military strategy in the region. The corridor follows rather closely the path of an ancient land bridge, the Royal Road, which was built by the Persian king Darius the Great in the fifth century BC. Darius built the road to facilitate logistics and communications throughout his large empire. It began in Susa, the ancient city of the Elamite and Persian empires, in present-day south-western Iran, near its border with Iraq. The corridor ran west to Babylon, then turned north along the Tigris through present-day Samarra, Tikrit, and Mosul past northeastern modern-day Syria and on to Sardis, the capital of ancient Lydia, which was one of the important cities of the Persian Empire.

Twenty-six centuries later, the Quds Force and its commander, General Qasem Soleimani, have secured a line of communication largely following that ancient route, connecting Iranian-led forces in the western front to their supply base in Iran. The Quds Force can now move personnel and materiel on land from Iran to Syria and Lebanon and the Israeli northern fronts. It still maintains its "air bridge" to Damascus International Airport and other Syrian airfields, but the land corridor enables the movement of heavy military equipment and guarantees continual supply even if major Syrian airfields are destroyed.

The Syrian Conflict

In Syria, Iran took decisive action to protect the Shia-Alawi regime of President Bashar al-Assad and defeat Sunni opposition forces. As a result, nearly eight years after the 2011 uprisings, the Assad regime is increasingly dependent on Iran. The Quds Force deployed tens of thousands of Shia militants—fighters from Lebanon, Iraq, Afghanistan, and Pakistan—to the Syrian battlefields. Its SLA, augmented by elements of specialized forces deployed from Iran, conducted complex military campaigns on behalf of Assad. The fall of

Aleppo in 2016, fought primarily between the Quds Force–led militants and the Sunni opposition, marked the beginning of the final victory of the regime. The Iranians and their proxies paid a heavy price in blood and treasure to make this victory in Aleppo possible. This investment gave Iran and the Quds Force unprecedented influence in Syria: over Bashar Assad himself, his extended family and tribe, and above all, the Alawi-Shia community that came to see Quds Force commander General Soleimani as their savior.

The absence of peace in Syria also allowed the Quds Force to gain unprecedented influence and the ability to shape the functioning of Assad's elite security and intelligence services, which are run primarily by Assad's extended family, his tribe, and the extended Alawi community. The Iranians saw an opportunity to turn Syria into a semi-client state, with all its geopolitical and future economic benefits. If the country fractured, Iran saw the same opportunity in an Alawi-led state, comprising the so-called good Syria.

Great risks accompany Iran's regional policies. In Syria, Iran wanted to parlay its victories against the opposition into a permanent presence in a country on Israel's doorstep; this was Khomeini's old dream. The Quds Force had some eighty thousand Shia fighters in Syria at the height of the civil war, and it kept close to fifty thousand militants in-country after Aleppo. In order to support those fighters and act as the principal ground force to open a front against the Israelis, the Quds Force needed to establish permanent basing on Syrian soil. This meant that the Iranians had to lease entire or partial Syrian military bases to house their own command-and-control facilities as well as their foreign militias. But this was Israel's red line; it could not accept the presence of Iranian-led forces a short distance from its frontlines on the Golan Heights. In May 2018, the Israeli Air Force (IAF) simultaneously hit all the Quds Force bases in Syria—sixteen of them—and apparently will continue doing so as the Quds Force rebuilds its structures.

There is a great deal of risk that continued Iranian presence in Syria could lead to a direct military conflict with Israel on Syrian soil, which could rapidly escalate beyond Syria. The Quds Force and the IRGC have put their forces on a collision course with Israel.

The fact that the Quds Force is establishing permanent basing to house hundreds of its own personnel, including general officers, and tens of thousands of forces under its command on foreign soil far from Iran, risking a direct conflict with a powerful military, suggests that the Quds Force's own doctrine on proxy war—operating in a gray zone, a state between war and peace, of limited military actions and not inviting conflicts with superior forces—is transforming rapidly into a hybrid warfare doctrine with strong preemptive features.

The Iraqi Conflict

Iran's position in post-Saddam, post-U.S. Iraq is strong. Iran has always maintained close relations with the Shia community in Iraq. When U.S.-led coalition forces invaded Iraq and toppled Saddam Hussein's regime in 2003, Quds Force senior officers crossed the porous border into a chaotic Iraq, bringing with them a large contingent of Iraqi exiles who had fought along-side the IRGC against their own country's military during the Iran-Iraq War of 1980s. The newly arrived Iraqis soon began organizing young Shias. Before long, the Quds Force and its allied Shia militia groups were staging a bloody war against the U.S. with the goal of pushing their troops out of Iraq. They sought to establish a Shia-led government modeled on the Iranian experience—an Islamic Republic of Iraq of sorts.

This war lasted until 2011, when the U.S. pulled out. The Quds Force–led Iraqi Shia militia forces were by then tens of thousands strong; further, the insurgency had made them well trained, well armed, and battle tested. The government in Baghdad was led by Shias, and the prime minister was especially close to Tehran. Iraq had effectively become a satellite state of Iran.

Then came the Arab Awakening. Iraqi Sunnis in predominantly Sunni regions of the country joined the movement and staged protests against the discrimination they had suffered at the hands of the Shia-dominated government in Baghdad. The movement spread to neighboring Syria. The Quds Force suddenly found itself defending friendly governments in Damascus, as well as Baghdad, against a growing and increasingly militant Sunni opposition. By the end of 2011, the Quds Force was on a war footing in Syria and had been forced to deploy its Iraqi Shia militias into Syria to help save Assad.

As the conflict spread throughout Syria, the Iraqi Sunni extremist group the Islamic State in Iraq (ISI), formerly Al-Qaeda in Iraq, also crossed the border into Syria. In the midst of a civil war, the group captured ungoverned territories and renamed its organization the Islamic State in Iraq and Syria (ISIS), using the Arabic acronym *Daesh*. In June 2014, ISIS forces crossed the border back into Iraq, joined by its fighters from the areas of Fallujah and Ramadi, and captured Mosul. They then staged their thunderous march along the now-famous land corridor running south from Baghdad. By summer 2014, Daesh had captured Jalula, a town only nineteen miles from the Iranian border. Iran was now at war with ISIS.

As ISIS marched across Iraq, the Quds Force mobilized all its forces to defend Baghdad; it sent Iraqi Shia militias fighting in Syria back to Iraq and deployed armored and artillery elements of the Iranian regular army, Artesh, to the Iraqi side of the border to stop the advance of ISIS. Eventually the Quds Force–led Shia militias, along with Iraqi and Kurdish security forces and U.S.-led coalition forces, rolled back ISIS and recaptured lost territories.

But risks accompanied the Iranian strategy. Soleimani and his cohort wanted to parlay the victory over Daesh into a permanent presence in Iraq, both directly and through their Shia militia proxies. But true to form for strongmen in the region, they overplayed their hands. Such moves risked arousing nationalist sentiment against foreign intervention. Iraqi Shias saw the Quds Force and its militia groups as the defenders of their government and their southern Shia region, spanning from Baghdad to Karbala, and Najaf to Basra. But as Iraqis, they considered the Quds Force commanders' presence and growing influence in their country an insult to their national sovereignty. These mixed feelings manifested in the 2018 parliamentary elections, the first since the defeat of Daesh, when the vehemently anti-Iran and pro-Iran coalitions (both led by the Shias) finished first and second, respectively.

The Quds Force now needs to balance its close relations with Iraqi Shia militia groups, who dominate some of the country's security institutions and government agencies, with the need to respect Iraqi national sovereignty. Its failure to do so, manifested in the parliamentary elections, does not bode well for its ability to strike the right balance in the future.

THE SOUTHERN FRONT

The Arabian Peninsula

The Arab Awakening gave the Quds Force another friendly government running a capital in the Arab World; it had allies in Baghdad, Damascus, Beirut—and now in Sanaa, Yemen's capital, as well. As protests spread to Yemen, they shook the country's political establishment—ultimately leading to the ouster of its president. The Quds Force's ally in Yemen, the Houthis, sought to take advantage of the country's chaos and significantly weakened central government to seize control of the country. In September 2014, Houthi fighters supported by significant elements of the Yemeni military still loyal to the ousted president captured Sanaa. The Quds Force immediately began planning to build an air bridge to Yemen to transfer advisers and advanced weaponry through Sanaa International Airport, which was now under Houthi control. The stage was set to build a potent force in the country, literally in the back yard of Saudi Arabia, the Islamic Republic's archenemy.

The Houthis were early supporters of the Islamic Revolution in Iran. Days after the victory of the revolution, three top leaders of the Houthi clan, including their current leader and his late father and brother, arrived in Tehran to personally congratulate Ayatollah Khomeini on his rise to power. The Houthis were Zaydi-Shias, and during their visit the leaders attended theological and political seminars in Qom, the seat of Shia power in Iran. When they returned home, they took with them the militant interpretation of Shia

Islam to which they had been exposed in Iran. These ideas shaped the doctrine of their movement in Yemen.

The newly created IRGC began training the Houthis to use advanced weaponry and organize armed formations from military bases in Iran. Thus thirty-five years later, the Houthis were well placed to take advantage of the power vacuum created once the Yemeni president was ousted. When the Houthis took control of Sanaa, they were highly trained, well armed, and ideologically committed fighters who had decades of experience staging uprisings against a central government. Throughout those years, they had received continued support from the IRGC extraterritorial branch and its successor, the Quds Force. The air bridge to Sanaa brought them highly advanced weaponry, including Iranian-made ballistic missiles, ASCMs, and explosive boats. Quds Force advisers and technicians also began upgrading the older Scud missiles that had come under the control of the Houthis for better accuracy and longer range. All these weapons would be eventually used against targets inside Saudi Arabia, including the Riyadh airport, and on Saudi and Emirati ships off the coast of Yemen.

The governments of Saudi Arabia and the United Arab Emirates were determined to stop the advance of another Iranian-backed proxy in Yemen, especially after an assertive new leadership came to power in Riyadh in January 2015. By March of that year, a coalition led by Saudi Arabia began a direct military intervention in Yemen: it closed the Sanaa airport, blockaded Yemen's ports, and ended Iran's overt arms supplies to the Houthis. The Quds Force, after four years of unopposed expansion of its forces in Syria and Iraq, now faced real opposition by the Saudis and the Emiratis. A proxy conflict for supremacy on the Arabian Peninsula was under way.

By supplying advanced weaponry and military advisers to the Houthis in the war against the Saudi-led coalition, the Iranians gained strong support from the Zaydi-Shia community in Yemen and also Zaydi-Shia communities across the border in Saudi Arabia. The Houthis also became increasingly dependent on the Quds Force to continue their war. But the determination of the Saudis, Emiratis, and their Yemeni allies to counter the Iranian influence on the peninsula has put the Iranians on a course of direct military conflict with Iran's Gulf Cooperation Council (GCC) neighbors, which are supported by the U.S. and other Western states. This conflict, on top of the current situation in Syria, has exposed the overstretched Quds Force–led forces in the face of superior hostile forces in two countries—both of which pose an existential threat to the Islamic Republic.

Bab el-Mandeb

Iran also seeks to exert power by consolidating influence over sea passages. Iran already controls the shipping through the Strait of Hormuz in the Persian

Gulf, a major chokepoint for global oil transport. Bab el-Mandeb, or the Mandeb Strait, is another key waterway of strategic interest to Iran. It lies off the coast of Yemen and serves as a shipping route that runs between the Mediterranean Sea and the Indian Ocean, cutting through the Suez Canal and the Arabian Sea. More than twenty thousand ships cross this twenty-mile passage annually. If Iran were to gain control of the Mandeb Strait in addition to the Strait of Hormuz, it would be able to cripple shipping in the eastern hemisphere. In order to achieve this end, the Quds Force has trained and armed the Houthis, providing them with its most advanced ASCMs, explosive boats, and floating mines. Quds Force leaders equipped the Houthis with these weapons in order to have them seize control of the Mandeb Strait, essentially transferring it to Iranian control.

The moves could not remain unnoticed. American, Saudi, and Emirati forces (along with other allies in the Arabian Peninsula) formed a coalition to guarantee the freedom of shipping through the Mandeb Strait. A Quds Force–led Houthi threat to the shipping through the strait would potentially trigger a major conflict in which U.S.–led coalition naval and air forces would target the Quds Force and its allies. This kind of intervention by a global power in the Yemeni conflict would further raise the stakes in an already brutal Yemeni conflict.

THE EASTERN FRONT: AFGHANISTAN

An April 1978 coup in Afghanistan brought a socialist faction to power, and the new government soon began a massive drive to modernize this traditional Islamic society. By October of that year, Islamists' opposition to the government had escalated into revolt. The Islamic Republic came to power in Iran a few months later, and the new government in Tehran took the side of the Afghani Islamists' anti-regime movement. The newly established IRGC and its extraterritorial branch began recruiting Afghan refugees in Iran, mainly Shia Hazaras, and sending them to then-makeshift military training camps near Tehran. There Iranians trained them to take arms against their country's government, seated in Kabul.

Islamist forces eventually eroded the central government's influence. In December 1979, the Soviet army invaded Afghanistan to defend the flailing central government. At this juncture, the conflict in Afghanistan became an anti-Soviet struggle by the American-backed Mujahedeen, the Afghan Islamist fighters. While the U.S. funded and armed the Mujahedeen in order to advance its Cold War interests of rolling back Soviet power, the Islamic Republic also entered the conflict on the side of the Islamists. The IRGC deployed the Afghan militias it had trained and armed to fight the government and its Soviet backers. Those Afghan militias became the first contingent of IRGC–organized foreign Shia militias to fight abroad to uphold the interests of the Islamic Republic and the Shia nation. Three decades later, the successors to those early militants, who were also mainly Hazara refugees in Iran, would form the Fatemiyoun brigades to fight in Syria under Quds Force command. This time, foreign Shia militants organized to fight for a different Iranian strategic goal: preserving the Assad regime.

Two successive Afghani Islamist governments, the Mujahedeen and then the Taliban, came to power in the wake of the Soviet withdrawal in 1989 and the subsequent fall of the Socialist government in 1992. Other Islamist extremists, like al-Qaeda and forerunners of Daesh, established camps in Afghanistan and plotted attacks against Western targets, including the attacks of 11 September 2001. Shia militias under Quds Force command participated in the U.S.-led military coalition to keep the Taliban out of the Panjshir Valley and create a buffer zone between the Taliban and the Iranian border. In another instance, alongside U.S. and British special forces, as well as the Mujahedeen, Shia militants fought to help liberate Herat.

As U.S. forces and their local partners succeeded in gaining the upper hand in the country, the Taliban became the principal anti-U.S. actor. The Islamic Republic forged a tactical coalition with the Taliban in order to counter American power. Tehran wanted to raise the cost of the American presence in Afghanistan, both in blood and treasure, in order to force the U.S. out of the country; the IRGC's strategy was to utilize the Taliban to bleed American resources.

The depth of Iran's ties to the Taliban became public in 2016 when a U.S. drone struck a vehicle transporting Taliban chief Mullah Mansoor from Iran to Baluchistan, in Pakistan.[4] Mansoor was in Iran to manage tactical cooperation for the Taliban's offensive against the U.S.-backed government. Later that year, three Quds Force officers were killed in a U.S. airstrike against Taliban positions in Farah Province, on the Iranian border.

Links between the Quds Force and Afghan Shia militias have remained close. The IRGC sponsors Afghan Shia militias by paying their recruits a regular salary and promising them the option of Iranian residency after a deployment to Syria.[5] Overall, the Quds Force has organized more than fifteen thousand Afghan Shia militants under the Fatemiyoun Brigade and deployed them to Syria to fight alongside pro-Assad forces against the Sunni opposition. These forces are now battle tested, having seen heavy combat in the Syrian cities of Aleppo, Daraa, and Palmyra. The Quds Force can, at any time it pleases, deploy the Fatemiyoun fighters back to Afghanistan, and it may choose to do so in a post-Syria conflict. Such a move would significantly increase Iran's leverage in the country: the militants might become a powerful force inside Afghanistan, following the Iraqi Popular Mobilization Forces (PMF) model.

THE RISE OF THE QUDS FORCE

Since 2011, the Quds Force has involved itself in all the region's major conflicts. The Quds Force's predecessor had modest beginnings in the Islamic Republic's early days, when its responsibilities amounted only to training dozens of Afghan Shia militants in makeshift camps near Tehran. Under this mandate, it recruited and organized Iraqi Shia refugees to fight under their command in the Iran-Iraq War of the 1980s. Since then, its activities have expanded to executing the IRGC's mission of advancing the Islamic Revolution with a ground force, the SLA, comprised of Shia militias from across the Middle East. The Quds Force currently has an estimated strength of 200,000 active and reserve combatants in Shia militant groups. These fighters are highly trained, well armed, and battle tested.

Commanding nationals of many regional countries in its pan-Shia ground force offers many advantages to the Quds Force. The Quds Force can deploy these combatants to many different battlespaces or keep them on reserve for operations in their respective countries. Augmented by specialized units of the IRGC and Artesh (such as the IRGC ballistic missile force), the Quds Force–led SLA is one the largest and most experienced hybrid fighting forces in the Middle East today.

Iran's unchecked push for primacy in the Middle East with its use of the SLA could put Iran on a collision course with the U.S., Israeli, Saudi, and Emirati militaries, and these potential conflicts could threaten the Islamic Republic's existence. On the other hand, a Quds Force–led operation kept under close control could be a major long-term advantage for the Islamic Republic.

The Quds Force is organized so as to enable it to outlast the Islamic Republic. The Quds Force can tap into vast business holdings outside Iran that are run by the country's nongovernmental Islamic foundations. These resources include banks, transportation companies, a cache of arms in many areas in the Middle East, a large network of associates across the globe, and above all, nearly 200,000 trained and armed youths committed to fight on its behalf. The Quds Force could continue serving as the command center for a vast Shia militant network with branches in almost all countries in the region.

THE RISKS

The successes of the Quds Force in Syria, Iraq, and Yemen have come with heavy risks. If unaltered, the Quds Force's and Hezbollah's establishment of a permanent presence in Syria—complete with a land corridor connected to Iran, military bases on Syrian soil, and creation of a robust missile force on the ground—will inevitably lead to conflict between the Iranian and Israeli militaries. It is inconceivable that the U.S. military would not to come to Israel's aid in the event of conflict with Iran breaking out.

In Iraq, the proximity of the Quds force and Iraqi Shia militias to the U.S. and allied forces is a major concern. Those militias have long disseminated the anti-U.S. ideology of the Islamic Republic. Many of them fought the Americans during the occupation years of 2011–2013. Any inadvertent or intentional move on the part of one of the nearly one hundred Shia militia groups in Iraq that harmed U.S. personnel and interests could put Iran on a collision course with the U.S. inside Iraq.

In Yemen, Houthi ballistic missile attacks on Saudi targets, including attempted attacks on Riyadh International Airport and the Royal Palace, are very aggressive and risky moves. Iran could ultimately be held responsible for these attacks, putting the Islamic Republic on a military collision course with the kingdom and its backers, including the United States.

The Iranian involvement in the current conflicts in the Middle East has generally benefited Iran and the Quds Force and has strengthened the SLA, but any miscalculation or unintended incident could result in a larger conflict involving major regional and global powers at a time when Iran, its economy, and its public can least afford it.

THE SHIA-SUNNI DIVIDE

The Sunni-Shia divide is an enduring source of friction and discord throughout the Middle East. Sectarianism is a common thread in all current conflicts. In Syria, the central contest is between the regime, supported by the Alawi-Shia community, and the Sunni opposition. In Iraq, Sunnis struggled against the Shia south and a Shia-dominated government in Baghdad. In Yemen, the Zaydi-Shia community is aligned with the Houthis in opposition to the Sunni-dominated former government.

Sectarian divisions are often sown as a tactic to polarize populations in support of larger geopolitical ambitions. The Quds Force's recruitment literature targeting young Shias for deployment to Syrian battlefields, for example, invariably states the urgent need to defend the Damascus shrine of Sayyidah Zaynab, the daughter of the first Shia imam, against Sunni attacks—even though recruits could be deployed to places nowhere near the shrine. Battle sites like Aleppo are often more than two hundred miles north of it.

Sectarianism has proven a powerful tool for recruiting and fighting. However, it is also liable to spark new conflicts that entangle those who sought to utilize it. For example, the Quds Force–led Shia militias created tremendous animosity within Sunni communities while clearing Iraqi towns liberated after the defeat of Daesh. The sectarian hatred that motivated the militias' actions led them to create a situation in which their continued presence in the area was untenable. Considering that the majority of Muslims are Sunni, Iran's hostile actions against the Sunni opposition in the current conflicts could further isolate Shias and their communities across the Middle East.

THE QUDS FORCE'S MILITARY CAPABILITY

The Quds Force is a military headquarters that gathers intelligence, prepares operation plans, provides logistics support, and conducts command-and-control functions for its military campaigns. The fighting brigades are provided by affiliated regular and asymmetric units. The infantry force is generally comprised of members of Shia militia groups deployed to a particular battlefield. The major militia groups also deploy their mechanized elements in the battlespace. Other ground force components—armor, artillery, UAV, missile, and special forces elements—provided by the IRGC and Artesh are deployed to the battlefield on temporary duty. The Quds Force uses allied air forces, Russian, Syrian, and occasionally Iraqi, for air support for its campaigns. Naval assets in the Yemeni theater are provided by the IRGC Navy.

With such an arrangement, Iran's military capabilities are put to use in support of the Quds Force's campaigns and are also used to deter rival militaries that challenge its operations outside Iranian borders. The cornerstone of Iran's deterrent and preemptive military strategies is the IRGC missile force. Iran fields thousands of ballistic and cruise missiles and hundreds of launchers. Iran's robust domestic R&D and military production capabilities are producing increasingly more accurate missiles with increasingly longer ranges. The use of seeker technology has increased the accuracy of its ASCMs. The latest generation of its high-precision ballistic missiles have multiple-warhead capability and can reach any target in the Middle East. Their precision is measured in a radius of yards.

The Quds Force provides these ballistic and cruise missiles to select Shia militant groups, including Hezbollah and the Houthis. It also manages a campaign dubbed "Precision Project" to upgrade its current inventories of rockets and missiles in order to increase their range and accuracy.

Iran produces high-precision ASCMs and unmanned explosive boats, which have been used against enemy ships off the coast of Yemen. Domestically produced UAVs support the intelligence, surveillance, and reconnaissance (ISR) capabilities of the Quds Force; allegedly, some have even been armed with missiles. Iran also develops and produces radar, satellite navigation systems, and other surveillance systems that are used in Quds Force campaigns. Iran's growing cyberwar capabilities are operational and have been used by Quds Force cyber units against targets not just in the region but globally.

Notwithstanding the importance of technological advances in weaponry, the reality of current conflicts in the Middle East is that they are still mostly proxy conflicts fought out on the ground by largely asymmetric forces. The transformation from gray-zone conflicts into offensive operations using advanced weapons is already under way. The proxy conflicts give the Quds Force the upper hand when waging war with infantry primarily comprised of local Arab Shia fighters, while the advanced weaponry will be increasingly necessary if the Quds Force takes offensive actions against regional powers like Israel or the Saudi-UAE coalition backed by Israel and the United States.

THE REGIONAL STRATEGY

Iran's long-standing strategy has always appeared to be pursuing leadership of Shia populations and expanding its regional influence while carefully limiting the extent of its aggression in order to avoid provoking full-fledged war with major powers. Leading the Shia nation according to a militant interpretation of Shia Islam was the cornerstone of Iran's Islamic Revolution. The founders of the revolution believed that the Islamic Republic's mission was to become the undisputed leader of Shias across the region, and as such a leader of the Islamic world. Today, the Quds Force's information operations attempt to prove that it fulfills this mission of fighting on behalf of all Shias.

In Syria, the absence of peace from 2011 to 2015 meant that the Alawi-Shia regime led by Assad remained dependent on the Iranian military to defeat its opposition. But avoiding a major war with the Sunni powerhouses who backed the opposition meant that the Quds Force deployed proxies— Hezbollah and other foreign Shia fighters, like Afghan militants—to the battlefields. The specialized elements of the IRGC and Artesh that augmented the militias, like the armor and artillery units, remained in the country on temporary duty for specific battles and only in support of Quds Force–led forces and were deployed back to Iran soon after the battles ended. In Iraq, a similar strategy was followed against Daesh: the Quds Force let local Shia militias do the fighting while prohibiting them from attacking the U.S.-led coalition forces, thus avoiding a major war with a superior force. Tacking between war and peace has become the preferred form of conflict for the Quds Force.

Information operations are a necessary tool in this strategy to show that the IRGC and the Quds Force are fighting for the interests of Shias across the region while not starting a major war.

The Quds Force–led victory in Aleppo, however, ended an important phase in the Syrian Civil War. The moderate opposition was all but defeated, and continuation of Assad's government became all but certain. The Quds Force, and the leadership of the Islamic Republic, saw an opportunity to parlay the defeat of the opposition into a permanent presence in Syria to counter the Israeli forces on its borders—an old dream of the Islamic revolutionaries. The doctrine of proxy warfare could no longer cover this changing strategy.

Absent a complete retreat by the Quds Force and foreign Shia militias from Syria, which is highly unlikely, the Israelis will take advantage of the fact that the Quds Force has exposed its forces to continued Israeli attacks on its bases. Rising tensions could lead to a direct military conflict between Iran and Israel on Syrian soil, where the Quds Force's old doctrine would no longer apply, pushing the Iranians toward a more aggressive, offensive strategy. Preemptive doctrine, as opposed to the long-standing military strategy of deterrence, has found many converts within the Iranian leadership.

The IRGC missile deterrence during a conflict with Israel has its own limits. In May 2018, the Quds Force launched twenty rockets at Israeli positions on the Golan Heights to retaliate for an earlier Israeli attack on one of its command-and-control centers and a weapons depot in northern Syria. The Quds Force probably expected a proportional response. Instead, the Israelis attacked sixteen Quds Force installations in Syria within the span of an hour, Israel's largest air operation since the Yom Kippur War of 1973.[6] These nonproportional attacks against almost all their installations in Syria caught the Quds Force unprepared; they were equipped neither to defend themselves against a large-scale, coordinated onslaught by their archenemy nor to launch a proportional retaliatory response. Limited wars do not always remain that; even carefully limited aggression can spiral into a full-fledged war against a superior force. The consequences of changing military strategy from defensive to offensive are enormous, a transition that could not possibly favor Iran.

THE POLITICAL STRATEGY

The core political strategy of the Quds Force has been to push its allies and proxies to seek leadership in areas with significant Shia populations. In Lebanon and Iraq, Hezbollah and the PMF (an umbrella organization of mainly Shia militias) have fielded candidates in the parliamentary elections with great success. Both organizations have significantly infiltrated the security institutions of their respective countries. Hezbollah is the de facto ruler of Lebanon, and the PMF is the largest political-military organization in Iraq. In Syria, the Quds Force's support was critical to keeping the Shia-Alawi–led government in power in Damascus; it also pushed for the creation of PMF-type organizations like the National Defense Forces, established by the IRGC Basij Force in 2012. Given the highly fragmented nature of politics in the country, the Quds Force has also prepared itself and its local allies to create an independent Shia-Alawi state in western Syria if Assad is ultimately unable to retain control of the entirety of Syria.

In Yemen, Quds Force support was critical if the Houthis were to hold on to power in Sanaa. The best-case scenario for the Iranians was the formation of a central government in which the Houthis played a key role, as Hezbollah does in Lebanon. But after the military intervention by the Saudi-Emirati–led coalition, there is a strong possibility the Houthis could be pushed back to their longtime northwestern stronghold of Saada and its surrounding areas. At the same time, the country is becoming increasingly chaotic. South Yemen will most likely declare independence and reestablish the pre-1990 state. The Quds Force has prepared itself and its allies for creating a Zaydi-Shia–led independent state in northwestern Yemen if the country fractures. The new state will be literally in the backyard of Saudi Arabia.

Chapter Two

The Shia Liberation Army

As the Middle East fell into chaos in the wake of the Arab Spring in 2011, the Quds Force and its cadre of highly trained, armed, and battle-tested Shia militias were positioned to take full advantage of the breakdown of the political order and the outbreak of civil war. Topping the list were thousands of Hezbollah fighters, veterans of three decades of bombing campaigns against Western targets and the 2006 war against Israel. There were also thousands of Iraqi Shia militants, led by veterans of the Iran-Iraq War of the 1980s and the deadly campaigns against U.S.-led coalition forces in Iraq from 2003 to 2011. Also at the Quds Force's disposal were hundreds of Afghan Shia militants, veterans of the war against the pro-Soviet Afghan government in the 1980s, along with thousands of their compatriots living in exile in Iran. Last, but not least, were the Yemeni Houthis, who by then had been waging a seven-year war against the central government and were the rulers of the de facto, autonomous, Zaydi-Shia–dominated northwestern region.

Faced with a rising Sunni militancy in the region and the prospect of losing a key Shia-friendly government in Syria, the Shia militant groups, under the guidance of General Qasem Soleimani's Quds Force, began forming a united front to safeguard their Shia interests and push their own brand of militant Islamist ideology across the region. Hezbollah, the Iraqi militias, the Afghan militants, and the Houthis formed the nucleus of the Quds Force–led SLA.[1]

Within five years of the start of the Arab Spring and the Syrian Civil War, there were nearly 200,000 Shia youths mobilized, trained, and armed by Quds Force–led militia groups. In 2016, the IRGC commander surprised the world by announcing the number of armed Shia militants mobilized by the Quds Force across the region: "The upside of the recent conflicts in the region is the mobilization of nearly 200,000 armed Shia youths in the countries of the region," said General Mohammad Ali Jafari, the IRGC commander, in a speech delivered on 12 January 2016.[2]

The SLA has become the Quds Force's principal ground force in battlefields across Syria and Iraq, and it is deployable to any conflict zone in the Middle East. The SLA is not your typical ragtag militia force; it acts as an advanced conventional land force. Its fighters are chosen by professional recruiters affiliated with the major militant groups based on strict military and ideological profiles. The new recruits are enrolled in regimented basic training courses in the region, and the best graduates are sent to Iran to attend one of the rigorous Quds Force boot camps. Their leaders are sent back to Iran, on up to five different occasions, for advanced and specialized training in areas such as cutting-edge explosives; anti-tank, anti-aircraft, and theater ballistic missiles; and UAVs. The fighters receive monthly salaries and wear IRGC–type uniforms with their distinctive unit insignia. Although there are no rank insignia, the groups adhere to standard military-type hierarchical policies and procedures.

When deployed to the battlefield, the SLA ground forces have their own armor, artillery, and UAV elements, with the most advanced groups also equipped with anti-tank, anti-aircraft, and ballistic and cruise missiles. If needed, their forces are augmented by specialized units from Iran on temporary duty to provide additional armor, artillery, UAV, and missile support. After the SLA and the Iranian units, the crucial missing link is air support. The Quds Force has used the friendly air forces of Russia, Syria, and Iraq in past battles to overcome this weakness. Standing up a modern air force for the IRGC is in the works as soon as restrictions on importing advanced military equipment, including aircraft, are lifted, authorized by a 2013 nuclear agreement between Iran and the major powers.

THE EARLY YEARS OF REVOLUTION AND FOREIGN SHIA MILITIAS

The Islamic Revolution triumphed in Iran on 11 February 1979. Within weeks, the anti-shah militants who had formed armed groups after the collapse of the shah's army had established the IRGC and its extraterritorial branch. The latter was charged with establishing relations with revolutionary movements across the globe and promoting the newly triumphant revolutionary Islamist ideology across the Muslim world. The first challenge facing the IRGC's extraterritorial branch was brewing unrest in neighboring Afghanistan, where the Communist Party had come to power in the previous year. The new government's secular policies and radical modernization reforms ───── ¹ ighly unpopular in rural Afghanistan. By April 1979, large parts of the ' were in open rebellion. The IRGC's response to the situation set a precedent that would define its extraterritorial operations for decades to come. It decided to build a fighting force from Afghan Shia refugees inside Iran and deploy them in Afghanistan under the command of IRGC senior operatives to fight the central government in Kabul and later the Soviet occupation army.

A makeshift training camp was set up north of Tehran by the IRGC, staffed by Iranian revolutionaries who had undergone irregular warfare training at Fatah military camps in Iraq and Lebanon before the victory of the revolution in Iran. The recruits, mainly ethnic Shia Hazaras, underwent basic training in weapons and irregular war tactics and were deployed to Afghanistan. By the time the Soviets invaded the country at the end of that year, about five hundred armed Afghan Shia militants had crossed the border to take part in the fight against the Soviet army and the pro-Soviet government in Kabul. They in turn recruited fellow Hazaras inside Afghanistan to join the fight.[3] Those fighters became the IRGC's first foreign Shia militias to be deployed on battlefields outside Iran, the forerunners of the Abuzar Brigade, which fought on the IRGC's side during the Iran-Iraq War and the Fatemiyoun Division that saw heavy combat in the Syrian Civil War.

During the decade-long fight against the Soviets, four major Shia militant groups emerged in Afghanistan, headquartered in Iran and all under IRGC command. The groups recruited and trained new fighters in predominantly Hazara regions. They were Sazman-i Nasr-i Islami-yi; Harakat-i-Islami; Sepah-e Pasdaran-e Afghanistan; and Shura-i Inqilab-i Ittifagh-i Islami-i.[4]

In the early days of the revolution, the nascent IRGC also recruited within the Iraqi Shia refugee community inside Iran, those who had fled the brutality of Saddam Hussein's regime. A makeshift training camp was set up for the Iraqis, separate but not far from the one set up for the Afghans. The newly trained Iraqi fighters were sent to the Iran-Iraq border region to take part in border skirmishes between the IRGC and the Iraqi army. By the time the Iran-Iraq War began in September 1980, more than one thousand Iraqi militants had undergone the IRGC training courses and had seen combat in the border fights. These fighters later formed the nucleus of two Iraqi militia groups to fight alongside the IRGC against their own country's military: the Badr Brigade, affiliated with the Supreme Council for Islamic Revolution in Iraq (SCIRI), and the armed wing of the Dawa Party. The IRGC's Iraqi and other foreign Shia militias suffered heavy casualties in the war. A recent report puts the number of foreign Shia militants wearing IRGC uniforms killed in action in the Iran-Iraq War at 4,565.[5]

Among the young founders of those early Iraqi militia groups were Hadi al-Amiri of Badr and Abu Mahdi al-Muhandis of Dawa, who two decades later would rise to prominence in post-Saddam Iraq.[6]

The IRGC's efforts to stand up Shia militias went beyond neighboring Iraq and Afghanistan and included all hot spots in the near abroad. Lebanon was a special case: many of the founders of the IRGC were affiliated with and in some cases part of the leadership structure of militant organizations active in the country at the time. Some had gone through Palestinian military camps in Lebanon. Some were veterans of the then-ongoing Lebanese civil war. In the first days of the revolution, leading Lebanese Shia militants visited the Islamic Republic, and the IRGC sent its delegation to Beirut. The IRGC was ready to establish a new group that would unite the more militant members of different organizations in the country, including the Shia members of Fatah, militant members of Amal, and even the Shia members of leftist organizations. The 1982 Israeli invasion of southern Lebanon accelerated these efforts, and Hezbollah was born. A 1,500-strong IRGC contingent was deployed to Lebanon to stand up the new organization. More than three decades later, Hezbollah is the jewel of the Quds Force–led SLA, transformed from a Lebanese resistance organization into the leading member of the Quds Force global network.

Relations with the Yemeni Houthis also started in the beginning days of the IRGC. A Houthi delegation headed by its spiritual leader and his sons visited Iran months after the triumph of the Islamic Revolution. The leaders spent a full year in Iran undergoing military and ideological training and took home with them a militant interpretation of Shia Islam. A decade later, and under the IRGC's guidance, they would stand up a new Shia-Zaydi movement, Ansar Allah, commonly known as "the Houthis."

In the first years of the revolution, the IRGC established close relationships with Shia militants across the Middle East. A number of Shia militant organizations were born in the period under the IRGC's guidance. Hezbollah in Lebanon, Iraqi and Afghan Shia militia groups, and Ansar Allah in Yemen formed the nucleus of the Quds Force–led SLA.

ARMING THE MILITIAS

A look at the SLA's weaponry tells the story of how the militia groups evolved into the ground forces of the Quds Force. During the 2003–2011 Iraq War, the Iraqi militias were using small arms and rockets. Their deadliest weapons were improvised explosive devices (IEDs), which are crude bombs used by insurgents against conventional military forces, and improvised rocket assisted mortars (IRAMs), which are a propane or fuel tank filled with explosives and propelled by a rocket booster. As the war progressed, they used explosive formed penetrators (EFPs), which have a charge designed to penetrate armor.

By 2016, in addition to these weapons, the Quds Force was supplying the groups with close-range ballistic missiles (CRBMs), anti-tank guided missiles (ATGMs), tanks, armored personnel carriers, artillery, UAVs, and man-portable air-defense systems (MANPADS). Groups were also armed with specialized weapons for their specified missions. Hezbollah carried tens of thousands of rockets, which were being upgraded for better accuracy and longer range. The Quds Force supplied the Houthis with ASCMs and unmanned explosive boats.

TRANSFORMATION TO A MULTINATIONAL EXPEDITIONARY ARMY

The growing conflicts in the region also transformed national militia groups into members of a multinational expeditionary army, deployable to battlefields outside their home countries under the command of the Quds Force. In Lebanon, Hezbollah evolved from what was advertised as a militant force defending Lebanese sovereignty against Israel into the SLA's premier mechanized division deployed to Syria to fight Assad's opposition. The Iraqi militant groups were deployed back and forth between Iraq and Syria to fight the opposition in Syria and the Islamic State, or Daesh, in Iraq. The Afghan militias, the Fatemiyoun Brigade, saw heavy combat in Syria. Hezbollah and Iraqi Shia militia advisers were deployed to Yemen to train and assist the Houthis, while the Houthis announced their readiness to fight alongside Hezbollah against Israel.

The multinational composition of the SLA does not lessen its effectiveness in acting as the Quds Force's principal ground force. In the Battle of Aleppo (2015–2016), Soleimani perfected the way of war for the SLA. Twenty-five thousand foreign Shia fighters were joined by elements of the IRGC's armor, artillery, theater ballistic missile, and UAV units and Artesh's special forces. The Russians provided air support. With these, Soleimani had the necessary conventional ground and air forces to retake Aleppo.

TRAINING THE MILITIAS

The training of the foreign Shia militants began in IRGC camps inside Iran soon after the revolution. The Afghan Hazaras and Iraqi Shias were trained in makeshift camps set up by the nascent IRGC before being deployed to Afghanistan and the border regions with Iraq to engage their governments. When the Iran-Iraq War started, the IRGC's camp in Karaj, near Tehran, became the training hub of anti-Saddam Iraqi militias to fight against the armed forces of their own country. The Iraqi survivors remained in Iran after the war ended in 1988. They became useful again in the 2003 invasion of Iraq by U.S. and coalition forces and the overthrow of Saddam Hussein. The Quds Force, which was organized as an independent expeditionary force based on lessons learned from the Iran-Iraq War, had a cadre of battle-tested

Iraqi militants and deployed them in Iraq during the chaos that followed the U.S. invasion. The Quds Force established an advanced explosive training camp for the Iraqi veterans, training the militants in anti-armor operations and the use of IEDs before their deployment. The militants not only engaged the U.S. and coalition forces inside Iraq but began a massive recruiting effort among the Shias of southern Iraq. The Quds Force established several training camps inside Iran to handle the rapid influx of trainees who were sent to the country by different Iraqi militia groups that had been stood up in post-Saddam Iraq. These camps were soon augmented with training facilities inside Iraq. By the time the United States withdrew its troops from Iraq, most members of the Iraqi Shia militia groups had undergone continued training and gained years of experience fighting the Americans.

In the 1980s while fighting the Iraqi army, the IRGC set up the militant Shia group known as Hezbollah in Lebanon. The founding members were participants in the Lebanese civil war and former Shia members of the Lebanese Amal and Palestinian Fatah militant groups, trained in their military camps, as well as other militants, including Shia members of leftist parties in Beirut. They were all battle tested in the brutal war that had begun four years before the victory of the Islamic Revolution in Iran. Many Iranian exiles of the shah's regime, including militant Islamists, were also trained in the Palestinian camps in Lebanon, Iraq, and Algeria. The Islamists among them joined the IRGC after the revolution and helped organize Hezbollah.

Since the founding of the Islamic Republic, the IRGC and then the Quds Force have kept close relations with the Zaydi-Shias in Yemen and in 1997 helped organize their political movement, the Ansarallah, commonly known as the Houthi movement. The Houthi leaders stayed in Iran for over a year immediately after the revolution and returned home armed with a militant interpretation of Shia Islam. Many Houthis also were trained in Quds Force camps inside Iran and returned to Yemen to participate in a ten-year insurgency against the Saleh government from 2004 onward.

The Quds Force training regimen inside Iran, and occasionally in Lebanon, starts with a basic skills and weapons course. Captured militants have reported that their basic training courses lasted from twenty to forty-five days. Conducting operations and tactics is the focus of advanced training courses, including training in logistics and support, explosives, and advanced weapons skills. The more advanced courses cover EFPs, mortars and rockets, tactics and warfare, and sniper skills.[7] The Quds Force also ran specialized training courses on anti-aircraft, cruise, and theater ballistic missiles for Hezbollah and the Houthis.

THE SLA IN PERSPECTIVE

The Iranians use the SLA as a key component of their regional project. In March 2017, the Iranian supreme leader, Ayatollah Ali Khamenei, said the "far reaching strategic depth of the Islamic Republic, particularly in (the Middle East), is of most significant progress in the last four decades."[8] The progress is particularly evident in terms of Quds Force–led SLA military victories on the battlefields in Iraq and Syria, Iranian dominance of Iraqi and Lebanese politics, and Iran's growing influence over governments in Damascus and Sanaa. Together this amounts to dominance and influence in four Arab capitals.

If the SLA is the manifestation of the Quds Force's military prowess in the region, its vast network of associates and supporters manifests its global reach. A large number of religious, cultural, and academic conferences that have popped up in Tehran or other major Iranian cities in the past decade provide the Quds Force with a pool of individuals influential in their communities who could be recruited to support its operations, some naively believing they are just defending the Shia cause. When the Syrian, Iraqi, and Yemeni civil wars broke out, many of those clerics, cultural figures, and academics strongly sided with Iran and supported the Quds Force operations in those conflicts.

The Quds Force network, with operators across the globe, controls over one hundred front businesses, including air, sea, and ground transport companies. The Quds Force also uses its local presence to store large caches of arms in Shia enclaves across the region. With over 100,000 active SLA members across the Middle East, a vast network of associates and supporters across the globe, front businesses, and caches of arms in the region, the Quds Force is organized to last for decades as the defenders of a militant political interpretation of Shia Islam and if necessary to outlast the Islamic Republic itself.

ORGANIZING THE SLA

The Quds Force's commander acts as the overall SLA commander and along with his senior officers provides operational command and advise-and-assist functions across the SLA divisions. Lebanese and Iraqi militant groups make up the core of the SLA.

Hezbollah

Founded by the IRGC in 1982 as a resistance movement against the Israeli occupation of southern Lebanon, the military wing of Hezbollah has evolved into the premier element of the SLA, deploying nearly ten thousand fighters in different theaters and battlefields in current conflicts and functioning as recruiters and trainers alongside Quds Force officers. A typical Hezbollah member wears insignia resembling the IRGC's and believes in the primacy of the *velayat-e faghih* religious doctrine and Khamenei's supreme leadership. Hezbollah also is a leading proponent of the Iranian-led political Shia Islam project, where militants like those of Hezbollah grab and maintain controlling influence over governments in countries with a significant Shia population.

The Quds Force maintains a joint command-and-control structure with Hezbollah. Soleimani frequently meets with Hezbollah's leader, Hassan Nasrallah, and his senior aides. Quds Force senior officers also participate in the decision-making process of Hezbollah at its highest levels regarding all military and terrorist operations carried out or supported by the organization. This practice began in the first days of the founding of Hezbollah, with the 1983 truck suicide bombings of the U.S. Marine and French barracks at Beirut International Airport, killing 241 U.S. and 58 French servicemen. Other terrorist attacks carried out by Hezbollah and its affiliates include the bombing of AMIA, the Jewish community center in Buenos Aires, that killed 85 people in 1994, and the 1996 truck bombing of Khobar Towers in Saudi Arabia, which housed members of the U.S. Air Force 4404 Wing, carried out by the Saudi wing of Hezbollah, killing 19 U.S. servicemen.[9] In 1997, the U.S. State Department designated Hezbollah a foreign terrorist organization (FTO).

On the military side, the deployment of nearly ten thousand Hezbollah fighters to Syria to fight Assad's Sunni opposition was closely coordinated between General Soleimani, Hassan Nasrallah, and their senior aides.

Iran provides the bulk of Hezbollah's budget, estimated at $1 billion a year. Hezbollah secretary general Hassan Nasrallah has said, "Hezbollah's budget, its income, its expenses, everything it eats and drinks, its weapons and rockets, come from the Islamic Republic of Iran."[10] Hezbollah also raises funds by receiving support from some members of the Lebanese Shia diaspora and by smuggling contraband goods, falsifying passports, trafficking in narcotics, and laundering money, as well as through credit card, immigration, and bank fraud.[11]

The Quds Force provides advanced weaponry to Hezbollah, including over 100,000 rockets and missiles.[12] It has now begun a massive upgrade program, referred to as the Precision Project, to improve the range and accuracy of its rockets, with production plants in Lebanon and Syria. Israel considers the Quds Force delivery of advanced weapons to Hezbollah and establishment of manufacturing plants to be direct threats to its security. It has launched numerous air attacks against the processing facilities for incoming weapons from Iran at Damascus International Airport and targeted convoys carrying weapons to Hezbollah. Israel has also launched air attacks against manufacturing plants associated with the Precision Project for Hezbollah's current rocket and missile arsenal.[13]

Al-Hashd al-Shaabi (the Popular Mobilization Forces, or PMF)

The Badr Organization, Kata'ib Hezbollah (KH), and Asa'ib Ahl al-Haq (AAH) form the core of the Quds Force–led PMF. Among the leading members of these groups are veterans of the Iran-Iraq War of the 1980s and the 2003–2011 Iraq War. After the 2011 breakout of the Syrian civil war, General Soleimani deployed major Iraqi Shia militia groups to Syria to fight Sunni militants opposing Assad's regime. When the Islamic State overtook Mosul in 2014 and declared an Islamic caliphate in territories captured on both sides of the Iraq-Syria border, Iraqi militia groups were redeployed to Iraq to stop ISIS's thunderous advance toward Baghdad and points south close to the Iranian border. That was when the PMF was born, an umbrella structure of predominantly Shia militia groups, with Badr, the KH, and the AAH leading its operations. In the post-Daesh period, the PMF focused its operations on the Iraq-Syria border regions, enabling the establishment of a land corridor connecting Iran through Iraq and Syria to Lebanon and the Israeli front on the Golan Heights.

The story of the Iraqi Shia militia groups fighting under the command of the IRGC and the Quds Force began in the early days of the Islamic Republic. The IRGC recruited militant Iraqi Shias who had fled Saddam Hussein's Iraq and become refugees in Iran. Some one thousand Iraqi recruits were sent to makeshift boot camps set up by the IRGC and deployed to the Iraqi border regions to take part in border skirmishes with the Iraqi army before the start of the Iran-Iraq War in September 1980. Those fighters later formed the nucleus of Iraqi Shia militia groups that were formed by the IRGC to fight their own country's army during the war with Iraq. One of the oldest of these groups was the Badr Brigade. It was organized in 1982 as the military wing of the Supreme Council of Islamic Revolution in Iraq (SCIRI), which was later renamed the Islamic Supreme Council of Iraq. The Badr Brigade fielded thousands of Iraqi Shia exiles on the battlefield. One of the brigade's leaders was young Hadi al-Amiri. The military wing of the Dawa party in exile in Iran was also organized to fight on the side of the IRGC. The group was led by Abu Mahdi al-Muhandis. Amiri and Muhandis would eventually become the two most powerful Iran-backed men in post-Saddam Iraq and the leaders of the PMF, the Iraqi component of the SLA.

The Iraqi Shia militants working under the IRGC were deployed back to Iraq in the chaotic days that followed the 2003 U.S. invasion of the country and the overthrow of Saddam Hussein's regime. The Badr Brigade, now renamed the Badr Organization, not unlike Hezbollah, conducted a two-pronged strategy. It conducted terrorist operations against the remnants of

Saddam's regime and later against the Sunni insurgency, while it joined the new Shia-led Iraqi state apparatus, especially the new security establishment, formed by the U.S. and coalition authorities.[14] By the time the Americans left Iraq in 2011, Badr was in control of the Ministry of Interior and its federal police. Badr fighters played a major role in defending Baghdad against the Islamic State, or Daesh, and were part of a Quds Force–led SLA that fielded some 100,000 men to battlefields inside Iraq. Badr chairman al-Amiri, who fought alongside the IRGC against his own country's military in the Iran-Iraq War and still reports directly to General Soleimani, now was projecting himself as the defender of Iraqi sovereignty and supporter of state institutions with ambitions to form the future Iraqi government.

Another group formed in the years of the U.S. occupation was the KH. Founded in 2007 by Abu Mahdi al-Muhandis, the KH became one of the most lethal militia units organized under the Quds Force. It fought hard against the U.S.-led coalition forces in the latter years of the occupation. In 2009, for its leading role in attacking U.S. and coalition forces in Iraq, the KH was designated by the U.S. State Department as an FTO. Its fighters were deployed to Syria after civil war broke out there in 2011, later to be deployed back to Iraq to fight the Islamic State.

Another group, the AAH, was organized in 2006 by the Quds Force from the pro-Iran militants of Muqtada al-Sadr's Jaysh al-Madhi group. As lethal as the KH, the AAH also conducted an anti-U.S. campaign and was notorious for its roadside bomb attacks during the occupation years. It also deployed fighters to Syria in 2011 and fought ISIS inside Iraq after their 2014 capture of Mosul. The KH and AAH, and their more than twenty thousand fighters, along with Badr, became key components of the PMF and the SLA.

Other major Iraqi components of the SLA include the Harakat Hezbollah al-Nujaba, which was founded in 2013 under the command of the Quds Force to fight in Syria, and later joined the PMF, fielding some ten thousand fighters to simultaneously counter Daesh and pro-Assad campaigns in the two countries. Kata'ib al-Imam Ali (KIA) is another example of a well-trained, well-supplied PMF group operating under the command of the Quds Force. It was founded in 2014 to check Daesh's advance in Iraq. Many other smaller Iraqi groups have also been organized by the Quds Force to conduct specialized operations. Among them was Saraya al-Khorasani, which was formed in 2015 and saw combat in Iraq, including battles near Samarra, Baghdad, and Kirkuk. The group also deployed fighters to Syria during the battle of Aleppo.

The KH and AAH, like their Hezbollah brethren, assist the Quds Force in recruiting and training Shia militants in Iraq, Syria, Lebanon, and Iran. In 2015, the Bahrain Interior Ministry accused the KH of training the Shia militant group Saraya al-Ashtar in their camps in Iraq and helping them smuggle explosives across the border into Bahrain.[15]

In 2016, the Iraqi parliament incorporated the PMF into the country's armed forces. The move recognized the fact that the PMF had evolved into an enduring Iraqi institution, which is among the most significant Quds Force accomplishments since Hezbollah established controlling influence in Lebanon.

Like Hezbollah, the PMF has evolved into a hybrid organization with political and military wings, controlling the country's security institutions and having a significant presence in the parliament and the executive branch.[16] Abu-Mahdi al-Muhandis, the principal Iran-backed man in Baghdad, and Hadi al-Amiri, the other Iran man, have directed the PMF's operations and are among the most influential figures in post-Saddam Iraq.

Fatemiyoun and Zaynabiyoun

In addition to Iraqi and Lebanese fighters, the SLA also incorporates Afghan and Pakistani Shia militants in its ranks. They form the Fatemiyoun and Zaynabiyoun divisions of the SLA, respectively, and both saw heavy combat in Syria. The Afghan fighters in particular have been groomed by the Quds Force for a long-term support role.

The Iranians have used financial aid and offers of Iranian residency to recruit Afghan Shias from the predominantly Hazara refugee community inside Iran.[17] Each fighter deployed to Syria, for example, is paid a salary of $300–$500 a month and is promised permanent Iranian residency for themselves and their immediate families as well as payment to their family if they're killed or severely injured in action.

At the height of their involvement in the Syrian civil war, the 2015–2016 Battle of Aleppo, the Afghan division had nearly ten thousand Shia fighters. The Pakistani division represented an estimated two thousand Shia militants. Some of those fighters were deployed on multiple occasions to battlefronts. In post–civil-war Syria, many of the Fatemiyoun and some Zaynabiyoun fighters are expected to be deployed to the Syria-Iraq border region to keep the land corridor linking Iraq and Syria open, fulfilling a major Quds Force strategy in the two countries. Those fighters will be based in military camps and forward bases controlled by the Quds Force in Syria.

Some of the Afghan fighters and most of the Pakistani fighters have been sent back to Iran and Pakistan, respectively, as the fighting in most of Syria loses its intensity. The Quds Force can redeploy these well-trained and battle-tested militants for future missions in Afghanistan and Pakistan and to intervene in the conflicts in the region.

The Houthis

The Zaydi-Shia Houthi militants operate in a country separated from Iran by the Persian Gulf, unlike the Shia militants in Lebanon, Syria, Iraq, and western Afghanistan whose enclaves have been linked by land bridges to Iran. This situation has created major logistical challenges for the Quds Force. Its lack of naval power meant it could not force its way into Yemen's seaports to deliver arms and personnel to the Houthis after the Saudi and Emirati forces blockaded the country's seaports in 2015. Its air campaign also faced a similar fate when the Yemeni airspace and airports were closed to its aircraft by the Saudi-Emirati coalition. The only routes that remained were traditional smuggling routes using dhows or a hybrid route to ship or fly arms and personnel into Oman for overland transfer into Yemen. But the dhows could not carry large caches of arms, and the overland route through Oman faced opposition in regions not controlled by the Houthis. The Quds Force's successes in Iraq and Syria, and its setbacks in Yemen show its limits in operating in territories where it does not enjoy the support of the central government and where land and air bridges cannot be built without being challenged by regional powers.

The tyranny of distance, lack of dependable air and land bridges, and hostile environment created by the regional powers meant the Quds Force could not deploy large numbers of Shia militias in support of the Houthi operations, and arms transfers to the Houthis were challenged. The Iranians, however, established working relations with the Houthis after the victory of the Islamic Revolution in 1979. The senior people in the Houthi movement, including its current leader, visited Iran and stayed in the country for over a year soon after the establishment of the Islamic Republic. Iran has trained and armed Houthis since then. When Sanaa fell to the Houthis in 2014, and until the 2015 blockade, the Quds Force undertook a massive air and sea lift to deliver advanced weaponry, including cruise and ballistic missiles, as well as unmanned explosive boats, to Houthi rebels. These weapons have been used by the Houthis against U.S., Saudi, and Emirati ships and in attacks against Saudi targets inside the kingdom, including the international airport and the royal palace in Riyadh in 2017.[18]

The challenges faced by the Quds Force in Yemen have affected its command-and-control structure, limiting its role in the tactical-level Houthi decision-making process. Continued senior-level contacts between Quds Force general officers and Houthi leaders, however, have ensured that the overall targeting strategy and the way of war are jointly coordinated and adhered to.

These shortcomings notwithstanding, the Quds Force regards the Zaydi-Shia Houthis as the main element of its SLA in the Arabian Peninsula. To have a well-armed, battle-tested, militant Shia force in the Saudi and Emirati backyards, and to have a degree of control over the all-important Bab al-Mandeb Strait, a pathway for international trade and a major chokepoint for oil transport along Iran's own Hormuz Strait, are two major factors in the Iranian calculus for regional hegemony.

SHIA OPPOSITION PARTIES IN THE REGION

In addition to its main core, the SLA, the Quds Force also supports a variety of Shia opposition parties across the region. In Bahrain, where the Shias constitute the majority of the population in a country ruled by Sunni royalty, the Quds Force sponsors militant Shia groups who have attacked government targets with arms and explosives transferred to the country by Quds Force operatives and affiliates, including Iraqi Shia militia groups. The Bahraini security forces have in recent years intercepted major shipments of arms and explosives, including a 2013 interception of a maritime shipment containing Iranian-made IEDs and grenades.[19]

The Quds Force also openly supports leading Bahraini Shia clerics in their opposition to Bahrain's king Hamad bin Isa Al Khalifa. In 2016, General Soleimani threated to annihilate the Bahraini regime if the government imprisoned Ayatollah Sheikh Ahmed Qassim, the leading Shia cleric and a political opposition figure.[20]

For the Quds Force, the eastern provinces of Saudi Arabia, especially Qatif province with its significant Shia population, form a target-rich environment. Hezbollah's affiliate, Hezbollah al-Hejaz (Saudi Hezbollah), was involved in terrorist attacks on Saudi soil with the goal of destabilizing the kingdom. In 1996, it targeted Khobar Towers, killing nineteen U.S. servicemen. The FBI investigation showed that the group detonated a 25,000-pound TNT bomb under "direct orders from senior Iranian government leaders."[21] The blast destroyed Building 131, home to U.S. Air Force personnel, and grievously wounded hundreds of additional U.S. servicemen. The FBI also revealed that the bombers were trained in Lebanon's Beqaa Valley, received their passports at the Iranian embassy in Damascus, and were paid $250,000 in cash for the operation by IRGC general Ahmad Sharifi. The Khobar bombing mastermind and the leader of Hezbollah al-Hejaz, Ahmed al-Mughassil, was arrested in Beirut in 2015 and was extradited to Saudi Arabia.[22] Mughassil's arrest was a significant blow to the Quds Force's efforts to expand the SLA network inside Saudi Arabia. In 2016, Saudi authorities executed Sheikh Nimr al-Nimr, a Qatif-based Shia cleric, on terrorism charges.[23] Sheikh Nimr reportedly had ties to Hezbollah al-Hejaz.

The recruiting of Shia militants in the near abroad has also extended to neighboring Azerbaijan, which boasts a majority Shia population. In 2012, Azerbaijani authorities detained twenty-two Shia Azeris and charged them with plotting terror attacks against U.S. and Israeli targets in the country.[24] The authorities said the detainees were working under orders from Iran. In 2017, Azerbaijani authorities arrested eighteen men, charging them with plotting to overthrow the government, saying the suspects' political movement was suborned by Iran.[25]

OUTREACH TO SUNNI MILITANTS

The founders of the Islamic Revolution believed their movement could spread across the region because their call—to push the U.S. and the West out of the Middle East and annihilate the Israeli government—resonated beyond sectarian divides. Soon after the victory of the revolution in Iran, Ayatollah Khomeini realized that the Sunni masses were not eager or ready to line up under a Shia imam. So the movement increasingly took on a sectarian Shia character. But the early revolutionary zeal lived on. In order to reach their anti-West, anti-Israel goals, the revolutionary organs of the country, led by the IRGC and the Quds Force, pushed for close working relations with Sunni militant groups active in the region. Hamas, Palestinian Islamic Jihad (PIJ), al-Qaeda, and the Taliban were seen as fellow revolutionaries whose efforts were against common enemies, particularly the U.S. and Israel.

Hamas, like the Islamic Republic, regards resistance against Israel as a core belief that motivates its base. The Quds Force has supplied arms to Hamas since the 1990s, including rockets used to hit Israel.[26] The bulk of the budget of the military wing of Hamas is reportedly provided by the Iranians.[27]

APPENDIX: IRAQI SHIA GROUPS

Whereas the Lebanese and Yemeni components of the SLA consist of a single group, Hezbollah and the Houthis, respectively, the Shia movement in Iraq has produced dozens of militant groups. Few among them are considered major fighting organizations, and they are comprised generally of groups that were affiliated with the IRGC and the Quds Force in the Iran-Iraq War of the 1980s, or the Iraq War of 2003–2011, such as Badr, the KH, and the AAH, or with Muqtada al-Sadr, like the Peace Companies. A number of these groups were also formed in reaction to the Islamic State's attack on Iraq, some after the anti-Daesh fatwa of Iraqi Shia spiritual leader Ayatollah Ali Sistani. Some of the groups were organized through splits within older and larger organizations. Some were created by the Quds Force to perform specialized tasks.

The following alphabetical list contains the names of the Iraqi Shia militia groups that have been active in Iraq and the region.[28] Most operate under the umbrella coverage of the PMF.

Abu al-Fadl al-Abbas Forces
Ansar Allah al-Awfiya
Asa'ib Ahl al-Haq
Badr Organization
Faylaq al-Karar Dar' al-Iraq
Faylaq Al-Wa'd al-Sadiq
Harakat al-Abdal
Harakat al-Nujaba
Harakat al-Shaheed al-Awal
Hezbollah al-Abrar
Hezbollah al-Ghalibun
Hezbollah al-Tha'irun
Hezbollah al-Mujahideen fi al-Iraq
Imam Ali Division
Jaysh al-Mukhtar
Kata'ib A'imat al-Baqi
Kata'ib Ahrar al-Iraq
Kata'ib al-Ahad al-Sadiq al-Jadid
Kata'ib al-Aqila Zainab
Kata'ib al-Fatah al-Mubin
Kata'ib al-Ghadab
Kata'ib al-Iman Ali
Kata'ib al-Imam Musa bin Ja'afaar
Kata'ib al-Imam al-Hussein
Kata'ib al-Jaysh al-Fatemi
Kata'ib al-Muqawama al-Islamiya fi al-Iraq
Kata'ib al-Qiyam al-Husseini
Kata'ib al-Shaheed Zayd al-Tha'ir
Kata'ib al-Tayyar al-Risali
Kata'ib al-Zahra
Kata'ib Ansar al-Hijja
Kata'ib Ansar al-Madhhab
Kata'ib Ansar al-Wilaya
Kata'ib Ansar Allah
Kata'ib Ansar al-Hijah
Kata'ib Assad Allah al-Ghalib
Kata'ib Dir' al-Wilaya
Kata'ib Hezbollah
Kata'ib Jund Allah al-Ghalibun

Kata'ib Rayat al-Huda
Kata'ib Rouh Allah
Kata'ib Sayyid al-Shuhada
Kata'ib Thawrat al-Abbas
Kata'ib Zaynab al-Kubra
Liwa al-Imam al-Hussein
Liwa al-Karama
Liwa al-Mu'ammal
Liwa al-Muntazar
Liwa al-Qa'im
Liwa al-Sadiqeen
Liwa al-Shabab al-Risali
Liwa al-Shahada
Liwa Ali al-Akbar
Liwa Ansar al-Marja'iyya
Liwa Assad Allah al-Ghalib
Liwa Dhu al-Fiqar
Liwa Fatyan Bani Hashim
Liwa Youm al-Qaim
Manzamat Ansar Allah
Martyr Sadr Forces
Mujahideen Army
Mujahideen of Iraq Brigade
Quwat al-Kadhimain al-Qitaliya
Quwat Zaynab al-Kubra
Saraya ad-Difa al-Shabi
Saraya al-Ashura
Saraya al-Imam
Saraya al-Jihad
Saraya al-Khorasani
Saraya al-Salam
Saraya al-Zahra
Saraya Ansar al-Aqeedah
Saraya Aqa'idiyoun

Chapter Three

The Years of Revolution and War

The revolutionary fervor in Iran reached its peak on 1 February 1979 when Ayatollah Ruhollah Khomeini returned to Iran after spending more than fourteen years in exile and told millions of his supporters that an Islamic state should replace a monarchy marred by corruption and dependence on foreign powers.[1] The shah had already left Iran, and on 11 February a popular uprising caused the collapse of his security forces. The Islamic Revolution had triumphed, not just in Iran but also for the whole region, as Khomeini reminded everyone.

During a speech in Tehran three days into the revolution, he called the members of the security forces who had left their posts and joined the uprising the "guardians of the revolution and the fighting sons of Islam."[2] The stage was set for the establishment of the IRGC, as guardian of the revolution, and the Quds Force, as the fighting sons of (Shia) Islam in the region.

The IRGC, aka the Revolutionary Guards, was set up in the early days of the revolution, bringing together various militant groups and individuals who supported Khomeini and his movement. The movement's doctrine incorporated two complementary and at times competing ideological beliefs: an Islamist tendency, manifested in Khomeini's *velayat-e faghih*, "Guardianship of the Jurist," which envisioned the establishment of an Islamic state led by the senior members of the Shia clerical establishment; and an Islamic interpretation of left-wing and anti-imperialist tendencies, which manifested itself in anti-U.S., anti-West, and anti-Israel beliefs. The IRGC was created to be the guardian of this new order. The extraterritorial activities of the IRGC, which was later organized under the Quds Force, sought to counter U.S. and Western presence and influence in the region, upend the established pro-Western political order in the Muslim World, and liberate Jerusalem (Quds).

Some of the movement activists in the newly established Islamic Republic had long-standing ties to revolutionaries and Islamist activists across the Middle East and championed their cause. Mostafa Chamran, the first deputy prime minister of the revolutionary government and later its minister of defense, was trained in Fatah's military camps and followed Fatah's leader, Yasser Arafat (Abu Ammar), to Beirut in the early 1970s. It was Arafat, and Fatah's military chief Abu Jihad, who introduced Chamran to the militant Shia cleric Musa Sadr. Chamran soon became Sadr's senior aide, and together they formed the Amal Movement as the voice of the Shia block in Lebanon.[3] Chamran, who had trained in irregular warfare with the Palestinians, in turn set up training camps for Amal members and other Shia militants coming from across the Middle East. The new political order in Iran raised Chamran's hopes and those of his comrades for a new beginning in the Muslim world. They were ready for a protracted struggle to defend Islam, upend the pro-Western political order in the region, and end the U.S. presence and influence.

In the first year of the revolution, the IRGC's extraterritorial branch, the precursor to the Quds Force, created one of the earliest renditions of a foreign legion of Shia militias to spread the movement in the region. According to a published intelligence assessment, by February 1980, only a year into the revolution and prior to the start of the Iran-Iraq War, the IRGC was providing training and arms to about one thousand Iraqi Shia militants in camps inside Iran.[4]

The early ambitions went well beyond Iraq. In the first indications of the new regime's vision to build a land corridor to Syria and Lebanon, Khomeini singled out the importance of Syria as a bridge for empowering the Shias of southern Lebanon.[5] Chamran, acting as a senior adviser to Khomeini, advocated strategic alliance with the Syrian regime to strengthen their foothold in southern Lebanon, calling the place "the holiest Shia outpost in the world."[6] These sentiments displayed the revolutionary leaders' early resolve to turn southern Lebanon into the western flank of a Shia nation in the Middle East.

SADDAM'S INTERVENTION

The September 1980 military invasion of Iran by Saddam Hussein's Iraq upended Khomeini's plans to parlay the momentum gained from the victorious Islamic Revolution to spread his movement across the region in short order. Saddam, fearful of the effect of Khomeini's ideology on his country's Shias (who formed the majority of Iraq's population), hoped to strike a fatal blow to the newly established Islamic state on his borders. But the invasion united all Iranians in defense of their homeland, and the Islamists and revolutionaries joined and led the fight against Saddam. The expansion of the revolution had to wait.

Chamran and his revolutionary comrades left their senior posts to form a vanguard brigade of volunteers to fight the Iraqi army and to show a new way of war combining revolutionary zeal and unconventional tactics. The unit soon became known to the Iranians and the Iraqis alike for its success in irregular warfare. Chamran was killed in action near Susangerd eight months into the war, in June 1981. But the way of war he had already unleashed would become the hallmark of the future Quds Force. Among the defenders of Susangerd at the time was an IRGC unit from Kerman, in southern Iran, whose young commander had gained a reputation for bravery. His name was Qasem Soleimani, and he would be the future commander of the Quds Force.

In May 1982, the Iranian city of Khoramshahr, which had been occupied by the Iraqis at the start of the war, was liberated. By the end of that year, the Iraqis had withdrawn all their forces from Iran and called for peace talks. For the Iranians, Saddam's withdrawal not only manifested a historic victory but also the end of the defense-of-the-homeland phase of the war. The movement activists, those who saw the spread of the revolution across the region as their main mission, and especially in Shia-dominated enclaves and outposts, could now focus on their ambitions.

SHIA IRAQ

Ayatollah Khomeini's victory in Iran brought senior Iraqi Shia clerics under Saddam's suspicion. Ayatollah Muhammad Baqui Sadr was assassinated in Baghdad in April 1980, and when war with Iran broke out, another senior cleric, Ayatollah Mohammad Baqir Hakim, fled to Iran to avoid assassination. Khomeini and the IRGC saw in Hakim a capable leader who could organize an Islamist movement directed at Saddam. In 1982, Hakim founded SCIRI. The organization, with IRGC guidance, established an armed wing, the Badr Brigade. Brigade members were recruited from Iraqi Shia dissidents living in Iran and Shia defectors from the Iraqi army.[7] In an apparent violation of the Geneva Convention on the rules of armed conflict, Iraqi Shia POWs were also recruited to join the Badr Brigade to fight against their own army.[8] The IRGC provided training, arms, and funding to the group, establishing it as a fully functional militia. When the Badr Brigade was deployed to the front, it set a precedent for the Quds Force's future way of war: using foreign Shia militias as its infantry force in regional conflicts.

The war ended in 1988, but the Badr Brigade stayed active, continuing its anti-regime activities in southern Iraq from its bases on the Iranian side of the border. It conducted forays into Iraq to attack Baath Party officials.[9] Although the brigade's efforts to ignite an Islamist movement inside Iraq to overthrow Saddam did not succeed, their unquestionable loyalty to Khomeini as their *velayat-e faghih*; their training and long years of combat experience as a militia unit engaged in unconventional warfare; their acceptance of the IRGC, and later the Quds Force, as their mother organization; and their dedication to the Shia cause made them a model proxy force for the IRGC–Quds Force. When the U.S. invaded Iraq in 2003, Badr fighters were among the first Iraqi refugees to enter Iraq in the chaotic days that followed the overthrow of the Saddam regime. Years later, they would become part of the Quds Force–controlled PMF, a predominantly Shia militia force and arguably the most powerful political-military organization in Iraq.

The IRGC also had other Iraqi militants under its command during the war years. The Iraqi Shias at the time were split into the followers of Ayatollah Muhammad Baqir al-Hakim, the founder of SCIRI and its Badr Brigade, and those who followed Ayatollah Baqir al-Sadr, a leading Shia theologian who supported the Dawa Party, an early Islamist organization founded in Iraq in the late 1950s. A number of Iraqi Shia dissidents affiliated with Dawa lived in Iran during the war,[10] among them Abu Mahdi al-Muhandis, who headed the party's armed wing, as well as political figures including Ibrahim Jafari and Nouri al-Maliki, future prime ministers of Iraq. Dawa's military wing was incorporated into the IRGC as a second Iraqi arm of its extraterritorial branch. Similar to the Badr Brigade members, the Dawa fighters received their funding, training, and arms from the IRGC. In 1983, Muhandis and his team landed in Kuwait and orchestrated bombing attacks against the U.S. and French embassies and Kuwaiti installations to punish their hostility toward the Islamic Republic. Muhandis was sentenced to death in absentia by a Kuwaiti court for his role. The Kuwait bombings carried out by the Dawa military wing, along with the bombings of the U.S. Marine barracks in Beirut carried out months earlier by Hezbollah, were the first coordinated large-scale attacks by the IRGC's foreign Shia militias against U.S. and allied targets.

By late 1982, the Iran-Iraq War had entered a new phase. The Iraqis had withdrawn from the Iranian territories and proposed peace talks. Khomeini and the Islamists, including and especially the revolutionaries, did not want peace. By taking the war into Iraq they hoped to ignite an uprising inside the country against Saddam that would lead to the eventual collapse of the regime. That did not happen. The Iranian armed forces—the IRGC and Artesh, the regular military—were seen not as liberators, but aggressors. The war dragged on for another six years, with hundreds of thousands killed and injured, before Khomeini accepted peace reluctantly, famously comparing it to drinking from a poisoned chalice.[11] He died less than a year later. But even with the fighting raging during those eight long years of war, the IRGC extraterritorial branch did not deviate from its main mission of spreading the movement across the region. Southern Lebanon was its prime target.

THE LEBANESE CONNECTION

While the war with Iraq was raging, the IRGC did not lose sight of turning southern Lebanon into a base for the Islamic Revolution. The large Shia community in Lebanon concentrated in the south, southern Beirut, and the Beqaa Valley was woefully underrepresented in the country's political system. In the early 1970s, the Amal Movement was founded to organize the Shias and act as their voice. When the Islamic Revolution triumphed in Iran, no less under a Shia cleric, the Lebanese Shias found new hope for gaining respect and power in their own country. The IRGC, from its early days, believed that Lebanon was fertile ground for spreading Khomeini's movement and acting as a launch pad to unite the Shias in the Arab world.

The Amal Movement was the IRGC's natural ally. One of its own, Mustafa Chamran, was a founding father of the organization and had served as the chairman of the organization's executive committee. But the Lebanese political landscape was difficult to navigate. The country was in the midst of a civil war; Musa Sadr had disappeared; Chamran was in Iran fighting the Iraqis; and the Amal Movement was fracturing from within. The internal struggles were political as well as ideological. The Syrian role in Lebanon was a matter of political contention within the organization.

Hafez Assad's Syria had intervened militarily in Lebanon on the side of the hard-right Christian Phalanges and against Arafat and the Palestinian-led coalition. Hussein el-Husseini, the Amal leader who had replaced Mousa Sadr after his disappearance, opposed Assad's growing meddling within his organization, pushing it to take sides against Arafat's Fatah. Husseini was eventually pushed out, and the leader of the pro-Syria faction, Nabih Berri, took the helm of Amal. The IRGC agents on the ground in Beirut did not want to offend Assad. Their long-term plans for the Levant required an alliance with Assad, who was after all an Alawi Shia. For the time being, they accepted Berri's leadership and tried to work with him even though they were probably aware of the widespread discontent among the rank and file for the new leadership's pro-Assad and anti-Palestinian policies.

There was also an ongoing ideological struggle within Amal. Musa Sadr viewed the Shia community in Lebanon as an integral part of the country's history and political system and wanted to work within that system to raise the power and influence of the local Shia community. Chamran saw the Shia community in Lebanon as part of a larger Shia community in the Middle East that could be organized as a force to drive out the U.S. and Israeli presence and influence in the region. After the victory of the Islamic Revolution in Iran, the differences within the organization took on a new and practical meaning. Iran's revolution gave them a clear choice: whether all Shias, including those in Lebanon, should accept Khomeini as their *velayat-e faghih*, religious and political leader, or whether they should remain a community within their respective nation states and follow their own local leaders. This was a question that would haunt the Shia activists across the region for years to come. Notwithstanding organizational incoherence on these major issues, the IRGC liaison officers in Beirut continued their training of Amal members to form an active militia force for future operations.

In July 1981, the first president of the Islamic Republic, Abolhassan Banisadr, along with Mujahedeen-e Khalq leader Masoud Rajavi, fled Iran after falling out with Khomeini and landed in Paris. Khomeini was angry at the French government's acceptance of Banisadr and Rajavi. In September, Louis Delamare, the French ambassador in Beirut, was assassinated in the city. A published intelligence assessment links the attack to the Amal Movement, making it the first known operation conducted by an IRGC–led Shia militia group outside the Iran-Iraq battlespace. [12]

In August 1982, Arafat was forced to leave Lebanon after the Israeli invasion and Syrian opposition to Fatah's presence in the country. A month later, the Phalanges, Assad's partners in the civil war, massacred hundreds of Palestinian refugees in the Sabra neighborhood of Beirut and the adjacent Shatila refugee camp. Berri's continued support of Syria in the face of the Israeli invasion, Arafat's expulsion, and the Sabra/Shatila massacre caused a break in relations between Arafat's Fatah and Berri's Amal, and the more militant Amal members began to look for a way out. The IRGC and the Iranian veterans of Chamran's training camps in Lebanon, militants like Jalaleddin Farsi, [13] who had replaced Chamran as the main liaison with the Lebanese Shia militants, also needed a radical partner to spread Shia militancy, setting the stage for a split within Amal and the creation of Hezbollah.

HEZBOLLAH IS BORN

With the victory of the Islamic Revolution in Iran, Chamran went home, becoming deputy prime minister in the interim revolutionary government and later the Islamic Republic's defense minister. The torch of organizing a militant Shia militia in Lebanon was passed to a core group of Iranian revolutionaries residing in Beirut, notably Jalaleddin Farsi, Chamran's lieutenant, and Mohammad Saleh Hosseini, a former aide to Sadr.

Back in Tehran, senior officials of the revolutionary government, some of whom had spent the formative years of their careers struggling for militant Shia causes in Lebanon—people like Chamran; Ali Akbar Mohtashemi, who would become the Islamic Republic's ambassador in Damascus; and Mohammad Montazeri, the son of the then–heir apparent to Khomeini—supported deployment of IRGC officers and personnel to Lebanon to create a militant Shia organization. The IRGC's operations chief at the time, Abbas

Zamani, better known by his nom de guerre Abu Sharif, was tasked to act as the IRGC liaison with Lebanese Shia militants.

In the summer of 1982, the IRGC dispatched a large contingent of its officers and personnel to Beqaa Valley, Lebanon's Shia-land, under the command of Mohsen Rafiqhdoost.[14] By November, Rafiqhdoost had left Lebanon to become Minister of the IRGC and was replaced by his senior aide, a young IRGC officer named Hossein Dehghan, who later rose to the rank of an IRGC *sardar*, or general officer, and who served as Iran's minister of defense. Dehghan was assisted by another IRGC rising star, Ali Reza Asgari, who would become the IRGC commander in Lebanon in 1984 but would defect to the West in 2007. With the IRGC's presence in the country, the stage was set to fund, arm, train, and lead the activities of a militant Shia organization in Lebanon.

By 1982, the differences between the more militant Islamist members of the Amal Movement and Berri had deepened. The IRGC encouraged the militants, probably a third of the organization, to break from Amal. Hussein Musavi, who was the main IRGC operative within Amal, led the rebellion. The militants split from the organization and formed Islamic Amal, the core of the future Hezbollah. Among the members making up Islamic Amal were reportedly a number of Iranian military officers serving with UNIFIL, the UN peacekeeping body in Lebanon, during the last days of the shah, who had sided with Khomeini and joined Amal's ranks.[15]

In the first days after the victory of the Islamic Revolution in Iran, Yasser Arafat, the leader of Fatah and the PLO, flew to Tehran to congratulate Khomeini.[16] Among Arafat's seventeen-person delegation that landed in Tehran was a young Fatah militant named Imad Mughniyah. The young Shia revolutionary was deeply committed to the Palestinian cause and was close to Fatah's military chief Abu Jihad, also known as Khalil al-Wazir. Abu Sharif, the IRGC operations chief, must have been impressed with the young man: two years later he sent Mughniyah, who was temporarily residing in Iran and had become close to the IRGC, back to Beirut to help organize the new militant Shia militia group.[17]

Mughniyah played a key role in convincing the Shia Lebanese members of Fatah who had strong Islamist tendencies to switch their loyalty from Arafat and the Fatah to Khomeini and the IRGC. The group split from Fatah and joined fellow Islamists who had formed Islamic Amal earlier that year to create a unified militant Shia militia group under the command of the IRGC. Individual Lebanese Shia militants, some even with past affiliations with the Left, also were recruited. By year's end, the IRGC operatives facilitated the transfer of the members of the new organization to an IRGC camp in the Beqaa Valley, under Dehghan's command, for military training and ideological indoctrination. Although the new organization did not formally announce its formation under the name *Hezbollah* until 1985, it had become a reality established by the IRGC from former Amal and Fatah Islamist militants and other Shia revolutionaries.

In the 1985 public announcement of its formation, Hezbollah announced its adherence to the *velayat-e faghih* doctrine, which meant acceptance of Khomeini as their supreme leader, and establishment of an Islamic state in the region. In its "Open Letter Addressed by Hezbollah to the Downtrodden in Lebanon and the World," Hezbollah emphasized the leadership role of Iran and put forward its organization vision:[18] "We, the sons of Hezbollah's nation, whose vanguard God has given victory in Iran and which has established the nucleus of the world's central Islamic state, abide by the orders of a single wise and just command currently embodied in the supreme Ayatollah Ruhollah al-Musavi al-Khomeini."

Notwithstanding who the Hezbollah secretary general was at any time, the IRGC's chief operative within the organization was Imad Mughniyah, a position he enjoyed until his assassination in 2008. To the Iranians, he was the real Hezbollah chief. Ironically, before joining Hezbollah he was not part of Amal or Islamic Amal but had spent his formative years as a militant with secular Fatah. A number of other Fatah members and some secular Shias who joined ranks with the Islamist movement also played important roles in the early days of Hezbollah.

Soon the trio of Dehghan, Mohtashemi—the Iranian ambassador to Damascus—and Mughniyah emerged as the guiding force behind Hezbollah's paramilitary operations. When Dehghan and Mohtashemi returned to Iran, other IRGC officers took their place. But the constant presence and the institutional memory of Hezbollah's military leadership was Mughniyah, whom the Iranian called by his nom de guerre, Haj Rezvan. Soon after its founding, Hezbollah succeeded in pulling off large-scale terrorist bombing attacks against the U.S. and Western personnel and interests as well as kidnappings and assassinations.

The IRGC had found its base in the promised land that was Lebanon, and Hezbollah was on its way to become the jewel of the IRGC's Shia militia army.

EARLY DAYS OF TERROR

The Quds Force and its predecessor, the IRGC's extraterritorial division, used the Shia militia organizations to conduct a number of terrorist attacks on foreign soil outside the war zones. The targets included American, Western, and Israeli personnel and interests as well as Iranian dissidents abroad.

The 1981 assassination of the French ambassador in Beirut by Amal operatives, as discussed above, is believed to be the first assassination of a Western official by an IRGC-led foreign Shia militia group.

In 1982, Hezbollah began a decade-long campaign of hostage-taking in Lebanon. The victims, mostly Americans and Western Europeans, were abducted by Hezbollah operatives between 1982 and 1992. Hezbollah mostly used the name *Islamic Jihad* to take responsibility for the kidnappings.[19]

There were 104 kidnapping cases reported during the period. Hezbollah's first hostage was David Dodge, president of the American University of Beirut, who was kidnapped in July 1982. He was first kept in the Beqaa Valley, then sent to Iran in 1983. Dodge spent three months in Tehran's notorious Evin Prison before being released, reportedly through Syrian intervention.[20] At least eight of the hostages were killed while in captivity, including William Buckley, a former CIA station chief in Beirut.[21] Imad Mughniyah, or Haj Rezvan, who oversaw Hezbollah's hostage-taking operations, was assassinated by the CIA outside Damascus in 2008.[22]

In 1983, there was a spate of bombing attacks against U.S. and Western interests and personnel organized by Hezbollah operating teams, under Mughniyah's command and under the name *Islamic Jihad*. In April of that year, they targeted the U.S. Embassy in Beirut, killing sixty-three people, including seventeen Americans.[23] The bombing was the first by newly formed Hezbollah, which became one of the first Islamist groups to use suicide bombing as an organizational tactic. Months later, in October 1983, Hezbollah conducted two suicide truck bombings of the U.S. Marine and French military barracks at Beirut International Airport. The attacks killed 241 U.S. Marines and 58 French soldiers. The Americans and the French had been part of the peacekeeping mission of a multinational force in Lebanon.[24]

In December 1983, Iraqi Dawa Party operatives, under the command of the IRGC, carried out a series of bombings in Kuwait City against U.S., French, and Kuwaiti targets, including the U.S. and French embassies, petrochemical plants, and Kuwait International Airport. Abu Mahdi al-Muhandis, then the leader of the IRGC-led Dawa military wing, directed the attacks. He was later convicted and sentenced to death by a Kuwaiti court.[25] Muhandis is currently operations chiefs for Iraq's PMF, the umbrella group for mostly Shia Iraqi militia groups that operate under the command of the Quds Force.

Islamic Jihad also took responsibility in 1985 for a suicide car attack against the emir of Kuwait, who narrowly escaped assassination.[26]

During the period, the IRGC's operatives began an assassination campaign against Iranian dissidents abroad, killing at least three between 1979 and 1984, including Shahriar Shafiq, the shah's nephew, in December 1979 in Paris; Ali Akbar Tabatabaei, president of the Freedom Foundation of Iran, in Bethesda, Maryland, in July 1980; and General Gholam Ali Oveisi, chief of the general staff of the Imperial Iranian Armed Forces, in February 1984 in Paris. Assassinations of Iranian dissidents continued under the Quds Force, with at least fifteen killings in the past three decades.

THE QUDS FORCE AS AN INDEPENDENT FORCE

The IRGC was founded in May 1979, three months after the victory of the Islamic Revolution. Ayatollah Khomeini in his directive establishing the IRGC called it a force to protect the revolution against internal and external threats. The newly formed organization soon created an intelligence component for covert operations abroad. One of the unit's first known projects was recruiting and supporting Hazaras, Afghanistan's predominantly Shia ethnic group, in opposition to the pro-Soviet Democratic Republic of Afghanistan. Many Hazara militants spent their formative years in Iran undergoing military and ideological training, forming various resistance groups, and going back to Hazarajat to fight the Soviets.[27] Three decades later, young Hazaras, some descendants of the veterans of the anti-Soviet campaign, some living as refugees in Iran, would make up the bulk of the Quds Force–led Shia militias fighting in Syria to save Assad.

In the 1980s, during the Iran-Iraq War, the intelligence unit became a full-fledged department within the IRGC, known as Department 900, which later morphed into the Special External Operations Department. During this period, the IRGC's expansion abroad was centered on establishing Hezbollah, Iraqi Shia militias, and unified Hazara militant groups. The war with Iraq ended in 1988, and in the postwar reorganization of the IRGC, extraterritorial operations and the associated components—recruiting, training, intelligence, and logistics related to operations abroad—became parts of an independent branch, known as the Quds Force. It inherited command over Hezbollah, Iraqi militias, and Hazara militant groups.

In its first decade, the revolutionary IRGC did not have any military rankings for its commanders and officers. Everyone wore non-camouflage green operational uniforms with no ranks, only an IRGC insignia, signifying the group's egalitarian culture. The commanders and officers who were captured by the Iraqis, also, were not treated based on their rank, as they would have been if they were so commissioned. In the postwar reorganization, IRGC commanders became commissioned as a brigadier general or brigadier general 2. The future Quds Force commanders Vahidi and Soleimani were commissioned as brigadiers. IRGC general officers also kept their honorific title *Sardar*, as in Sardar Brigadier General Qasem Soleimani. As the IRGC grew in personnel, it promoted some of its brigadiers, including Soleimani, to the rank of major general. If the officers had performed their haj duty, the annual pilgrimage to Mecca, they could also be called, affectionately, by their first name with the honorific preface *Haj*, as in *Haj Qasem* for Soleimani.

In the postwar era, the Quds Force was organized under the command of Brigadier General Ahmad Vahidi, who would serve as the inaugural commander from 1988 until 1998. He would later become defense minister in the Ahmadinejad administration.

Afghanistan

Vahidi's command coincided with the Soviet withdrawal from Afghanistan, the collapse of its socialist government, and the start of civil war in that country. Vahidi supported the unity of Hazara groups and the formation of Hezb-e Wahdat under the leadership of Abdul Ali Mazari, a figure closely linked in the past to the IRGC. Vahidi was also a supporter of the Farsi-speaking Tajiks of Panjshir as well as their legendary leader Ahmad Shah Massoud and his military commander Mohammad Fahim, the future vice president of Afghanistan, during that tumultuous period in Afghan history. Many future senior officers of the Quds Force spent their formative years advising and arranging for arms transfer to their favorite Mujahedeen factions during the Afghan civil war.

Iraq

In Iraq, under the direct leadership of the newly independent Quds Force, the Badr fighters led thousands of Iraqi army defectors in the 1991 uprising in Basra and Karbala, the Shia commercial and religious centers in Iraq, respectively.[28] Although the uprising spread in the country, from the south to the Kurdish region, it did not prompt a revolution and overthrow the regime, and the Badr fighters returned to Iran after the uprising was crushed. In 1996, in one of the earliest uses of Shia militias as its ground force, a Quds Force–led task force, which included some five thousand Iraqi defectors organized under the Badr banner and supported by IRGC's artillery and armor units, was inserted in the battles of Erbil and Sulaymaniyah on the side of the Patriotic Union of Kurdistan (PUK) led by Jalal Talabani against Masoud Barzani's Kurdish Democratic Party (KDP) during fierce Kurdish factional fighting in Iraqi Kurdistan.[29] Talabani lost Erbil, but with the help from the Quds Force–led Shia militias was able to occupy Sulaymaniyah.

Former Yugoslavia

The Vahidi era also coincided with the Yugoslav wars. The Quds Force actively supported the Bosnian (predominantly Sunni) Muslims during the war. It supplied significant amounts of weapons, ammunition, and military equipment to the Muslims during the Bosnian war of 1992–1995. The Quds Force also deployed a large contingent of senior officers and Hezbollah advisers to Bosnia to train, advise, and assist Alija Izetbegovic's Muslim forces on the frontlines.[30]

Yemen

After the victory of the Islamic Revolution in 1979, a number of Yemeni Zaydi-Shias visited Iran. Among them was Hussein al-Houthi, a leader of the Zaydi sect, who visited Iran in the early 1980s along with his brother Abdul-Malik al-Houthi and their father, Badreddin al-Houthi, the spiritual leader of the group.[31] They attended ideological and security training in Qom, Iran's center of Shia scholarship. Their stay in Iran, especially in Qom, "shaped the revolutionary outlook,"[32] and they brought home a militant interpretation of Shia Islam. The IRGC kept close ties with the Houthi leaders throughout the 1980s and 1990s. In 1997, the Quds Force urged Hussein al-Houthi to leave the Haq party and form his own group, which would be later named the Ansarallah, using Hezbollah as its model.[33] Within seven years of the founding of their new movement, the Houthis rose up in rebellion against the Yemeni central government. Hussein al-Houthi was killed in the fighting and replaced by his brother Abdul-Malik, who would prepare the Houthis to eventually take over the country's capital, Sanaa. Throughout that period, Abdul-Malik could count on the Quds Force for training, arms, and financial aid.

Terrorism

During General Vahidi's era, the Quds Force continued its suicide bombing and assassination campaigns. In July 1994, a suicide bomber exploded at the Jewish Mutual Association (AMIA) community center in Buenos Aires, Argentina, killing eighty-five people and wounding three hundred. The Argentine judiciary later issued international arrest warrants for General Vahidi, the Quds Force commander at the time, and other Iranian and Hezbollah suspects in connection with the bombing.[34]

In June 1996, Hezbollah in the Hijaz, or the Saudi Hezbollah, detonated a truck bomb adjacent to a building in the Khobar Towers housing complex in the city of Khobar, Saudi Arabia. The eight-story structure housed members of the U.S. Air Force. Nineteen U.S. servicemen and a Saudi national were killed in the bombing, with hundreds of personnel of many nationalities wounded. In 2006, a U.S. court found Hezbollah and the Islamic Republic guilty of orchestrating the attack.[35] The mastermind of the attack, Ahmed al-Mughassil, was arrested in 2015 by Saudi authorities. He was believed to have been living in Beirut since the attack.[36]

The assassination campaign on foreign soil continued. The killings were either directed by Quds Force operatives, or the Quds Force assisted other Iranian intelligence agencies' operatives with the logistics. The attacks in this period began in Vienna in July 1989, with the assassination of the chairman of the Democratic Party of Iranian Kurdistan, Abdul Rahman Ghassemlou, and his aide. In April 1990, Kezem Rajavi, from Mujahedeen-e Khalq's National Council of Resistance of Iran and former ambassador to European offices of the UN, was assassinated in Switzerland. Shapour Bakhtiar, the shah's last prime minister and the head of the National Resistance Movement of Iran, was assassinated in France in August 1991. Fereydoun Farrokhzad, an Iranian artist and dissident and brother of legendary Iranian poet Forough Farrokhzad, was assassinated in Bonn, Germany, in August 1992. In September 1992, Sadegh Sharafkandi, chairman of the Democratic Party of Iranian Kurdistan, along with two other Kurdish leaders and Nouri Dehkordi, another Iranian political activist serving as adviser and translator to the Kurdish delegation, was assassinated at the Mykonos Restaurant in Berlin. In total, twelve people were assassinated on foreign soil during this period.[37]

SOLEIMANI TAKES COMMAND

General Qasem Soleimani, or Haj Qasem, took command of the Quds Force in 1998. He began by reorganizing the force, establishing a clearer organizational vision and mission. He inherited Shia militant groups in Lebanon, Iraq, Afghanistan, and Yemen. The militia groups were acting as separate organizations in their own country or sub-region. Soleimani's vision was to create a unified SLA under Quds Force command.

The Iran-Iraq War had showed Soleimani that Sunni Arab countries stood behind Iraq. Iran's only Arab ally was Shia Alawi–led Syria. The SLA was to safeguard the interest of all Shias in the region. In fact, the war changed one of the underlying tenets of the Islamic Revolution, uniting all Muslims against foreign powers and their local allies. Khomeini's movement became the unifier of all the Shias, and the Quds Force–led SLA would become the guardian of the Shia nation.

Soleimani significantly increased the funding, arming, and training of the Shia militias, opening additional training camps in Iran. The militias would act as the Quds Force's infantry in future conflicts. To him, reliance on a militia force was not out of weakness but was Iran's preferred way of war in future conflicts, shaped by their irregular characteristics. His unconventional ground force, the militias, would be augmented by conventional elements from the IRGC and Artesh. Their armor, artillery, missile, UAV, and special forces units would be deployed on temporary duty to individual battlefields if necessary and when possible. The IRGC missile force could provide defensive cover for the Quds Force to deter enemy retaliation against its operations. The missing link was tactical air cover, something Soleimani was determined to acquire, or if that was not possible then to borrow, in future conflicts. Soleimani created the doctrine of expeditionary warfare for the Islamic Republic.

Within a decade, Soleimani had mobilized an army of 200,000 armed Shia youths hailing from many countries of the Middle East to serve as the principal ground force of the Quds Force in regional conflicts: the SLA.

"The upside of the recent conflicts in the region is the mobilization of 200,000 armed Shia youths in the countries of the region," said General Mohammad Ali Jafari, commander of the IRGC, in an address commemorating the death of a Quds Force officer in Syria.[38]

THE PRE-9/11 PERIOD

The al-Qaeda attacks on New York and Washington in September 2001 were the start of a series of earth-shattering events that shook the Middle East. What followed included the U.S. invasion of Afghanistan and Iraq, the Arab Spring, the civil war in Syria, the rise of ISIS (Daesh), and the war in Yemen. Soleimani's doctrine would be put into practice and tested during those conflicts. But in the three-year period before 9/11, Soleimani's first years in command, the Quds Force faced different challenges.

In August 1998, the Taliban seized the Iranian consulate in Mazar-e-Sharif in Afghanistan, killing ten Iranian diplomats and an Iranian journalist working for the Islamic Republic News Agency. Earlier, the Taliban had captured the city to retaliate for the killing of thousands of their prisoners by Hazara and Uzbek forces, which were generally considered to have close links to the Iranians. Iran deployed some seventy thousand troops along the Afghan border. Mediation by the UN defused the situation, but the Quds Force began reactivating Afghan militia brigades that had seen action in the anti-Soviet war and the civil war in Afghanistan, as well as the Iran-Iraq War, in anticipation of a coming conflict with the Taliban. Three years later, Soleimani deployed Afghan Shia militias under the command of his senior officers to Herat to fight the Taliban and help liberate the city, ironically in coordination with U.S. forces, which invaded Afghanistan in retaliation for 9/11.

To the west of Iran, Soleimani continued to strengthen the Badr militias, still residing in Iran, to conduct clandestine operations in southern Iraq and the Basra area against Saddam's regime. One of the Quds Force's key Iraqi operatives, Mustafa Sheibani, was later said to have established Badr beyond southern Iraq and in Baghdad itself. Badr was also instructed by the Quds Force to take up operations against Mujahideen-e Khalq (MEK), which had its headquarters in southern Iraq.

This is the period during which Sheibani and his group began transferring EFPs made in Iran into Iraq. The weapons were designed to penetrate armor in the fight against Saddam. A few years later, when Saddam was overthrown by the Americans, the EFPs became the Shia militia's weapon of choice against U.S. forces in Iraq.

The post-9/11 period would open the gateway for the Quds Force to enter Iraq and Afghanistan.

Chapter Four

Gateways to Afghanistan and Iraq

On the morning of 11 September 2001, a Tuesday, al-Qaeda attacked the United States. The Islamist terror group hijacked four passenger planes, crashed two into the World Trade Center's twin 110-story towers in New York City, crashed the third plane into the Pentagon, and were flying the fourth plane toward Washington, DC, when it crashed into a field in Pennsylvania after its passengers overpowered the hijackers. The terrorist attacks killed 2,996 people, injured over 6,000 others, and caused over $10 billion in infrastructure and property damage.[1] They were the deadliest attacks on American soil in U.S. history. Osama bin Laden, the leader of al-Qaeda, later claimed responsibility for the attack.[2]

On October 7, less than a month after 9/11, the United States, with help from the United Kingdom and the Northern Alliance, an umbrella opposition group operating in northern Afghanistan and backed by Iran, launched Operation Enduring Freedom to dismantle al-Qaeda and to overthrow the Taliban. Preliminary preparation for a possible direct military operation in Afghanistan against al-Qaeda had been under way before 9/11; the administration of President George W. Bush had planned to present an ultimatum to the Taliban to hand over bin Laden and senior al-Qaeda operatives. They were suspected of masterminding the 1998 U.S. Embassy bombings in Dar es Salaam, Tanzania, and Nairobi, Kenya, and had sought a safe haven in the Taliban's Afghanistan, where they had fled from Sudan two years earlier. The 9/11 attacks made the military operation inevitable.

Days after the 9/11 attacks, the CIA deployed a high-powered team of specialists, including Farsi-speaking operations officers, a Special Activities Division officer, and an expert on paramilitary operations, along with additional specialists, to act as liaison with the Northern Alliance. The Northern Alliance was also reeling from a loss at the hands of al-Qaeda, having lost its legendary commander Ahmad Shah Massoud in a Taliban-orchestrated suicide bombing attack just two days prior to 9/11. By 26 September, the CIA's Northern Afghanistan Liaison Team reached Northern Alliance headquarters in the Panjshir Valley, north of Kabul.[3] Present alongside the Northern Alliance commanders were senior Quds Force and IRGC special operations officers who would play a key role in planning and coordinating joint anti-Taliban operations. The Quds Force, the Iranians, and the Shia Hazara militia group under their command would join the U.S.-led coalition and Northern Alliance forces in pushing back the Taliban in the northern and western regions of Afghanistan.

THE BATTLE OF HERAT

The Herat operations began in October with U.S. airstrikes hitting targets in and around Herat, including tanks, communications facilities, and underground networks in order to soften the Taliban defenses. The Quds Force and IRGC Special Operations Forces, along with senior Hazara Shia militia commanders, clandestinely entered Herat on 12 November 2001. Their mission was to start an insurrection in the city against the Taliban. A U.S. Special Operations detachment had been inserted by helicopter near Herat the day before. As the public uprising against the Taliban started, the Hazara militias, Northern Alliance fighters, and the U.S. detachment, all under the command of Ismail Khan (popularly known as the "Lion of Herat" for his groundbreaking role in the anti-Soviet campaign to liberate Afghanistan) entered the city, with the Taliban forces fleeing to the mountains along the Iranian border, leaving behind several abandoned tanks. Among the Taliban prisoners taken on that day were Chechen and Arab volunteers.

The planning and coordination efforts had started in mid-September in several locations, including Tehran, between the Iranians, the Americans, and the Northern Alliance leaders. Herat was liberated with effectively no bloodshed. The Hazara brigade would later form the nucleus of the Afghan Fatemiyoun and become a major component of the SLA.

THE QUDS FORCE IN THE POST-9/11 PERIOD

Within a month of the attacks on 11 September, Operation Enduring Freedom had overthrown the Taliban's Islamic Emirate of Afghanistan, and al-Qaeda's leaders had fled the country. By December 2011, a new interim government was in place, chosen by an international conference convened in Bonn, Germany. Among the Iranian delegation in Bonn were senior Quds Force officers. Hamid Karzai was a compromise candidate acceptable to the Western as well as the Iranian delegations. Soleimani, just three years into his command, saw a golden opportunity for the Quds Force to expand its presence beyond the Hazara community and transform western Afghanistan—Herat, Farah, and Nimruz provinces—with its significant Shia population into an arc of influence linked to Iran by a 582-mile border. The Karzai government would reopen the gates of Afghanistan to the Iranians.

Iran's honeymoon with the United States did not last long. On 29 January 2002, in his State of the Union address to Congress, President George W. Bush announced that Iran, alongside Syria and North Korea, was a member of the "Axis of Evil." The news sent a shockwave through the Pasteur Institute, the seat of *velayat* (the Office of the Supreme Leader), in Tehran. Khamenei had repeatedly warned the Iranians could not trust the Americans. Bush's speech fulfilled that warning. A year later, when the United States invaded Iraq and overthrew Saddam Hussein, another shockwave hit Pasteur, this time with the fear that Iran would be the next target.

To avoid such an outcome, the Khatami government in Tehran agreed to begin negotiations with major European powers, with America's blessing, on his country's nuclear program and other outstanding issues, even being willing to cut a so-called grand bargain to normalize relations with the U.S.

Soleimani and his Quds Force had a different take on the turn of events. The U.S. invasion had opened Iraq's gateway for them and their Iraqi comrades-in-arms, the Badr and Dawa militants who had been trained, armed, and funded by the Quds Force and had eight years of combat experience fighting their own country's army alongside the IRGC. Within a span of eighteen months, Iran's enemies on its eastern and western borders, the Taliban and Saddam's regime, had been overthrown by the Americans, and the Quds Force put in motion a long-term strategy to bring Iraq and Afghanistan under its arc of influence, aided by the Shia Iraqi militias and Shia Afghan militants.

IRAQ'S WIDE-OPEN GATES

The day 20 March 2003 was the eve of the Iranian New Year. Offices were closing and people were preparing for the two-week celebration of Norouz. At the Quds Force headquarters, the new year was full of promise. The United States had invaded Iraq earlier that day and Saddam's regime was on the verge of collapse, something the Iranians had not come close to achieving in eight years of bloody war. The Quds Force moved fast. The Badr Organization and Dawa Party leaders and fighters who were stationed in Iran were deployed into the chaos that followed the invasion of Iraq.[4] Those Iraqi militants were veterans of the Iran-Iraq War, having fought alongside the IRGC against their own country's military.[5] General Soleimani, the commander, and some of his senior officers also crossed the border into post-

Saddam Iraq. The Iraqi returnees soon launched a campaign to recruit Shia youths, organize them as a resistance force against the U.S. occupation, send them across the border to receive military training inside Iran, and then return to Iraq to fight the Americans.

In 2004, a year after the invasion, the Iraqi Shia militants staged an uprising against the American military presence in the country and unleashed deadly attacks on U.S. and coalition forces in the form of roadside bombs. Their now-infamous IEDs would eventually claim the lives of around two hundred U.S. servicemen.[6]

Badr Organization

By 2004, the Quds Force had developed a two-pronged strategy in Iraq. Militia IEDs and other attacks on U.S. and coalition forces were to raise the cost of occupation in order to push them out of the country while control of Iraqi security institutions would ensure long-term influence in the country. The Badr Organization was Soleimani's preferred vehicle for achieving the latter goal, while more militant splinter groups were to take on the Americans.

Soleimani used the post-invasion chaos to have loyal militiamen infiltrate the Iraqi army, security, and intelligence institutions. The U.S.-controlled Coalition Provisional Authority (CPA) Order Number 2 made the job that much easier. In May 2003, the American administrators of post-Saddam Iraq disbanded the country's military and security apparatus and began to organize new structures instead. The Badr Organization wasted no time pouring "volunteers" into the new army and security organizations, which were badly in need of new hires. It also used the CPA's de-Ba'athification policy to infiltrate other government agencies that had been decimated after expulsion of anyone suspected of being a Ba'ath Party sympathizer.

The IRGC had stood up, funded, armed, and trained the Badr Corps (later the Badr Organization) inside Iran since 1982. The Badr Corps had fought for eight years alongside the IRGC against the Iraqi army; it had led uprisings in Basra and Karbala; and it had been used as the Quds Force's ground force during the Iranian intervention in factional wars in Iraqi Kurdistan. The Badr Organization had proven its loyalty to Iran, its belief in *velayat-e faghih*, and its acceptance of the IRGC–Quds Force supremacy. Between 2003 and 2005, sixteen thousand Badr-led militants and new recruits were incorporated into Iraqi security forces (ISF) units at the Ministry of Defense and Ministry of Interior like the new Iraqi army and the federal police force.[7] The Badr cadres, with years of combat experience, occupied senior positions within the Iraqi security establishment even though Badr leaders continued to directly report to General Soleimani.

A decade later, after ISIS had taken control of parts of Iraq, the Quds Force used its operatives at senior positions of the ISF to establish a militia organization, the PMF, mainly composed of Shia militia groups under its direct control, not only to fight ISIS but to formally incorporate it into the ISF, giving the Iranians an unprecedented degree of control over the ISF.

The Mahdi Army

Shia cleric Muqtada al-Sadr founded the Mahdi Army—Jaysh al-Mahdi— upon his return from a trip to Iran in June 2003, three months after the U.S. invasion of Iraq. Muqtada was building a militia force for the Sadrist Movement, a religious populist movement founded by his father, Grand Ayatollah Mohammad Sadiq al-Sadr, and his father-in-law, Grand Ayatollah Mohammad Baqir al-Sadr. Following his return from Iran, Muqtada al-Sadr called upon Sadrists to join his Mahdi Army, which they did in droves. The goal was to raise the cost of the occupation of Iraq and eventually expel the American and coalition forces from Iraq.

Muqtada had accepted the Iranians' help, but his relations with the Quds Force were problematic. His father was an ardent Shia Arab activist, and his teachings on the importance of Arabism and tribalism to the identity of Iraqi Shias ran counter to Khomeini's pan-Shia, anti-nationalist ideology. Muqtada also did not believe in Khomeini's *velayat-e faghih* over all Shias, including Iraqi Shias. But his strong passion against the occupying powers, especially the Americans, prompted him to accept assistance from the Iranians, who for the same reasons were ready to help a movement whose ideology ran counter to theirs.

In April 2004, members of the Mahdi Army carried out simultaneous attacks in Baghdad's Sadr City, Najaf, Karbala, and Kufa, targeting U.S. and coalition forces.[8] Soleimani provided arms and advisers to the Mahdi Army. While the uprising was crushed by the end of April, Muqtada and his movement had proven to be significant forces in the anti-occupation movement.[9] The Mahdi Army also positioned itself as a distinctly Iraqi phenomenon, founded independently of the Quds Force and pursuing its own goals.[10]

The Quds Force had kept direct contact with more radical elements within Muqtada's organization, likely without his knowledge. It became obvious to Soleimani that on religious matters, Sadrists overwhelmingly were followers of Grand Ayatollah Ali Sistani, the most senior and influential Shia cleric in the country, a reality in stark contrast to be the adherents of Iran-based *velayat-e faghih*, or accepting the leadership of Iran's supreme leader on all matters religious, political, and ideological. Muqtada had by then become a powerful political leader in his own right, as evident in an August 2005 march involving an estimated 100,000 of his supporters in the streets of Baghdad. Soleimani had lost all hope that he could now accept Khamenei's supreme authority as the religious leaders of Hezbollah had done two decades earlier.

In 2004, pro-Iran fighters among the Sadrists, led by Qais Khazali, the principal Quds Force operative within the Mahdi Army, began acting independently of Muqtada. The Khazali brigade continued to fight U.S. troops into the summer of 2004 despite Muqtada's cease-fire orders. For the Quds Force, the way ahead became the model used by the IRGC two decades earlier. The establishment of Hezbollah became possible when IRGC operatives inside the Amal Movement and the Fatah organization in Lebanon staged a split within those organizations, encouraging the pro-Iran Shia militants to join a new paramilitary group, the Party of God, or Hezbollah. In early 2006, most of the fighters loyal to Khazali split from the Sadrists to join a new Shia militia group, the League of Righteous People, or Asaib Ahl al-Haq (AAH).

Asaib Ahl al-Haq

The Mahdi Army's principal Quds Force operative, Qais al-Khazali, led the split within the Sadrists, becoming the leader of the new militia group, the AAH.[11] He soon became known in occupied Iraq for managing arms smuggling operations from Iran, forming death squads during the 2006–2007 sectarian violence in the country, conducting assassinations and kidnappings, and attacking U.S. forces in Karbala in January 2007. The AAH eventually took credit for over six thousand attacks on U.S. and coalition forces in the five-year period between its formation in 2006 and the American troop withdrawal in 2011. The AAH became known as Iraq's largest "Special Group," a term used by the Americans to designate Quds Force–led Shia militia groups. At least two hundred U.S. servicemen were killed by the Shia militias, mainly in IED and EFP attacks. Khazali was captured by coalition forces in Basra in March 2007, along with a senior Hezbollah member who was acting as an adviser to the AAH. In response, the AAH kidnapped a British IT consultant, Peter Moore, at the Iraqi Finance ministry in May, and negotiated the release of their leader in exchange for Moore's freedom. Khazali was freed by the pro-Iran Maliki government in January 2010. Four members of Moore's security detail were also kidnapped with him but were later killed by the AAH. Their bodies were recovered in 2009.

The Iraqi government also allowed the return of senior Quds Force Iraqi operative Mustafa al-Sheibani, a former Badr commander, whose claim to fame was setting up the Sheibani Network, smuggling IEDs and EFPs from Iran into Iraq. Sheibani had fled to Iran during Saddam's era but returned to Iraq after Saddam's overthrow along with many IRGC–affiliated Iraqi Shia militants. In 2006, evading capture, he fled back to Iran after an arrest warrant was issued for him. Maliki overlooked those warrants and allowed Sheibani back into Iraq in December 2010. Sheibani promptly joined the AAH, which had been formed during his stay in Iran, and became one of the group's senior military leaders.

Among significant actions by the AAH were an attack in October 2006 on Camp Falcon, a U.S. military forward base outside Baghdad, and a January 2007 attack in Karbala where AAH fighters infiltrated the U.S. Army's headquarters, killing one soldier and abducting and later killing four more. The AAH also waged political campaigns. In 2012, the AAH famously distributed over twenty thousand posters of Iran's supreme leader, Ayatollah Khamenei, throughout Iraq, with their members forcing workers at different municipalities to display the posters or face retribution.

During its height of activities before the U.S. troop withdrawal, the AAH was estimated to have 1,000–3,000 fighters under its command in Iraq. The group members periodically were sent to Iran for advanced military training. The Quds Force also funded the group. The AAH smuggled arms and explosives into Iraq through the Quds Force–led Sheibani Network. During this period, the group was organized into five brigades, each with its area of responsibility: southern Iraq, west Baghdad, east Baghdad, central Iraq, and a Lebanon brigade that fought alongside Hezbollah in the Lebanon-Israel War in 2006. In January 2012, after the U.S. withdrawal, Khazali declared victory over the Americans. By then the Syrian civil war had begun and many AAH fighters were deployed to Syria by the Quds Force to save Assad.

Kataib Hezbollah (KH)

Abu Mahdi al-Muhandis was chief of the military wing of the Dawa Party during his exile years in Iran in the 1980s. His claim to fame was his orchestration of bombings in 1983 of the U.S. and French embassies in Kuwait City, for which he was convicted in absentia in Kuwaiti courts and sentenced to death. He fled to Iran after the bombings. The IRGC commanders, impressed with his Kuwaiti operations, made him commander of the Badr Corps. Badr was the most militant organization of the Shia Iraqi exiles in Iran and the military wing of SCIRI, which was itself started by the IRGC. When General Soleimani crossed the border into Iraq after the overthrow of Saddam Hussein in 2003, Muhandis was his most senior aide among the Badr and Dawa leaders who accompanied him. They wasted no time in organizing militant Shia youths to fight the Americans. In 2005, during the first post-Saddam elections, Muhandis was elected to the Iraqi parliament. In 2007, under Soleimani's guidance, he founded an elite Shia militia organization called Kata'ib Hezbollah (KH).[12] From its founding until the withdrawal of American forces from Iraq, the KH conducted the most lethal attacks against U.S. and coalition forces in Iraq.[13] After the U.S. troop surge in Iraq in 2007, the KH came under increasing pressure from the U.S. and coalition forces, and news of Muhandis's involvement in the Kuwaiti bombings two decades earlier came to light later that year after media reports. Muhandis had to flee to Iran once again. He would return to Iraq only after the U.S. troop withdrawal in 2011.

Muhandis's long affiliation with the Badr Organization, serving as its first commander during the exile years in Iran, continued during the occupation years in Iraq. His deputy commander at Badr, Hadi al-Amiri, replaced him as the organization's commander. Together, Muhandis and Amiri were Soleimani's top men in Iraq. Years later, when ISIS attacked Iraq, they formed Iraq's PMF, an umbrella group of mostly Shia militias, later making it part of the ISF, giving the group legitimacy and the Quds Force a leading role in the county's security establishment.

THE WAR YEARS: 2003–2011

What General Soleimani saw as a golden opportunity was the beginning of all-out irregular warfare against the foreign occupation of Iraq. In Soleimani's mind, the occupiers in the Middle East were the U.S. and Western forces. He did not consider the Quds Force or Iranian proxy groups occupying forces in Iraq, or in Syria, or elsewhere in the region since he believed forces affiliated with the Iran-based Islamic Revolution had historic legitimacy to defend Muslim lands against the West irrespective of national boundaries. Now after more than two decades of training Shia militia forces in the camps inside Iran, and after deploying these forces to battlefields during the war with Saddam and involving them in terror attacks across the Middle East, the IRGC and the Quds Force were ready to test their clout in an anti-U.S. campaign in Iraq.

In the months immediately after the 2003 invasion, the Iranian government had concerns about Bush's intentions toward Iran. It seemed as if the Islamic Republic was next on an invasion list that already included Afghanistan and Iraq. But the post-invasion chaos and lack of effective governance that prevailed in Iraq convinced them that the U.S. would not have the will or the force to invade Iran. For Soleimani, the time was ripe to hit the Americans hard, with the idea that the rising costs of the war would push them out of Iraq and the region once and for all. Although his rosy expectations were not realized, as the Americans kept their forces in the region even after withdrawing from Iraq in 2011 and returned to Iraq in 2014 to fight Daesh, his analysis that the U.S. had lost any appetite to fight Iran proved to be right.

Soleimani's two-pronged strategy of hitting the U.S. and coalition forces while also hollowing out Iraq's new security forces produced confusion, as probably intended, among U.S. officials. The Badr Organization planned to integrate its militias into the ISF, including the new army, the federal police force, and intelligence. Because of that it largely held its fire against the American forces who were setting up those new security institutions, prompting the Americans to consider Badr and its leader, Hadi al-Amiri, a more moderate force and potential ally, especially when other Shia militia groups began attacking U.S. forces. The fact that the Quds Force controlled not just the Special Groups but also the Badr Organization must have escaped the Americans. Amiri directly reported to Soleimani throughout the war. The information Amiri shared with his newfound friends, the Americans, or military strategy and tactics he discussed with them during the war, was cleared by the Quds Force and its commander.

Amiri's militias were not absent from the battlefields during the period. The effective cease-fire with the Americans allowed them to launch a bloody campaign against their Sunni rivals and Baathist supporters, especially in the security forces and intelligence establishment.[14] Revenge killings against Baathists became a major part of Badr's operations.[15]

The year 2006 became the bloodiest year of the war, when U.S. casualties caused by the Iranian-made IEDs spiked and the death toll of U.S. soldiers reached three thousand. The organization most responsible for the deadly IED and EFP campaign against the Americans was the AAH. It worked closely with the Sheibani Network and other former Badr commanders to smuggle the IEDs and EFPs from Iran into Iraq. By the time the Americans withdrew from Iraq, the AAH claimed credit for some six thousand attacks on U.S. and coalition forces, earning itself the American designation of Iraq's largest Special Group.

A year after the founding of the AAH, the Quds Forces stood up a niche Shia militant group, the KH, headed by its principal operative in Baghdad, Abu Mahdi al-Muhandis, to conduct the most lethal attacks against the U.S. and coalition forces as their most trusted Iraqi militia group. The group received state-of-the-art Iranian weaponry, including improvised IRAMs, to cause catastrophic damage and inflict mass casualties.

Between Badr, the AAH, and the KH, General Soleimani was exceptionally able to launch and sustain operations in Iraq, including eliminating the Baathists, attacking U.S. and coalition forces, and staffing the country's new security institutions with militias under his direct control.

In February 2007, President Bush publicly admonished the Quds Force for providing the sophisticated IEDs that had harmed U.S. troops in Iraq.[16] U.S. forces had already begun targeting selected Quds Force operations and commanders in Iraq. In December 2006, a U.S. Joint Special Operations Command (JSOC) task force found and detained Quds Force brigadier general Mohsen Shirazi and his chief of staff in the Baghdad compound of SCIRI leader Abdul Aziz al-Hakim. Under protest from the Iraqi government, JSOC released the Quds Force officers a week later. This was at a time when hundreds of U.S. troops were being killed by IEDs planted by Shia militia groups under the overall command of General Soleimani. The episode demonstrated the degree of control the Quds Force exerted over the Iraqi government.

Hakim was the brother of Shia leader Mohammad Baqir al-Hakim and had replaced him as leader of SCIRI when Mohammad Baqir was assassinated in Najaf in the early days of the U.S. invasion of Iraq. In December 2003, Abdul Aziz al-Hakim was appointed by the U.S.-controlled Coalition Provisional Authority to be president of the Governing Council of Iraq and became the top Iraqi executive of the country under U.S. occupation, replacing Saddam. His SCIRI took control of Iraq's Interior Ministry and its federal police force as well as units within the new Iraqi army, set up by the U.S. military. Even with his obvious and publicly known background as Iran's operative, Abdul Aziz was the U.S.'s top choice to head the first post-Saddam government. In early December 2006, Abdul Aziz al-Hakim was greeted by President Bush at the White House. It was after his return from Washington that JSOC operators found Quds Force General Shirazi at his compound in Baghdad.

On 11 January 2007, the JSOC's Delta operators arrested five Quds Force officers in an Iranian compound in Erbil, the capital of Iraqi Kurdistan. Nine days later, AAH fighters penetrated the U.S.–Iraqi Karbala Provisional Joint Coordination Center, using black SUVs and wearing U.S. uniforms to gain access to the compound. They killed five U.S. soldiers before escaping the scene.[17] The U.S. military in Iraq accused Iran and the Quds Force of orchestrating the attack in retaliation for the arrests. A U.S. military spokesman said the Quds Force knew of and helped plan the attack on the Karbala compound.[18]

In March 2007, the British military detained Qais Khazali, the AAH chief responsible for the Karbala killings of the five U.S. servicemen. In May of that year, AAH operatives kidnapped British contractor Peter Moore at the Iraqi Finance Ministry and asked for Khazali's freedom in return for Moore. The captors killed Moore's four bodyguards who had been kidnapped along with him. The British finally agreed to the exchange, and Khazali was let out of prison on 30 December 2009.[19]

THE SURGE

In January 2007, the White House announced the deployment of an additional twenty thousand soldiers to Iraq in what became known as "the surge" to fight the rising insurgency. In February, General David Petraeus became the commander of the U.S. and coalition forces in Iraq to implement the surge. The focus of the operation was countering Sunni militants and securing neighborhoods in major cities. But Petraeus knew he had an Iranian problem as well. A new task force, known as Task Force 17, was established by JSOC to counter Quds Force activities in Iraq. The task force succeeded in arresting a number of the militia. Each time an arrest was made, however, the news traveled to Prime Minister Nouri al-Maliki's office, and under protest from the Iraqi government the detainees were handed over to the Iraqis and then released within a day or two.[20] It soon became clear to Soleimani that there was little political will in Washington to confront Maliki for his close ties with the Iranians, and the Quds Force was convinced that it could continue its operations without much cost to its organization and its militia force.

Encouraged by the turn of events even under the surge, the KH launched an IRAM at a U.S. military base southeast of Baghdad in February 2008, killing one American civilian and wounding many others.[21]

After the KH attack, Soleimani sent a now-famous text message to Petraeus through Iraqi President Jalal Talabani: "Dear General Petraeus, you should know that I, Qasem Soleimani, control the policy for Iran with respect to Iraq, Lebanon, Gaza, and Afghanistan. And indeed, the (Iranian) ambassador in Baghdad is a Quds Force member. The individual who's going to replace him is a Quds Force member."[22]

The message sought to convey to the American commander that the Quds Force, rather than the Iranian Ministry of Foreign Affairs, determined Iranian policy in the region, and if Petraeus wanted to avoid further attacks on U.S. forces he needed to directly negotiate with Soleimani. Apparently the message did not have much impact on the Americans. Petraeus's forces launched a crackdown against the KH in summer 2008 in retaliation for the IRAM attack, arresting thirty of its members. The group's senior leaders relocated temporarily to their safe haven on the Iranian side of the border.

In July 2010, U.S. General Ray Odierno, who replaced Petraeus in September 2008 as the U.S. commander in Iraq, told reporters in Baghdad that the KH was behind the threats against U.S. bases in the country.[23]

In June 2011, during the American withdrawal from Iraq, three U.S. soldiers were killed in a rocket attack at a U.S. base near the Iranian border. U.S. military commanders in Baghdad and the Pentagon blamed the mounting death toll on the growing sophistication of weapons that the Quds Force–controlled Shia militias were using, including powerful rockets, armor-piercing grenades, and jam-resistant roadside bombs smuggled in from Iran. The chief spokesman for the U.S. military in Iraq said at the time that the Quds Force–led Shia militias were the primary threat to the Americans.[24] In the same month, the KH accepted responsibility for launching a rocket attack on a joint Iraqi-U.S. military base in eastern Baghdad, killing six U.S. servicemen.[25]

"[Shia militia group] leadership lives in Iran, they are directly trained by the Quds Force, and are supplied by them," said a U.S. military spokesman.[26]

HEZBOLLAH

During the Iran-Iraq War in the 1980s, Lebanese individuals had volunteered to fight on the side of Iran against Saddam's army. Hezbollah, in those formative years, was too focused on the Lebanese scene and its civil war to participate as a unit in the Iran-Iraq war. When the Americans invaded Iraq in 2003, the situation changed. Hezbollah had matured into a top fighting force in the region. The Quds Force used its advisers, who were Arabic speakers, to help train Iraqi Shia militia groups inside Iraq as well as in its military training camps in Lebanon. But Soleimani did not deploy any Hezbollah units in Iraq. Hezbollah's main focus, he believed, should continue to be Israel. The Israelis had ended their occupation of southern Lebanon in 2000, which had boosted the morale of Hezbollah and the Quds Force, as southern Lebanon finally belonged to them. Soleimani wanted Hezbollah and its leader, Hassan Nasrallah, to use southern Lebanese territory to launch continued attacks on Israel. At the same time, he wanted Hezbollah to fortify its defenses against possible Israeli counterattacks.

Between 2000 and 2006 when Israel launched its counterattack against Hezbollah, the Quds Force sent hundreds of engineers and materials to Lebanon to help Hezbollah construct heavily fortified bunkers in southern Lebanon, which proved priceless during the 2006 Israeli bombing of Hezbollah's positions.[27] Soleimani also increased the delivery of missiles and rockets to Hezbollah during the period, including advanced weaponry that they used repeatedly against targets inside Israel. Starting in 1995 and running up to the Israel-Hezbollah war in 2006, the Quds Force armed Hezbollah with thousands of missiles and rockets, including Oqab missiles, delivered in 2005; Arash, Nuri, and Hadid rockets; short- and medium-range pieces of artillery; and rocket transporters and launchers. The Quds Force also supplied Hezbollah with C-802 ASCM and trained its operators. Two of those missiles were used by Hezbollah in an attack on an Israeli frigate during the 2006 war. During the period, Hezbollah fighters went through intensive training by IRGC and Quds Force officers at camps in Lebanon and in Iran on the advanced weaponry supplied to them.[28] The arms and training received by Hezbollah and the fortification of their defensive positions helped them counter the Israelis during the 2006 war. Israel's apparent lack of preparedness for the war against a much-improved enemy made the outcome inevitable, and during the war and for the months following it the Quds Force resupplied Hezbollah with weaponry used in the war and helped repair damage to its military infrastructure. To this day, the Quds Force and its Shia militias point to 2006 as their shining moment against Israel.

Economically, Iran also provided a lifeline to Hezbollah. In a February 2007 interview, Nasrallah said that Iran was supplying his group with monetary aid in addition to weapons.[29] Nasrallah was preparing the public for a future announcement on the subject. In a speech broadcast by Hezbollah's TV station, Al-Manar, on 24 June 2016, he said, "We are open about the fact that Hezbollah's budget, its income, its expenses, everything it eats and drinks, its weapons and rockets, are from the Islamic Republic of Iran. . . . As long as Iran has the money, we have money. . . . Just as we receive the rockets that we use to threaten Israel, we are receiving money. No law will prevent us from receiving it."[30]

In using foreign proxies to achieve its anti-U.S., anti-West, and anti-Israel agenda, the Quds Force thrived in the chaos of Iraq and Lebanon, setting the stage for the creation of its SLA, which would dominate the upcoming civil wars in Syria, Iraq, and Yemen.

Chapter Five

Uprisings, Civil Wars, and Insurgencies

On 17 December 2010, Mohamed Bouazizi set himself on fire in Tunisia to defend his dignity after abuse by the authorities and by doing so ignited dormant anger across the Middle East against autocratic and corrupt rulers in what would come to be known as the "Arab Spring."

On 14 January 2011, the Tunisian president was forced from office after an intense campaign of civil resistance. The uprising spread to Egypt and Yemen later that month; to Libya and Bahrain in February; and to Syria in March, with sustained street demonstrations in many other Arab countries.[1] Regimes were toppled in Tunisia, Egypt, Yemen, and Libya. By 2014, the chaos-fed insurgencies had engulfed Iraq, Syria, and Yemen. Bouazizi's self-immolation had set the entire region on fire.

The Islamic Republic of Iran and its Quds Force followed the earth-shattering developments closely. The fall of unfriendly governments, particularly in Yemen, presented opportunities for the Iranians. But they saw the potential for an unmitigated disaster if the Shia-dominated governments in Syria and Iraq, countries that were essential parts of the Shia arc of influence in the region, were to collapse. The Arab Spring was an occasion for sense-making in Iran. Should the country stick to its long-standing military strategy of deterrence, or did the new developments in the region necessitate more aggressive policies, a new preemptive and offensive military strategy?

SYRIAN CIVIL WAR

By December 2011, Assad's situation looked bleak. Hezbollah's Nasrallah traveled to Iran for an urgent meeting with Supreme Leader Ayatollah Khamenei. He told the ayatollah that Assad's forces were losing the fight and his regime could be toppled.[2] The Iranians took the warning seriously. It was only two years before that the massive anti-government Green Movement inside Iran, the precursor of the Arab Spring, had to be brutally suppressed by the IRGC and its Basij forces to save the regime. The wounds of the Iranian people had barely healed, and leaders of the Green Movement remained under house arrest. It was very possible the Arab Spring would become a Persian phenomenon as well. The defeat of the Syrian army and the Assad regime would have also upended the Islamic Republic's strategy in the Levant and would have cut its link to Lebanon and rising Hezbollah. So for the security of Iran's allies, and for the security of the Iranian regime itself, the Quds Force saw its role in preserving the Syrian regime as absolutely imperative.

Prior to the start of the uprising in Syria, a number of Quds Force senior officers and hundreds of Quds Force and IRGC specialists had been stationed in Syria helping to train the army and managing supply routes of arms and money to Hezbollah.[3] In late March 2011, Quds Force general Soleimani rushed to Damascus for a meeting with President Bashar al-Assad. The uprising needed to be suppressed, he counseled Assad, and he offered the resources of the Quds Force, its Shia militia units, and the whole government of the Islamic Republic to contain and defeat the opposition. Assad's mood was noticeably lifted.[4] Close relations between Syria and the Islamic Republic predated the civil war. Syria was the only Arab country that sided with Iran during the eight-year Iran-Iraq War in the 1980s. The Assad government was dominated by the minority Alawis, recognized by the Islamic Republic as a branch of Shia Islam. A year prior to the outbreak of the Syrian uprising, Assad hosted Iranian president Mahmoud Ahmadinejad and Hezbollah leader Hassan Nasrallah in a high-profile gathering demonstrating the Iran-Syria-Lebanon Shia axis, bonded by "deep and brotherly ties."[5] The Iranians saw the uprising as a "mischievous act of the Americans and Zionists" and saw the need for a forceful suppression of the uprising.

Senior officers of the Quds Force, especially those with prior experience in the country, were deployed to Syria. Hundreds, and soon thousands, of Hezbollah fighters were deployed across Syria to act as the ground force for the Quds Force–led operations in the country. The IRGC's Basij Force personnel were sent to advise and assist Syrian anti-riot security forces in quashing street demonstrations. Quds Force–affiliated Iranian airliners began transferring weapons and equipment to the Syrian police and military. The IRGC provided UAVs for ISR missions. The IRGC's special forces were deployed to advise and assist their Syrian counterparts. Iran also provided Assad with sophisticated technology to monitor email, cell phones, and social media. Iran developed these capacities in the wake of the 2009 Green Movement, establishing a "cyber army" to track down opposition online.[6]

Soleimani wanted to defeat the opposition decisively in those very early stages. But the opposition had its vote and did not fold as soon as wished by the Iranians.

The uprising in Homs was of particular concern to Soleimani in the early days of the conflict. A spike in Quds Force–supported arms and materials for the Syrian government was observed in early 2012. The lethal assistance helped the Syrian army launch an unprecedented offensive to crush the opposition in Homs.[7] The opposition leaders, citing high-ranking defectors from the Syrian army, also confirmed the presence of hundreds of Quds Force and IRGC advisers, security officials, and intelligence operatives in the battlefields, along with a flow of Iranian weapons, surveillance equipment, and cash to the country.[8] By mid-2012, Iran had shipped hundreds of tons of military equipment, including guns, rockets, and shells, to Syria through an air bridge connecting Iranian airports to Damascus International.[9] In October 2012, the Syrian rebels displayed a captured Iranian drone.[10]

The opposition forces captured 48 Iranian operatives, among them 14 Quds Force officers, including a general officer and 6 colonels, in Damascus in August 2012.[11] In January 2013, at intense pressure from Soleimani, the Syrian government agreed to swap 2,130 opposition fighters inside its prisons for the 48 captured Iranians.[12] The episode exhibited the extent of the Iranian military involvement in Syria not only to foreign audiences but also to the Iranian public that had been kept largely uninformed of the Quds Force's operations in the country. As the war continued, Iranian media announcements, mainly in newspaper obituary sections, of memorial services for fallen Quds Force officers and other military personnel in Syria, offered a window into the expanding Iranian role in the conflict and the rising casualties, though exact counts remained a state secret.

The assistance from the Quds Force and its affiliated Shia militia groups, including Hezbollah and major Iraqi militant organizations, was not enough to prop up the Syrian forces and counter the opposition. By March 2015, four years after the conflict began, Assad's forces controlled roughly one-sixth of the Syrian territory.[13] In a July 2015 TV interview, President Assad blamed manpower shortage as the greatest challenge to his government's war efforts.[14] Soleimani was also worried by the low morale among the Syrian soldiers.[15] He was ready to boost the number of Shia militias as well as support elements from the IRGC, Basij, and the Artesh. But to launch a major offensive against a resilient opposition, he needed air support. The Iranian Air Force, with its aging fighter jets, could not launch combat operations that far from its borders. The Syrian air force was small and already overworked. He needed a major partner to prevent Assad from a major defeat.

On 24 July 2015, Quds Force commander General Qasem Soleimani flew to Moscow to meet with Russian president Vladimir Putin.[16] They planned a dramatic escalation of Russian and Iranian involvement in Syria to save Assad. Before he left the Kremlin, Soleimani committed to fully activating the Islamic Republic's expeditionary army in Syria. Putin would provide air and artillery firepower and special forces in support of Quds Force–led operations. For Soleimani, the big prize was Aleppo, Syria's largest city. He would launch a major offensive to encircle Aleppo and eventually recapture all parts of the city held by the opposition. The strategy aimed to secure the Shia Alawi–dominated region from the Mediterranean coast to the M5 Highway, linking Damascus to Homs and Hama, with Aleppo at its northern end. Controlling Aleppo would provide defensive buffer zones for the security of the Alawi land and the survival of Assad's regime.[17] In the period after regaining control of Aleppo, the Quds Force was to be the guarantor of the security of Alawistan or its independence if Syria fractured.

Soleimani returned to Tehran to plan the Battle of Aleppo, which would involve the Quds Force's biggest operation after five years of military involvement in Syria. Quds Force personnel, including a significant number of general officers, would assemble near Aleppo to lead the operation. Soleimani increased the Quds Force–led Shia militias deployed to Syria to a historic high, including brigades of the Foreign Legion. The Haydariyoun—comprised of the top-tier Iraqi Shia militia groups Kata'ib Hezbollah, Asa'ib Ahl al-Haq (the Badr Organization), Harakat al-Nujaba, and Kata'ib Sayyad al-Shuhada—contributed more than five thousand battle-tested fighters to the force over the course of the conflict.[18] In addition, Hezbollah deployed some eight thousand fighters to Syria,[19] with many participating in the Battle of Aleppo. Also participating were the Fatemiyoun and Zaynabiyoun brigades, the former comprised of nearly five thousand Shia Afghan militants, mostly recruited inside Iran from among the Afghan Hazara refugee community,[20] and the latter comprised of an estimated two thousand Pakistani militants. Soleimani also deployed a cadre of some two thousand IRGC and Basij personnel from among their elite divisions and brigades on temporary duty to Syria to join more than five hundred personnel already in the country in support of Quds Force operations.[21] The IRGC contingent included elements of artillery and armor units, and its temporary headquarters was set up near the battlefield. Elements of Artesh special forces were also deployed to Syria on temporary assignment to take part in the fighting. The airlifting of equipment and personnel to Syria began well in advance of the first Russian airstrikes in September 2015.

After more than a year of intense fighting, the last opposition strongholds in Aleppo fell on 26 December 2016. The Quds Force–led forces, under the direct command of General Soleimani, scored their biggest victory in more than five years of war. The defeat of the opposition in Aleppo became the turning point in the country's civil war in favor of the Assad regime. More than 250 Quds Force and IRGC servicemen were killed in action between 15

October 2015, when the ground offensive began, and 26 December 2016, when Quds Force–led forces occupied all of Aleppo. Among the Iranian casualties were ten Quds Force and IRGC general officers. The Quds Force–led Shia militias, including Hezbollah and the Iraqi, Afghan, and Pakistani fighters, also suffered high casualties in the Battle of Aleppo.

The Sunni Arab opposition defeat at Aleppo became the beginning of the end of their uprising against Assad. The pro-regime forces, assisted by the Quds Force–led Shia militias and Russian air support, turned their attention to territories held by ISIS in the east and the al-Qaeda Syrian affiliate, the al-Nusra Front, in Idlib. In parallel with their efforts, the Kurdish People's Protection Units (YPG)–led Syrian Democratic Forces (SDF), backed by a U.S.-led coalition, launched the biggest operations of the war against ISIS and excised them from their capital, Raqqa. Less than a year after the fall of Aleppo, Syria seemed to be fracturing into three autonomous zones: A strong Assad-led state, which would be a smaller version of the former Syrian state, ruling over most of its territories; an autonomous Kurdish state; and Arab Sunni–dominated zones in Idlib, the south, and ungoverned territories.

The post-Aleppo Syria presented strategic challenges for the Quds Force. Soleimani had to make a decision on the extent and the nature of the Iranian military presence in Syria. If defeating the opposition was his goal when he began deploying forces to the country at the start of the civil war, the victory in Aleppo pretty much achieved that purpose; logically he should have begun to disengage from active combat, pull out most of his forces, and leave behind advisers embedded with Syrian military units. But Soleimani had other plans in mind. He now wanted to parlay his victory over the opposition into a permanent base in Syria to counter the Israelis, the official raison d'être for the existence of the Quds Force.

The change in strategy, from countering Assad's opposition to countering Israel, was a doctrinal transformation. Iranian military strategy had for long been based on deterrence and a defensive posture, with a preference for fighting in a gray zone: using proxies, gaining influence through limited military operations, and avoiding direct conflict with powerful militaries. Countering Israel in Syria required a radically different approach. Proxies by themselves were not powerful enough to challenge Israel; engaging the Israeli forces at their northern front could easily spiral out of control; and the Quds Force required major reinforcement by the IRGC and Artesh to engage a powerful military in a direct military conflict. The doctrine of proxy war in a gray zone was not adequate for the new strategy.

The Quds Force's experience soon proved the point. In May 2018, the Quds Force fired a number of rockets at Israeli military installations in the Golan to retaliate for an earlier Israeli attack on one its facilities in Syria. Within hours, Israeli missiles hit all Quds Force installations in Syria, killing scores of Iranians and foreign Shia militants and destroying command-and-control centers, UAV bases, weapons depots, and military equipment. Soleimani could not retaliate; his forces in Syria that were good enough to defeat the Sunni opposition were no match for Israel. Iran was in need of a new strategy or a drawdown of its forces in Syria. The presence of Quds Force personnel and their Shia militias under the old arrangement only exposed then to further Israeli attacks. For Soleimani, this was the time to make sense of what he wanted to achieve in Syria and how to do it.

THE BATTLE FOR IRAQ

The 2003 U.S. invasion of Iraq and the fall of Saddam's government upended the Sunni-led political and security structures of Iraq. In the power vacuum that followed, the Quds Force deployed hundreds of officers to the country. Soleimani was one of the first to arrive. With him came the leaders of the Iraqi militant organizations who lived in Iran, many of whom had fought against the Iraqi army during the Iran-Iraq War in the 1980s alongside the IRGC. Soleimani saw a golden opportunity in the new Iraq to sponsor Shia militias in order to counter the growing influence of the United States as well as grow Iran's influence in the country. In 2004, the Shia militants staged an uprising against the American military presence in Iraq and unleashed a wave of deadly attacks on U.S. and coalition forces. By the time the Americans left Iraq in 2011, the Shia militia organizations, under Soleimani's command, had staged more than six thousand attacks on U.S.-led coalition forces in the country.

Iranian influence in Iraq reached a peak in 2012 and 2013. The Iranian-backed militias operated in parallel to the Iraqi Security Forces (ISF) while reporting directly to Soleimani. The Iranians succeeded in reinstating Iraqi prime minister Nouri al-Maliki even though his coalition lost the parliamentary elections to a moderate, non-sectarian block. Iranian operatives like Hadi al-Amiri, the chairman of the Badr Organization, which was set up by the IRGC in Iran in 1982, held key posts in the government. When the U.S. withdrew all its troops from Iraq at the end of 2011, the Iranians believed they had achieved all of their objectives. U.S. influence in the country was severely diminished. The Americans failed in their attempts to keep a residual military force in Iraq to train and advise the new ISF. Iran managed to keep the friendly government in Baghdad in power. The Quds Force organized, funded, and armed a number of Shia militias who acted as a parallel security institution to the Iraqi armed forces. In December 2013, two years after the U.S. withdrawal, Iraq looked increasingly like an Iranian satellite state, and Qasem Soleimani finally emerged from the shadows as the single most influential figure in Iraq.

ISIS, the successor to Al-Qaeda in Iraq, also came back home to Iraq in 2003 in the chaotic post-occupation days along with Soleimani and the Shia militants. Nearly destroyed by the time the Americans left the country at the end of 2011, ISIS received a new lease on life when the Syrian civil war broke out in the same year. The remnants of ISIS quickly set up shop in chaotic Syria and its ungoverned territories while maintaining a small presence inside Iraq. Within two years, the Arab Spring entered Iraq, with street demonstrations across the country, especially in Sunni-dominated Anbar province. Opportunistically riding the wave of anger and feeling of despair among Sunni communities for being left out and punished by the Shia-dominated Maliki government, ISIS fighters entered Fallujah. On 4 January 2014, Fallujah and parts of Ramadi fell to ISIS. The insurgents then began their lightning advance along the Euphrates in the Sunni heartland toward Baghdad.

For Soleimani, the real shock came later. On 9 June, Mosul fell to ISIS. In a colossal intelligence failure, the Quds Force and its allies, including Hezbollah, with all their influence and intelligence-gathering capabilities in both Iraq and Syria, failed to detect the movement of hundreds of ISIS insurgents crossing the border from Syria into Iraq and hundreds more fighters leaving the Fallujah area to join their comrades to march into Mosul, Iraq's second-largest city. After Mosul, ISIS began its thunderous advance along the Tigris on a northern front toward Baghdad. Tikrit fell on 11 June. By summer 2014, ISIS had captured large swaths of Iraqi territory. In August, its fighters overran Jalula, only nineteen miles from the Iranian border.

"[On 11 August 2014], the terrorist and takfiri [Muslim fanatics who accuse other Muslims of apostasy] forces are near our border," said a message from the general staff headquarters of the Iranian armed forces sent to subordinate units.[22]

In recalling those fateful August days, the commander of the Iranian army ground forces said, "Daesh had recruited local supporters and had planned a series of (suicide) bombings inside Iran as a prelude to Daesh forces reaching the borders."[23]

Artesh deployed five infantry brigades, artillery and armor elements, and special forces just across the border of Iraq to stop the ISIS advance into Iranian territory.[24] Simultaneously, the Quds Force surged hundreds of personnel and thousands of tons of weapons and equipment into Iraq to prevent the advance.

Iran was at war with ISIS. The insurgents were severely undermining Iranian and Shia interests in Iraq. Just prior to the ISIS advance, Iraq appeared to be a secure Iranian satellite state. In a short time, the country had been transformed into a battlefield, with Baghdad, the Shia south, and the Iranian border threatened.

After the situation at the border and around Baghdad had been stabilized, the Quds Force–led Shia militias moved to an offensive posture and conducted operations against ISIS positions in the east and central Iraq. By year's end, Amirili, Jurf al-Sakhr, Balad, Miqdadiyah, and Jalula had been liberated. By then, the presence of Quds Force personnel inside Iraq had grown significantly, as had the personnel of supporting elements of the IRGC, Artesh, and intelligence units. Iranian forces were based in Baghdad, Najaf, Karbala, the Samarra-Balad corridor, Camp Ashraf, Taji, and the border town of Khanaqin. The Iranians also operated out of the airports in Baghdad, Kirkuk, Sulaymaniyah, and Erbil. Soleimani was back in control.

Days after the fall of Mosul, Soleimani was in Baghdad to stand up a foreign legion of Shia militias to counter ISIS, the largest Shia army ever assembled in modern history. Shia militia groups sponsored by Soleimani during the U.S. occupation days formed the nucleus of a new umbrella group to act as the headquarters for an Iranian-led Shia militia effort against ISIS, groups like the Badr Organization, the AAH, and the KH. There were new militias forming as well, comprised of new Shia volunteers and recruits. Together they formed the PMF, a new Iraqi security institution under Iranian control. The PMF became the main ground force element of the war against ISIS.

The stage was set for Soleimani's way of war. His counterinsurgency model was built around the strength of the Quds Force–led Shia militias operating under the banner of the PMF. In the initial phrase, Soleimani decided on his next battle. In the preparation phase, senior Quds Force officers and Shia militia commanders planned their military operation well in advance, drafting battle plans, addressing personnel issues, and arranging logistics. Quds Force officers and militia commanders then congregated near the battlefield to oversee the operation. IRGC drones provided ISR support. Preparatory fire began the operation to soften ISIS positions. PMF-led ground forces, supported by ISF, advanced on one or more axis toward the target. The IRGC as well as Iraqi specialized elements like artillery and armor units were deployed. Artillery barrages hit the targets. Close air support was provided by the Iraqis and on one occasion at Jalula by the Iranian air force. In some battles, like the Battle of Tikrit in April 2015, U.S.-led coalition forces also provided air support and artillery fire power against ISIS targets in and around the battlefield. In some battles, Artesh provided special forces troops. Other Iranian personnel filled specialized combat roles, such as combat engineering. IRGC Aerospace Force could use short-range ballistic missiles (SRBMs; Zelzal variants), and medium-range ballistic missiles (MRBMs; Fateh-110 variants). The clearing operation, the last stage of the fight, involved PMF militias and ISF conducting post-operation clearing to remove pockets of ISIS resistance. Iranian and Iraqi artillery and armor units departed the battlefield. The Quds Force–led militias readied themselves for the next battle.

SECTARIAN AND ETHNIC FAULT LINES

The conflict in Iraq exposed sectarian fault lines. The rise of Iranian influence in Iraq, the Quds Force and its Shia militias, had turned the significant Sunni population of the country practically into second-class citizens. The newly formed PMF was controlled, managed, and mostly manned by Shia militia groups loyal to Iran, with a token representation of Sunni groups. The PMF's own record during clearing operations in cities with significant Sunni populations, in places like Jurf al-Sakhr which fell in the early days of war, pointed to attacks by the Shia militia on Sunni civilians, burning or occupying their homes, expelling them from the city, and preventing the return of those who had fled ISIS.[25] On the larger governance issues, PMF Iraqi commanders Abu Mahdi al-Muhandis and Hadi-al-Amiri showed little political will to advance national reconciliation with the Sunnis. This type of behavior confirmed and solidified preexisting notions among the Sunnis that the Iranians had transformed Baghdad and Shia southern Iraq into their zone of influence and that the Iraqi state was nothing but a vassal state of Iran. If these fault lines continue to exist or grow in the post-ISIS period, the prospect for rebuilding a unified Iraq becomes increasingly less likely.

The conflict also exposed ethnic fault lines. In 1916, Great Britain, France, and Russia redrew the map of the post-Ottoman Middle East, establishing the modern borders of Iraq and Syria among other deals that collectively became known as the Sykes-Picot Agreement, without giving the millions of Kurdish inhabitants of those lands a homeland of their own. In 2017, more than one hundred years after the date, the inhabitants of the Iraqi Kurdish region voted overwhelmingly for the independence of Kurdistan and its separation from Iraq in a referendum held in Kurdish-led regions.

Reports coming from Erbil in the days prior to the vote pointed to a critical issue: the Kurds were in reality voting to separate more from Iran than from Iraq. The Kurdish Regional Government (KRG) was particularly concerned by the growing influence of Iran and General Soleimani in the country. Soleimani and many Quds Force and IRGC general officers were veterans of a brutal suppression of Iranian Kurdish rebellion during the first years of the Islamic Revolution, and four decades later they were warning the Iraqi Kurds not to hold a referendum on independence. But the Kurds in Iran marched on the streets of the country's Kurdish-dominated cities in support of the referendum. The vote was the beginning of a years- or decades-long process for the Kurds—not just in Iraq but also in Syria, Turkey, and Iran— to reorganize their relationships with their respective capitals and among themselves. The Quds Force played a central role in preventing a Kurdish independence that was otherwise likely in both Iran and Iraq, and this will remain a major ethnic fault line in all four countries for years and decades to come.

POST-DAESH IRAQ

By 2017, all the major cities in Iraq that had been captured three years earlier by ISIS had been liberated. The Quds Force–led Shia militia forces played a major role in the liberation of Tikrit, Fallujah, Ramadi, and Mosul. Concurrent to its campaign against ISIS, the Quds Force also worked to secure permanent control over the Iraqi government's security institutions. In the early days of the war, Soleimani sponsored the creation of a new security institution parallel to the country's conventional military to act as an umbrella organization or headquarters of the predominantly Shia militia groups that would be effectively under Iranian control: the PMF. Abu Mahdi al-Muhandis, the Iraqi intermediary to the Quds Force, and Badr chairman Hadi al-Amiri, who along with Muhandis served as an IRGC officer during the Iran-Iraq War, became the leaders of the PMF—Muhandis as the organization's operations commander and Amiri, the chairman of its largest component, as the nominal boss of the Shia militia groups. Amiri's Badr Organization also dominated Iraq's interior ministry and its federal police force. The trio of Soleimani, Amiri, and Muhandis became the face of Shia forces, with their photos and selfies on battlefields trending on social media.

The creation of the PMF was a paradigm shift in relations between Tehran and Baghdad. The Iranians now controlled a security institution in Iraq with a force of up to 100,000 Shia militia fighters that outranked the ISF in size by 2 to 1.

The defeat of Daesh and controlling the PMF were unqualified successes. But Soleimani probably overplayed his hand. While the Iraqi Shias accepted his leadership during the fighting, not all of them could accept Iranian dominance over Iraqi security institutions and their government. For most Shias, they were Iraqis first. Soleimani's total lack of attention to this reality proved to be nearly disastrous. In the 2018 Iraqi parliamentary elections, the first in post-Daesh Iraq, the Shias split into two camps, either approving or disapproving of the Iranian military's continued presence in Iraq in the post-Daesh period. Muqtada al-Sadr's list of candidates opposing Iran's presence received the greatest number of votes, followed by a list of PMF-supported candidates. This intra-Shia division, as manifested in the elections, could undo in time Iran's long-term strategy in Iraq. Soleimani and other senior leaders in Iran may be trying to make sense of the division and to seek policies more suited to the new realities on the ground.

YEMEN: AN OPPORTUNITY AGAIN

In September 2014, Soleimani was in Baghdad planning Operation Ashura to retake Jurf as-Sakhr when the news of the fall of Sanaa, the Yemeni capital, reached him. His rebel comrades, the Houthis, had captured the city. Soleimani saw a "golden opportunity" in the fall of Sanaa: a Shia-led government was in control of the capital of a country bordering Saudi Arabia, the main geopolitical, cultural, and sectarian rival of the Islamic Republic of Iran. The Quds Force could now stand up a Shia expeditionary force in the Saudis' backyard.[26]

The Houthis were followers of the Zaydi branch of Shia Islam and for many years had kept a close relationship with the Quds Force. The leaders of their movement had visited Tehran and Qom during the first days of the Islamic Revolution and had brought back home a militant interpretation of Shia Islam. With guidance from the Quds Force, they had created a political party, Ansarallah, using Hezbollah as their model.[27] The Quds Force provided training, arms, and financial support to the Houthis for years before the fall of Sanaa.

After the capture of the capital and its international airport, IRGC-controlled Mahan Air began daily flights to Sanaa, delivering arms and cash to the Houthis.[28] Quds Force senior officers flew to Sanaa to train, advise, and assist the mission. Operatives from Hezbollah and major Iraqi Shia militia groups also joined the effort.

In 2015, a new assertive leadership in Saudi Arabia decided to challenge the Quds Force in Yemen. The new monarch, King Salman, and his son, Deputy Crown Prince Mohammad bin Salman, who was put in charge of the Yemen portfolio, decided to counter Quds Force plans to stand up a Shia Houthi–led government on Saudi borders. The UAE and the GCC joined the anti-Iran coalition.

After years of unimpeded intervention in Iraq and Syria, the Quds Force faced concerted opposition by Sunni Arab countries. The coalition closed the Yemeni airspace and seaports to Iran. Without a shared border, and with the airport and seaports blocked, standing up a full expeditionary force in Yemen similar to efforts in Iraq and Syria became logistically challenging for the Quds Force. Soleimani did not have freedom of movement to deploy battalions of Shia militants and IRGC ground force personnel and equipment to the country. The expeditionary model of the Quds Force's way of war, developed in Iraq and Syria, was showing its limits. Without a shared border and facing a hostile environment, and without logistical capability to deploy as many officers, operatives, and militia members as necessary into a foreign land far from its immediate surroundings, the Quds Force was forced to limit its involvement to deploying only dozens of officers and trainers, and smuggling weapons to its local allies. It is also unknown if the Houthis wanted all the foreign militias deployed to Yemen because of the lack of a Quds Force capability to manage a full-scale involvement. Soleimani had to redefine the term "near abroad" in this case. He could operate unimpeded in the very near abroad with friendly governments, as in Iraq and Syria; operate more limitedly in the very near abroad without the consent of the local government, as in Afghanistan; and operate only with great difficulty in the not very near abroad and especially in a hostile environment, as in Yemen.

After the Saudis bombed the Sanaa airport and cordoned off the Yemeni air- and seaports to Iranian cargo planes and ships, the Quds Force launched concerted efforts to smuggle weapons into Houthi-controlled areas beyond the tons of weapons already delivered to the Houthis prior to the Saudi and Emirati intervention. The Iranians built potent maritime capabilities, including coastal defense missiles, radar systems, mines, and explosive boats that had migrated from the Persian Gulf.[29] By late 2016, the Houthis posed a grave danger to the security of the Bab al-Mandeb, the strait linking the Red Sea and the Gulf of Aden, one of the two naval chokepoints in the region—along with the Strait of Hormuz in the Persian Gulf—closure of which could seriously disrupt international commerce. The Houthis also used Iranian-supplied anti-ship missiles to hit UAE and Saudi naval vessels and threaten U.S. naval forces in the area.[30]

Clashes between opposing forces backed by the Saudi-Emirati coalition and the Iran-Houthi network could escalate into an all-out conflict. The coalition is intent on driving the Houthis back to their stronghold of Saada, which will require major battles at the port city of Hudaydah (Yemen's major Red Sea port) and Sanaa (the capital), both captured by the Houthis in 2014. If the Houthis threaten the Bab el-Mandeb in response to coalition advances in Hudaydah and Sanaa, the U.S. naval and air forces could get involved to enforce the free flow of commerce in the strait.

The preferred end state for the Quds Force in Yemen is likely regional powers' acceptance of the Houthis as an important part of the Yemeni state and a major partner in any future government, not unlike Hezbollah in Lebanon. But that's probably not what the Saudi-Emirati coalition has in mind. Soleimani might need to prepare plans for an autonomous Zaydi-Shia sub-state in northwestern Yemen. That possibility will look more likely as the civil war comes to an end, with the Yemenis in the south expecting to declare independence, reestablishing South Yemen, and the internationally recognized Yemeni government-in-exile taking control of Sanaa and central Yemen. The Houthis' choice could then be to establish an autonomous region in the northwest. The latter is appealing to the Iranians for another reason: the rump Houthi state would still be bordering Saudi Arabia, giving them a presence in the backyard of their nemesis.

THE RISE OF THE QUDS FORCE

The politically active anti-shah Iranian émigré community in the 1960s and 1970s was largely under the influence of leftist revolutionary movements in places like China, Vietnam, and Cuba. Even the Islamist activists among the community used leftist paradigms and instilled them with Shia doctrines to build their ideological constructs. They believed toppling the shah required the creation of a Vietnamese-type National Liberation Army and years or decades of armed struggle. But the shah left the country not long after huge crowds of demonstrators began marching on the streets and chanting "Death to the Shah!" Ayatollah Khomeini returned to Iran to fill the void. The Imperial Armed Forces provided helicopter and protection to move the Ayatollah from the scene of chanting mobs surrounding him in celebration on the first day of his return. Ten days later, as the pro-Khomeini demonstrations morphed into an uprising, the shah's military issued a proclamation of its neutrality and stopped fighting, and the Islamic Republic was born.

In the revolutionary fervor of those early days, the Islamists within Khomeini's inner circle, who had accompanied him back to Iran, took the first steps to create a people's army to defend the revolution against what they expected would be a U.S.-led coup by the remnants of the shah's military. The name given to the new organization was the *Islamic Revolutionary Guards Corps* (or Sepah). As fears of a coup subsided, the militant Islamists created a specialized unit within the IRGC to be the Islamic Republic's conduit to revolutionary movements across the globe. They also wanted to use the unit to counter U.S. and Western influence and presence in the region, upend the established pro-Western political order in the Muslim world, and destroy the state of Israel. That unit would later become the Quds Force.

In December 1979, ten months after the victory of the Islamic Revolution, the Soviet Union invaded Afghanistan. The U.S.-supported Mujahedeen waged war against the Soviets and its local allies, the socialist government of the Democratic Republic of Afghanistan. The war and the chaos that followed opened a major opportunity for the IRGC to enter the neighboring country and recruit militant Shias, especially among the Hazaras, the country's largest ethnic group, to fight the Soviets and the socialist government. The militia group became the IRGC's first foreign militia group involved in conflict outside Iran's borders, in the "near abroad." The Hazara militias would become not only a model for the IRGC's militia development but a large part of the future Quds Force's Shia Liberation Army (SLA) during the Syrian civil war.

Then Saddam's Iraq invaded Iran in September 1980. The IRGC recruited Shia Iraqis who were living in exile in Iran to form militia groups, the Badr Brigades and Dawa Party military wing, to fight the Iraqi military. After the war, they continued harassing Saddam's forces in Shia southern Iraq. The major break for the Quds Force came in 2003 when the United States invaded Iraq and overthrew Saddam Hussein. Iraqi militant groups were deployed into a chaotic post-invasion Iraq and formed the nucleus of the Iraqi Shia groups under Soleimani's command who would fight the Americans and their allies in the country.

The IRGC–Quds Force's major victory came not in Afghanistan or Iraq of the 1980s and 1990s but in Lebanon with the establishment of Hezbollah. Iranian militants with experience in Fatah military camps in the country before the revolution were among the founders of the IRGC. Now as senior members of the revolutionary organization, they returned to Lebanon and forced a split by militant Shias within the Amal Movement and Fatah to form Hezbollah. The organization grew rapidly, absorbing many other Shia militants outside Amal and Fatah, including Shias with leftist tendencies. With cash, weapons, and advisers provided by the IRGC, and later the Quds Force, the organization would eventually morph into the SLA, with a political wing that would control the Lebanese government.

The genesis and the contours of the SLA had become evident. Hezbollah, the Iraqi Shia militias, and the Hazara Afghan militants would form the nucleus, acting as the Quds Force's ground forces in major battles to come. Soleimani was thus well prepared to enter and shape the conflicts in Syria in 2011, Iraq in 2014, and Yemen also in 2014.

The other side of rising is falling. The Quds Force commander and the Iranian senior leaders might have overplayed their hand: alienating half of the Shias in Iraq because of their heavy-handed interference in Iraqi politics, setting themselves up for a major regional conflict in Yemen, given the Houthi attacks on Saudi soil, and allowing themselves to be cornered in Syria by exposing their personnel and the forces under their command to Israeli attacks without adequate strategy and military might for an effective deterrent and retaliatory response. Short of a significant drawdown or withdrawal of their forces from the three countries, they need a new strategy to adopt to the changing political landscape in the region.

Chapter Six

Land Corridor to Syria

From the early days of the revolution, Ayatollah Khomeini and his cohorts wanted to spread their political and militant interpretation of Islam and Shi'ism throughout the Middle East and especially in countries with significant Shia populations. The dream was to spread Khomeini's revolution, organize Shia militants, and link Shia enclaves across the region. The extraterritorial branch of the newly founded IRGC was tasked to implement the strategy. Four decades and many wars and insurgencies in the region later, the Quds Force, the extraterritorial branch originally named for Jerusalem, would organize and arm hundreds of thousands of militant Shia youths and establish a land corridor linking Iran through Iraq to Syria, Lebanon, and Israel's northern fronts.

The forty-year effort began on the streets of Dahieh, a predominantly Shia southern suburb of Beirut, where the IRGC recruited Shia members of Fatah, militant members of Amal, and other Shia militant youths to organize the Party of God, Hezbollah. On the military front, this group would become the jewel of the Quds Force–led Shia militant organizations in the Middle East, and on the political front, the de facto ruling party of Lebanon.

With Lebanon in the win column, the Quds Force needed to establish its influence and presence in Iraq and Syria to establish the idea of a Shia nation unified by its militant anti-Western and anti-Israeli ideology. The overthrow of Saddam Hussein's regime paved the way for installation of a Shia government in Iraq, with the Quds Force wasting no time in introducing Iraqi militant groups—trained and battle-tested during their fight on behalf of Iran against their own country's military during the eight-year war between the two countries—into the new Iraq. They began to recruit militant Shias to fight the Americans and their allies until their departure from the country eight years later. The rise of Daesh and the Shia militia's fight against the

The Quds Force, which successfully led the war against the Sunni opposition to the Assad regime, has changed its strategy and is directing its forces to counter the Israelis at their northern fronts, raising the specter of direct military conflict with Israel.

Sunni militants solidified the Quds Force's position of power and influence in the country, pushing Iraq close to becoming a de facto satellite state of Iran.

The missing link between Iraq and Lebanon was Syria. When the Arab Spring reached that country, it provided an opportunity for the Quds Force to establish its presence and a position of influence in Syria similar if not quite the same as what it had achieved in neighboring Iraq. It mobilized tens of thousands of Hezbollah fighters, Iraqi Shia militiamen, and Afghan and Pakistani militants to defeat the Syrian opposition to save the regime. The Quds Force–led Shia army, and the deft leadership of its commander, General Qasem Soleimani, helped change the trajectory of the civil war in Assad's favor and paved the way for his eventual control of strategic swaths of land reaching Iraq to the east, Lebanon to the west, and Israel to the south. Khomeini's dreams of a contiguous Shia nation under his militant teachings were being realized, if only three decades after his death.

Reaching that goal did not come easy. The opposition was fierce and four years into the civil war the regime was on the verge of collapse. In mid-2015, the Syrian government was in control of only 17 percent of the country.[1] Soleimani and his Shia army could not save Assad and needed help. On 24 July 2015, Soleimani flew to Moscow to seek the support of Russian president Vladimir Putin.[2] They struck a deal for a dramatic escalation of Russian and Iranian military involvement in Syria. Putin would provide air and artillery firepower and special forces in support of Quds Force–led operations in the country. Soleimani committed to fully activate the full force of the Islamic Republic's expeditionary army in Syria, to include the deployment of the IRGC and Artesh specialized units—armor, artillery, UAV, and special forces—on temporary duty to Syria in support of the Quds Force–led land forces of Shia militias. The full entry of Russia turned the trajectory of the civil war.

THE ARAB SPRING AND SYRIA

The self-immolation of Tunisian street vendor Mohamed Bouazizi on 17 December 2010 set off a chain of events that would upend the Middle East and North Africa in what would come to be known as the Arab Spring. The entire world watched as the fire Bouazizi set spread from Tunisia, with the popular overthrow of President Ben Ali, to Egypt, with the ousting of Hosni Mubarak.

In March 2011, Syrian security forces detained a number of young men accused of painting anti-government graffiti on their school walls in the city of Daraa. Encouraged by the demonstrations happening across the Middle East, protesters used this detainment as a catalyst to protest the injustice of Syria's security apparatus. Security forces opened fire on the demonstrators of Daraa, killing four. The protests soon enveloped Syria's capital, Damascus, and its most populous city, Aleppo, with demonstrators demanding more civil rights as well as political reform.

Only days after the first protests, Quds Force officers arrived in Syria. On 18 May 2011, the U.S. government reported that Mohsen Chizari, the Quds Force third-in-command, was training the Assad regime's security services to suppress the demonstrations. Delving into their own experience suppressing popular protests during Iran's 2009 Green Movement, they provided Assad's security services with weapons and surveillance technology. Quds Force officers also trained and advised Assad's forces on how to monitor email, cellphones, and social media.

Iran has supported the Syrian regime of Bashar al-Assad and his father, Hafez al-Assad, since the early 1980s with money and arms. In multiethnic and tribal Syria, the Assads represent the minority but powerful Alawi religious sect. The touchstone of the Alawi doctrine is the deification of Ali, the son-in-law of Prophet Mohammad, and the first imam of the Shias. The main Shia concern about the Alawi beliefs is that Ali is only the first imam and not the incarnation of Allah. Alawis in turn believe the Shias fall short of comprehending Ali's divinity. But the belief in Ali creates a bond for the Iranians strong enough to consider the Alawis part of the Shia community. To cement those special relations, the Alawis took concrete steps to patch up their differences with the Shias and establish a strong bond with the newly founded Islamic Republic of Iran. In 1982, the Alawi leaders declared themselves to be Twelver Shias, as their brethren in Iran and Lebanon.[3] That was good enough for the Iranians to regard Assad's Syria as a Shia-governed entity.

This religious bond added to the importance of Assad's Syria as a crucial ally for the Islamic Republic, a member of its "axis of resistance," along with Hezbollah, in any confrontation with Israel and the U.S. The Sunni opposition, even though it represented the majority in Syria, had to be defeated to save Assad. The immediate task for Soleimani's Quds Force and its Shia militias was to secure Damascus and Alawi-dominated western Syria, the economic heartland of the country, stretching from the Mediterranean coast to the Orontes River, with Aleppo and the southern suburbs of Damascus forming its defensive perimeter. Early in the conflict, the Iranian calculus was to save "Alawistan" if the country fractured.

CREATING A SECTARIAN NARRATIVE

From the start of their military intervention in the Syrian civil war, the Iranians officially offered a sectarian narrative of the conflict. They described their mission as "defending the shrine" and labeled the Quds Force personnel and their militias in Syria "Defenders of the Shrine." The shrine is the Sayyidah Zaynab Mosque, located in a southern suburb of Damascus, and according to Shia tradition, it houses the grave of Zaynab, the daughter of Ali, Shia's first imam. The narrative represented the civil war between the Assad regime and the opposition as a sectarian conflict between Shias, the defenders of the shrine, and the Sunni opposition. The Quds Force also named the battalions of its foreign militants in Syria after Zaynab and Fatimah, the daughter of the Prophet who was also the wife of Ali. The Pakistani Shia militants were organized as the Zaynabiyoun Battalion, and the Afghan Shia militants as the Fatemiyoun Battalion. The Iranian media described the Quds Force personnel and foreign Shia militants killed in action in Syria as being martyred in "defense of the shrine" even though there was no fighting at or anywhere near the shrine throughout the civil war and the majority were killed in Aleppo, some two hundred miles from the shrine.

The Iranian insistence on describing the civil war as a Shia-Sunni sectarian conflict has its roots in the dominant doctrine of the Islamic Republic. The Shia Islamic Revolution in Iran was not about one country but the whole Middle East, with the goal of creating a revolutionary movement across the region to defend Shia interests. It was natural for the Quds Force, the lead agency of the Islamic Revolution for implementing this doctrine, to view the conflict in sectarian terms, as Shias defending an Alawi-dominated government against a predominantly Sunni opposition.

THE QUDS FORCE TO THE RESCUE

From the very early days of the civil war, the Quds Force established an airlift to Syria to deliver arms and equipment to pro-regime forces and to deploy Quds Force personnel and Shia militias to the country. Two Iranian airlines, Mahan Air and Iran Air, were used extensively to augment the Iranian military's own transport aircraft in establishing an air bridge to Damascus. In September 2011, a random inspection of one of the aircraft by Turkish authorities found a shipment destined for Syria containing assault rifles, machine guns, explosives, detonators, 60mm and 120mm mortar shells, and other items. As the war progressed, Iran sent more and more sophisticated weaponry to pro-Assad forces. In 2013, Reuters reported that the weekly flights to Damascus contained arms including UAVs, cruise missiles, and surface-to-surface ballistic missiles. Even so, a year into the civil war, the Assad regime was on the brink of bankruptcy and defeat. Aside from weapons and equipment, the Iranians also provided much-needed cash and oil. Iran also funded the deployment and operations of foreign Shia militias, including Hezbollah and militant organizations from Iraq, Afghanistan, and Pakistan to fight the opposition. Throughout the civil war, Iran spent some $7 billion annually to prop up the regime.

The introduction of Hezbollah fighters and other foreign Shia militants into the conflict was a game changer. Assad's army was losing its troops due to casualties and defection and was unable to contain the uprising. Hezbollah began deploying battle-tested fighters to Syria from the first year of the war. They first saw combat in Syria during the siege of Homs, which started in May 2011 and lasted for three years. They were part of a task force led by Quds Force and IRGC senior officers, which also included the Badr organization and elements of other Iraqi Shia militia groups. The siege resulted in withdrawal of the opposition forces from the city, a pattern that repeated itself throughout the war, with the pro-regime forces surrounding population centers under rebel control to create hardship and famine among the local population, forcing the opposition to negotiate an agreement with the regime for withdrawal of their forces and the civilian population from the devastated town.

The next major battle was Aleppo, which began in mid-2012 and lasted for more than four years. Aleppo, arguably the most important battle of the war, is discussed later in this chapter. Some 25,000 Quds Force–led fighters under the command of General Soleimani saw action in Aleppo at different times during the four-year battle, including fighters from Hezbollah, Iraqi Shia militia groups, and Afghan and Pakistani militants. Other major battles for Hezbollah included the recapture of al-Qusayr, a major Syrian town on the Lebanese border lost to the opposition early in the war. In May 2013, some two thousand Hezbollah fighters, accompanied by a number of Quds Force officers acting as advisers and supported by elements of the Syrian army and the newly instituted National Defense Forces (NDF; a government militia group under the guidance of the IRGC's Basij Force), attacked the Free Syrian Army (FSA) at al-Qusayr. After two weeks of heavy fighting, Hezbollah captured the city in the first major military victory by pro-regime forces over the opposition. In the final days of fighting, Hezbollah and the FSA negotiated an evacuation plan for the rebels and civilians to leave the city through a narrow corridor without being attacked. The agreement became a model for future battles, with the rebels withdrawing from the battle-space when faced with superior pro-regime forces and the regime effectively depopulating Sunni-dominated towns and deploying pro-regime forces to control the abandoned areas.

Hezbollah maintained its significant involvement throughout the Syrian civil war. By 2015, it had upward of 8,000 fighters in the country and had lost up to 1,500 fighters in combat. The Quds Force also deployed thousands of Iraqi Shia militants to fight in Syria. Among them were fighters from the Badr Organization, the KH, the AAH, Kata'ib Sayyid al-Shuhada, and Harakat Hezbollah al-Nujaba. Other Iraqi groups like the Peace Companies/Promised Day Brigades also were deployed to Syria. In the battle of Aleppo, some five thousand Iraqi fighters took part. Afghan and Pakistani Shia militants also were recruited and deployed in significant numbers to Syria. Thousands of foreign fighters lost their lives in the Syrian conflict.

THE BATTLE OF ALEPPO

Soleimani returned to Tehran after his now-famous Kremlin meeting with Putin in summer 2015 to plan for the Battle of Aleppo, the Quds Force's biggest operation ever. Its personnel, including a significant number of general officers, assembled near Aleppo to lead the fight. He also deployed a cadre of some two thousand IRGC and Basij personnel from among their elite divisions and brigades on temporary duty to Syria to join more than five hundred personnel already in the country in support of Quds Force opera-tions in Aleppo.[4] The IRGC contingent included elements of artillery and armor units, and its temporary headquarters were set up near the battlefield. Elements of Artesh special forces were later deployed to Syria to also take part in the fighting. The airlifting of equipment and personnel to Syria began well in advance of the first Russian airstrikes in September.

Soleimani surged the foreign Shia militants deployed to Syria to a historic high. Hezbollah increased their number of fighters to eight thousand.[5] The number of Iraqi Shia militants was increased to five thousand.[6] At times referred to as the Haydariyoun, the Iraqis were the top-tier and battle-tested Shia militant groups the KH, the AAH, the Badr Organization, Harakat al-Nujaba, and Kata'ib Sayyad al-Shuhada. Also participating were the Fate-miyoun and Zaynabiyoun brigades. The Fatemiyoun comprised nearly ten thousand Shia Afghan militants, mostly recruited inside Iran from among the Afghan Hazara refugee community.[7] Human Rights Watch reported that the Quds Force hired Afghan refugees in Iran as mercenaries, giving them monthly salaries and a promise of permanent Iranian residency for them-selves and their families.[8] The program was likely in violation of the Geneva Convention for protection of refugees. The Zaynabiyoun comprised an esti-mated two thousand Pakistani militants. Most of these fighters saw action in Aleppo.

The Battle of Aleppo became the first test of Soleimani's enlarged Shia expeditionary army. The army included foreign Shia militias from Lebanon and Iraq, Pakistan, and Afghanistan acting as the frontline infantry supported by some two thousand specialized elements of the Iranian armed forces, including artillery, armor, and ballistic missile units deployed on temporary duty to the battlespace. Iranian UAVs were deployed as enablers of the ground forces to improve ISR; direct ground movements; facilitate artillery, air, and ballistic missile strikes; and improve battlefield awareness. Elements of the Syrian army also joined the fighting. And Russia provided the critical air support.[9]

In December 2016, after some of the most intense fighting in the civil war, Aleppo fell to the Quds Force–led pro-regime forces, who took full control of the city for the first time since 2012. In an evacuation deal worked out by Soleimani, 35,000 residents of Aleppo, mainly Sunnis, including some armed opposition fighters, left the city for neighboring Idlib province, which was under the control of anti-regime forces.[10] Meanwhile one thousand Shias were evacuated from the besieged majority-Shia towns of Al Fu'ah and Kafraya in Idlib province.[11]

Ironically, the fall of Aleppo drove opposition forces of different political stripes out of the city and into Idlib, one of the few remaining bastions of anti-regime forces. There, al-Qaeda affiliate the al-Nusra Front (ANF) had forced a merger with many opposition fighters to form Hay'at Tahrir al-

Sham (HTS). The group became the largest and most powerful armed group in the area. The more moderate opposition groups leaving Aleppo joined Ahrar al-Sham (AAS), a coalition of jihadist forces concentrated close to the Turkish border. The HTS and AAS could muster many anti-regime fighters in Idlib, making another major battle with the Quds Force–led forces inevitable, a battle at the scale of Aleppo if not larger.

The Battle of Aleppo itself began with a lightning offensive by the Quds Force–led forces. On 30 September 2015, Russia began massive strikes against opposition forces using its fighter jets and sea-based cruise missiles. Iran had given Russia permission to use Iranian airspace for its aircraft en route to Syria and for cruise missiles fired from Russian warships on the Caspian Sea near the Iranian coast.[12] The strikes lasted two weeks and softened opposition defenses before Quds Force–led ground operations began.[13] On 7 October, Soleimani launched his offensive in the vicinity of Aleppo.[14] The opposition was uniquely vulnerable in Aleppo City, relying on a single primary line of communication with the outside world: the M5 Highway that linked the city to Damascus. Soleimani wanted to cut the highway and surround the opposition in their city stronghold. Encircling Aleppo would eventually force the opposition to retreat from the city, Soleimani hoped, as it had happened in Homs five years earlier, where the Quds Force–led Shia militias were involved in the siege of the city in late 2011, leading to a general retreat by the opposition forces.

Soleimani's forces began to capture the rebel-held towns and villages in the southern countryside of Aleppo. By mid-November, the strategic town of al-Hadher, a key opposition-held town, fell. So did the town of Tal al-Eis, overlooking the Aleppo-Damascus highway. A second Quds Force–led column advanced northeast of Aleppo to break the siege of Kweires Airfield. By mid-December, the Quds Force captured the strategic town of Khan Touman, which sat on the M5 Highway and at the time was one of the few remaining towns held by the opposition south of Aleppo. By capturing the town, the Quds Force cut the primary opposition supply route from the provincial capital of Idlib province to Aleppo City. Soleimani felt he was on the verge of encircling Aleppo, and the fall of Aleppo was now in sight.

SETBACKS IN ALEPPO

On 6 May 2016, fighters led by the ANF recaptured Khan Touman.[15] Soleimani had taken the town less than five months earlier during the initial Russian-enabled offensive. The IRGC's 25th Karbala Division, based in the northern Iranian province of Mazandaran, whose elements were deployed to Khan Touman on temporary duty, and other Quds Force and IRGC personnel defending the town, suffered heavy casualties and had to retreat from the area. Twenty-one IRGC and Quds Force personnel, including two general officers, were killed in action. The Quds Force–led militias defending Khan Touman suffered significant losses. Eighty Hezbollah and Iraqi Shia fighters were killed.[16] The group Harakat al-Nujaba alone lost eleven fighters that day. Khan Touman became the single most devastating defeat to date for Soleimani in Syria. The blow came less than a month after Iran's regular military, Artesh, lost four officers, including a commander of one of its elite special forces units, while defending the town of Tal el-Eis, which Iranian-led forces had captured early in the Aleppo offensive.[17]

The collapse of Iranian-led defenses in Khan Touman and Tal el-Eis was partly due to inaction on the part of less well-trained and disciplined militias—a problem that has haunted and will continue to haunt Soleimani's foreign legion. Afghan, Pakistani, and some Iraqi fighters were at times unmotivated and difficult to control, disobeying orders and causing battlefield setbacks. Putting together a foreign legion of Shia militias to act as the Quds Force's frontline infantry seemed at times pure genius because of the ability to avoid costly foreign deployment of IRGC forces and dodge high casualties in wars not so popular or even widely known inside Iran. Most importantly, the organized militias gave the Quds Force a long-term mechanism for intervening in wars and insurgencies in the region to defend and expand militant Shia interests. But the concurrent conflicts in the region pushed the Quds Force to field tens of thousands of fighters to battlespaces far too quickly for thorough training, as the Khan Touman and Tal el-Eis setbacks showed.

ARTESH IN ALEPPO

During the surge to retake Aleppo, Soleimani broadened the Quds Force's support elements and deployed units of Iran's regular army, Artesh, on temporary duty to the battlespace. In April 2016, Artesh's special forces units, the elite 65th Airborne Brigade and the 45th Takavar Brigade, were deployed to Aleppo, the regular army's first foreign operation since the 1980s during the Iran-Iraq War. Artesh fought hard and suffered casualties in the Battle of Tal el-Eis, and the battle resulted in the addition of Artesh to Soleimani's way of war. Its specialized units would join battles along with IRGC and Basij units.

FINAL VICTORY IN ALEPPO: REDRAWING THE MAP OF CONFLICT

For a period in mid-2016, notwithstanding earlier expectations of a quick end to the fighting in Aleppo, the Quds Force seemed to be operating on shaky grounds. Following the recapture of Tal el-Eis and Khan Touman, the opposition retook villages in the southern suburbs of Aleppo that had been earlier captured by Soleimani's forces, including Kalasah, Zaytan, and Birmah, and were closing in on the strategic town of al-Hather, arguably the biggest prize of the Quds Force's previous victories in the Aleppo theater. The fall of al-Hather would have meant that the opposition had regained almost all territory lost during the Quds Force–led original offensives south of Aleppo.

Soleimani needed help and called on Russia to intensify its bombing campaign to cut opposition communications lines. Russia's continued bombardment of opposition positions in the area allowed the Quds Force to renew its efforts to push back the opposition and bring Aleppo under siege. It took six more months of intense fighting before Aleppo fell. "Our victory is imminent," Soleimani reportedly said when the Shaykh Sa'id neighborhood of Aleppo fell to his forces on 12 December. On 18 December, the opposition signed off on an evacuation deal, leaving the Quds Force–led forces in charge of the whole city. Opposition dreams of controlling Aleppo in a new Syria, born during the demonstrations on the streets of the city five years earlier, ended that day when they were forced to abandon their hometown and become refugees in their own country.

Soleimani's victory in Aleppo decisively changed the trajectory of the conflict in favor of the regime. The fall of Aleppo was the fall of the opposition as we knew it. The future of Syria still remained unknown, but the victory in Aleppo gave the upper hand to Assad and Soleimani in drawing the post-conflict map of Syria. Although it is highly unlikely that the old Syria will be resurrected, with significant swaths of territories remaining under de facto self-rule in places like the Kurdish north, the Aleppo victory created a strong state based in the Alawi-dominated western part of the country, controlling all major population centers of old Syria. Soleimani doggedly pushed his Aleppo plans and delivered a decisive victory. In the annals of Iranian military history, Qasem Soleimani will probably go down as one of the most brilliant military tacticians in the country's modern history.

The collapse of the opposition and loss of Aleppo, however, like any victory based on a sectarian approach, created the roots for future conflicts. Many Sunnis saw the victory as the final push by the Quds Force–led Shia forces to complete the displacement of Sunni communities in Syria and to see Iran-led forces as the biggest obstacle to settling the conflict in Syria. The Quds Force and its Shia militias are seen as the source of a new sectarian militancy in the country, with the opposition calling on all concerned, including the U.S., to form a coalition to counter their move beyond traditionally Alawi-dominated western Syria, the power base of the Assad regime.

IRANIAN CASUALTIES

The Quds Force advances in Aleppo proved to be costly. In the first two weeks of the Aleppo offensive alone, thirty IRGC servicemen were killed in action.[18] The early casualties included Brigadier General Hossein Hamadani, a former commander of Iranian forces in Syria and the most senior IRGC officer deployed to the country to help Soleimani. He was killed in Kweires, near Aleppo, during the first days of the operation.[19] The IRGC also suffered major casualties in the battles for Nubl and Zahra. Forty IRGC servicemen were killed in action, including five general officers, five colonels, one lieutenant colonel, one major, two captains, and five lieutenants.[20] The announcements of IRGC deaths and funeral ceremonies published in the Iranian media shed light on the extent of the IRGC deployment to Syria, which the government had wanted to keep a secret. The Saberin, the IRGC's elite special forces brigade, lost its former commander, Brigadier General Farshad Hosouni-Zadeh, on 12 October 2015 in the vicinity of Aleppo.[21] Other deployed IRGC units lost senior personnel between mid-October and early November 2015. They included the 1st Hazrat Hojjat Brigade based in Khuzestan;[22] the 8th Najaf Ashraf Division based in Isfahan;[23] the 33rd Mahdi Airborne Brigade in Fars;[24] the 15th Khordad Artillery Group;[25] the 43rd Imam Ali Engineering Group;[26] and the Basij's Imam Hossein battalions.[27]

The Iranian media reported in May 2016 that more than 250 IRGC servicemen, including more than 10 general officers, had been killed in action during the Quds Force–led Aleppo offensive, which began in October 2015. The high number of IRGC officers killed in action indicated the full combat role of IRGC personnel who were deployed to Syria in a capacity far beyond that of any other to train, advise, and assist the mission. Along with the Iranian casualties, there were significant numbers of Hezbollah, Iraqi, Afghan, and Pakistani fighters killed during the Aleppo offensive.

POST-ALEPPO OPERATIONS

On 7 June 2017, two terrorist attacks occurred simultaneously in Tehran. Four terrorists belonging to Daesh opened fire in Iran's Parliament building, and a suicide bomber detonated a bomb at the mausoleum of Ayatollah Khomeini. In total, the attacks left 17 civilians dead and 43 wounded. It was the first attack by Daesh inside Iran, and the IRGC responded with overwhelming force against an ISIL camp in the Syrian Deir ez-Zour governorate. On 18 June, the IRGC fired six surface-to-surface ballistic missiles from domestic bases.

In early November, the Quds Force–led Shia militias and Syrian army units, backed by Russian air support, recaptured most of Deir ez-Zour, which sits on a highway to Damascus, beginning their campaign to retake eastern territories lost during the war.

The principal Quds Force campaign after Aleppo, however, was to establish a land corridor linking Syria and Iraq. There are three major land routes linking the two countries. The southern route, which is the best route, connects Baghdad to Damascus through a major highway, but it runs through the Syrian border town of Al Tanf. U.S.-led coalition forces and elements of the Syrian armed opposition maintain a military base at Al Tanf. In 2017, a mechanized column of Quds Force–led militias attempted to approach the town but withdrew after U.S. forces took positions to defend the base and downed an Iranian UAV. The second option is a northern route, linking Mosul to the YPG-controlled Kurdish region in northern Syria. The Quds Force does not have a real working relation with the Syrian Kurds as it does with the Iraqi Kurds. Ideologically, the Syrian Kurdish militants, the YPG, are closer to their brethren in the Kurdish Democratic Party of Iran (KDPI), which the Islamic Republic considers an archenemy. The third option, in the midsection of the border, connects the Iraqi border town of al-Qaim to Syria's Abu Kamal and on to Deir ez-Zour. Soleimani chose this route to establish a land corridor. His militia forces took control of al-Qaim in Iraq and after intensive fighting took Abu Kamal on the Syrian side of the border in late 2017. The building of a land corridor via this route remained a strategic priority for the Quds Force.

THE IRANIAN PROJECT IN SYRIA

After the fall of Aleppo, the Quds Force focused on moving east to control territories bordering Iraq. The move enabled Iranian-led forces to establish a land corridor in the heart of the Middle East, from Iran through Iraq and Syria to Lebanon, the Mediterranean, and the Israeli northern fronts.

As part of its Syria project, the Quds Force began to establish permanent bases on Syrian soil for its forces and those of Shia militias kept in country for the long haul. The force, estimated at 25,000 strong, will help maintain regime gains against the opposition during the civil war and will be Iran's permanent vanguard force stationed near the Israeli northern fronts, fulfilling an old dream of the Islamic revolutionaries.

The Quds Force began using the Tiyas Military Base, also known as the T-4 Airbase, Syria's largest, in Homs Governorate, west of Palmyra, as its UAV operations center in Syria. The Iranian drones stationed there have a range of 600–900 miles, and the airfield is approximately 130 miles from the Israeli fronts on the Golan Heights and 140 miles from northern Israel. The

UAVs at the base have ISR as well as attack capabilities. The Quds Force also houses elements of its Shia militia force in and immediately around the base and uses mobile air defense systems to protect its personnel and UAV assets.

The Israelis, however, consider permanent basing for Iranian-led forces a threat to their security red line. In February 2018, an Iranian UAV flew from the T-4 airfield over Israeli territory on an apparent ISR mission over Israeli military formations in the tristate region linking Israel, Jordan, and Syria. The Israelis shot down the UAV, and in further retaliation the Israeli Air Force (IAF) launched an attack on Iranian positions at the airbase, including its UAV operations center. In April 2018, the IAF again struck Iranian and Shia militia positions at the airbase with air-to-ground missiles. IRGC colonel Mehdi Dehghan, commanding officer of the IRGC UAV unit, was among the casualties of the attack.

In a delayed attempted retaliation, the Quds Force fired twenty rockets toward Israeli installations on the Golan Heights. Only four reached the Golan, and they were all intercepted by Israeli anti-missile defense batteries. Israel wasted no time in retaliating in a major way, unproportioned to Iran's own failed retaliatory attempt. In a short period of time, Israel staged missile attacks against sixteen Quds Force installations in Syria, nearly all of its installations, destroying command-and-control centers, UAV facilities, and weapons depots, killing a score of Iranian military personnel and foreign Shia militias. The Quds Force was not prepared, or equipped, to stop the attacks. Proxy warfare operating in a gray zone can defeat the opposition but has its limits confronting a powerful military.

The Quds Force is also establishing plants in Syria to upgrade Hezbollah's thousands of rockets, making them more accurate and increasing their range—the so-called Precision Project. The upgraded rockets will pose a higher threat to Israel; hence establishing the Precision Project plants is Israel's second red line, and the IAF routinely attacks them as they are built. The third Israeli red line is the Quds Force's delivery of weapons to Hezbollah using a Syrian airfield to transport weapons from Iran and land routes to transport them to Lebanon. In the recent past, Israel has launched dozens of air strikes, hitting storage depots at Syrian airfields, including Damascus International Airport, and convoys carrying the weapons to Lebanon.

Iran and Israel are clearly on a collision course in Syria. The Quds Force's plans to maintain forces permanently in Syria, including near the Israeli front positions (notwithstanding Israel's red line against the Quds Force's plans to establish military bases in Syria); to continue with its Precision Project to upgrade Hezbollah's rockets; and to facilitate the flow of arms from Iran to Hezbollah make future direct military conflict between Iran and Israel in Syria almost inevitable.

Foreign Legion

The Quds Force's proxy army in Syria will have both Syrian as well as foreign components. Syria's NDF stood up by the IRGC Basij Force in the early years of the conflict and, led by Iranian officers, is projected to be a 100,000-fighter-strong popular mobilization force with a structure similar to Iran's Basij Force. Then there may be non-Syrian militia groups led by the Quds Force, projected to include groups totaling some 25,000 fighters divided into four nationally based brigades: a Hezbollah brigade totaling some 8,000 battle-tested fighters; the Iraqi Haydariyoun, a brigade of some 3,000 fighters from Iraqi Shia militia groups who are members of Iraq's PMF; and the Afghan Fatemiyoun and Pakistani Zaynabiyoun brigades, totaling some 14,000 fighters.

Iranian Units

Senior officers, including general officers, of the Quds Force are deployed to lead the NDF and foreign militias in Syria. Elements of specialized units of the IRGC and Artesh will be deployed on temporary duty under Soleimani's command to help train, assist, and advise the Quds Force's foreign legion and take part in military operations as needed. They will total upward of two thousand uniformed personnel deployed at any given time. Also, non-uniformed Iranian members of the Quds Force, the IRGC, and their intelligence units will be deployed to Damascus to set up a "Syrian Hezbollah" modeled after its Lebanese counterpart and to act as the political arm of the Iranian project in Syria. Hundreds of these operatives have already been deployed to Syria and live with their families mainly in the Sayiddah Zaynab district of Damascus, with many of them receiving dual Syrian citizenship.

Permanent Military Basing

To house its non-Syrian militias and its own uniformed officers permanently deployed to Syria, the Quds Force needs to build military bases in the country. Even though the Iranians routinely deny their intention to build permanent military bases in the country, a BBC report on 10 November 2017 revealed the construction of a Quds Force base near the village of al-Kiswah, south of Damascus, complete with satellite images showing the site under construction. The base reportedly would be able to house some eight thousand militia fighters. The Israelis have made it clear that constructing such bases to house Iranian personnel and foreign Shia militias in Syria is crossing an Israeli red line. On the night of 1 December, the IAF conducted air strikes and partly destroyed the construction sites. In 2018, the IAF also launched attacks against the Quds Force operations center at T-4 Airbase near Palmyra.

Soleimani now faces a dilemma. If he shelves his plan for permanent basing in Syria, fearing an Israeli attack, his overall project in Syria, which calls for the permanent presence of some 25,000 Shia fighters and some 2,000 Iranian uniformed officers in the country, will suffer a major blow. But building these bases will certainly invite Israeli attacks, which the Quds Force, or the Syrian military, is not equipped to counter. Meanwhile, Israeli senior officials insist that their red lines are serious and they will not let the Iranians cross them.

Building Indigenous Plants for Accurate Rockets

For many years, the IRGC has supplied rockets to Hezbollah for use against Israel. In the recent past, the Quds Force has begun a project to construct indigenous military-industrial facilities in Syria, as well as in Lebanon, to produce highly accurate rockets for Hezbollah. The project, dubbed Precision Project by the Iranians, will also upgrade Hezbollah's current inventory of older rockets into the accurate ones necessary to target specific facilities inside Israel. The Precision Project is another red line for Israel, in addition to the construction of permanent basing. The IAF has been targeting these plants in Syria and Lebanon, reportedly with a high degree of success. As the Quds Force builds them, they are attacked by the Israelis. As in base construction, Soleimani and the Iranian leadership need to make a hard decision on the fate of this project.

Naval and Air Bases

A land corridor connects Iran to the Mediterranean, allowing the Iranian military easy access to any future Iranian naval base and adjacent air base in Syria. In October 2017, the chief of the joint staff of the Iranian military, General Mohammad Baqeri, visited Damascus, reportedly to discuss an Iranian proposal to build the bases. Raz Zimmt, a Tel Aviv–based Iran expert, reported in November that the Syrian government, perhaps with Russian backing, so far has refused to grant Iran's request.[28] It is expected that the Iranians, having played an instrumental role in saving the Assad's regime, will continue their push to secure naval and air bases in Syria.

SYRIAN POLITICAL LANDSCAPE

The Syrian civil war has turned into a tangle of competing interests involving many domestic and foreign actors with few areas of commonality for reaching a negotiated settlement. Eight years of war has shown there are no easy military solutions to the conflict, and the cost of political inaction is enormous. More than 500,000 Syrians have been killed, nearly 6 million have become refugees in foreign lands, and 6 million more have been internally displaced. Whole cities have been destroyed. UN Security Council Resolution 2254, adopted unanimously in December 2015, calls for a cease-fire and political settlement in Syria, and Geneva peace talks offer a venue for peace negotiations between the Syrian regime and the opposition under the auspices of the United Nations. The major actors in the conflict have varying interests and hence different positions on a political settlement.

MODERATE OPPOSITION

The opposition to Assad was born at the height of the Arab Spring, with hundreds of thousands of Syrians marching on the streets calling for an end to a four-decade-old dictatorship. The uprising soon faced a brutal military crackdown by a regime determined to keep its grip on power. To counter the security forces, armed groups across the country were formed, many led by Syrian military officers who had defected to the opposition. The country was engulfed in civil war. And both sides sought and accepted foreign assistance.

The ideologically moderate opposition depended on support from a U.S.-led coalition. In August 2013, the Syrian government deployed chemical weapons on opposition forces in the town of Zamalka, a suburb of Damascus. Hundreds of people, including non-combatants and children, were killed in the attack. The U.S. government announced that the regime had crossed a red line. But President Obama decided at the eleventh hour not to take expected retaliatory action against the regime for engaging in chemical warfare. The decision manifested a lack of resolve by the U.S. administration to engage pro-regime forces in support of the opposition, the beginning of a downward spiral for the moderates. Two years later, Russia's direct military intervention in Syria in support of pro-regime forces and the Quds Force–led operation to defeat and push out the opposition from Aleppo changed the trajectory of the civil war in favor of the pro-Assad forces.

The moderate opposition is partly organized under the banner of the Free Syrian Army (FSA). The FSA was originally formed by a large group of Syrian military officers and soldiers who defected to the opposition in the early days of the civil war and started the armed struggle against Assad. But the original FSA brigades continued their existence independent of each other: some joined other groups, and some entered into larger opposition coalitions. Today, approximately two hundred smaller groups identify themselves with the FSA, more in the spirit of pioneer rebels than as members of an actual army. After the regime's victory in Aleppo, the major moderate groups were based at a corner of Idlib province on the Turkish border, or in the south, in the Deraa and Quneitra region near the border with Jordan. And there is no contiguous land corridor connecting the forces in the north and the south.

The southern front, near the border with Jordan, is isolated geographically and subject to control from Amman. Because Jordan seeks stability along its border with Syria, the group is reluctant to undertake major military action against the regime and therefore is ready to negotiate with the regime for a political solution to the conflict. The Idlib groups face opposition from pro-regime forces, including Quds Force–led militia forces as well as extremists like the ANF, which dominates the scene in the province. With their very survival threatened, they also seek a negotiated political solution with the regime. Some of the Idlib groups are headquartered in Istanbul and run the risk of being under the patronage of Erdogan's Turkey, who could use them in military operations against the Syrian Kurds instead of fighting the Syrian regime.

THE JIHADISTS

The extremist (or Jihadist) groups have ironically, with the exception of Daesh, expressed willingness to be part of a negotiated settlement. But the real goal seems to be using their apparent willingness for negotiations to improve their chances of attaining influence among the larger opposition and presenting themselves as necessary for the peace process to succeed. The two major Jihadist groups represent the non-Daesh extremist bloc in the civil war. The more powerful extremist coalition, based in Idlib province, is the HTS, which is led by the ANF, the local affiliate of al-Qaeda. Its rapid growth has been made possible in large part due to the government's tactic of cutting deals with opposition groups after a long period under siege or when they face imminent military defeat in a battle to leave the area to the regime and be transported, along with their families, by now-infamous green buses and other means to Idlib province. The ANF can provide the newcomers with safety and a means to continue fighting and in some cases can force them into submission by attacking them militarily with a superior force. The other extremist group, also based in Idlib, is the AAS. This group has been fragmented as of late after serious disagreement inside the group on supporting or rejecting the peace talks. Both groups are expected to seek and receive financial support from GCC patrons but at different points in time were in talks with the government to have their status in Idlib recognized by the regime in lieu of avoiding attacks on pro-regime forces elsewhere. The long and complex Syrian war can make even ideological extremists into transactional actors.

ISIS, or Daesh, as a movement capable of establishing a caliphate and controlling major population centers on both sides of the Iraq-Syria border, has been defeated. After the loss of Raqqa, the Syrian territories under its control are limited to pockets along the Iraqi border. But the organization still enjoys the support of a significant number of foreign fighters as well as newcomers recruited through social media and remains a threat in Syria and in the region.

THE KURDS

The Syrian Kurds throughout the civil war have kept their focus on protecting and expanding their de facto autonomous region in northern Syria, named Rojava.[29] The region is predominantly populated by Kurds divided into three cantons. The Jazira in the northeast and Kobane in the central north are adjacent to each other. The third canton, Afrin, is in the northwest corner of Syria, separated from the two other cantons by a small but predominantly Arab region. The Syrian civil war gave the Kurds a golden opportunity to attempt to establish Rojava as a political entity, and for the time being a proto-state of former Syria. They also created a coalition with friendly Arab tribes and groups to jointly administer a mixed-ethnic area within Rojava and eventually link the eastern and western parts of Rojava through establishing their administration of the Arab region separating the two.

The ultimate goal was to create a contiguous Rojava state across all the northern territories of Syria. But the project brought strong opposition from the Turks. The Turkish military along with their Syrian Arab allies moved against YPG positions in Afrin and by March 2018 had taken control of the city of Afrin, the region's capital. The Turkish move at least for the time being has stopped the Rojava unification project and put Kurdish post-conflict plans on hold.

The YPG and its Kurdish-Arab umbrella organization—the SDF—took control of Arab territories north and east of the Euphrates, including Raqqa, the former capital of Daesh; parts of Deir ez-Zour; and territories east of the river to the Iraqi border, in all accounting for a third of the land mass of former Syria. The YPG has enjoyed a strong working relation with the U.S. since President Obama intervened militarily in the battle of Kobane in September 2014 to break the ISIS siege of the city, which had been controlled by the YPG from the beginning of the civil war. The YPG has since acted as the main land force for the U.S.-led coalition's anti-Daesh activities in Syria, which defeated ISIS and drove them out of Raqqa and almost all the territories under their control in Syria. YPG control of the territories north and east of the Euphrates, supported by the U.S., prevented the Quds Force–led pro-regime forces from filling the vacuum in the post-Daesh period.

The Turkish state is determined, however, to roll back the YPG's advances and stop the creation of a Kurdish state in Syria. The Turkish attack on Afrin in 2018 and its attempt to retake major population centers within Rojava, including Manbij, manifested Turkish resolve to fight the Kurdish ambitions at any cost.

REGIONAL AND INTERNATIONAL ACTORS

Iran

The Iranians came to Assad's rescue and became the first foreign power to intervene militarily in the Syrian civil war. The Islamic Republic is committed to endure a protracted conflict in the country in order to achieve its strategic goals. From the Iranian point of view, the Quds Force and Hezbollah should have freedom of movement and be able to maintain military bases of their own in post-conflict Syria. As in Iraq, the Iranians want to have their proxies exercise wide influence in the Syrian state security institutions, including the NDF and its internal security apparatus. Finally, they want to preserve the pre-conflict boundaries and establish a land corridor connecting Syria to Iran. The Iranians see the continuity of the Alawi-dominated regime as essential to achieving those goals. Hence, they are not in any hurry for a political settlement in Syria, knowing full well that they would be unable to achieve their goals through an agreement with other stakeholders. The Iranians see the military option in defeating opposition forces as the only viable path forward. Such an outcome would also check the influence of the U.S., Turkey, and their allies in the future Syria and would prevent the establishment of an autonomous Kurdish proto-state in northern Syria. Above all, the Islamic Republic wants to be regarded as a protector and advocate of Shia interests and influence in the region and as a major regional player. But the longer the conflict continues, the less chance the Iranians will have of reaching most of their strategic goals, and they might be forced to settle for much less.

Russia

The Russian military intervention in the Syrian conflict came late but was meant to ensure that the Syrian regime scored major military gains against the opposition in order to cement its position as the dominant power in the country in post-conflict Syria. Russia, like Iran, opposes partition of Syria and will not push any political settlement that calls for autonomous zones and proto-states in the new Syria. Russian positions will force Syria to adopt a military option in resolving major issues in the conflict in the short term with the expectation that such circumstances will push all interested powers into a political settlement highly in favor of the current regime.

The Gulf Cooperation Council

Saudi Arabia, the UAE, and other Arab states of the gulf refuse to accept Iranian military involvement in Syria and will attempt to limit Iranian influence. The GCC countries will continue their support of Sunni groups to counter Iranian support of the Alawi-dominated government in Damascus. Iran and the GCC view the situation in Syria, and indeed in the entire region, from diametrically opposed positions and are locked in a zero-sum contest, with any gain by the Quds Force–led Shia militia forces or the Sunni opposition groups supported by the GCC seen as a loss to the other side. The GCC would be amenable to a political settlement in Syria but will not accept Iran's maximalist positions. The outcome of the contest between the two blocs, including the proxies supported by each side, will in large part determine the future of Syria.

Turkey

The Turks' main goal in Syria is to counter Kurdish ambitions and their drive to create an autonomous state of their own: less emphasis on Assad, more on the Kurds. Toward that end, they are ready to form strategic or tactical alliances—including their preference that the Assad regime take control of the Kurdish region—in their drive to crush Rojava. The outcome of the confrontation between Turkish security forces and YPG–led SDF forces will in large part determine the fate of YPG's Rojava project and the future of an independent or autonomous Kurdish region in post-conflict Syria.

The Way Ahead

Competing goals of the main regional actors will continue fueling seething proxy wars in Syria. The Quds Force–led Shia militia forces, supported by the Syrian and Russian military, are organized in a way to engage in protracted and enduring conflict against their opponents. The main challenge to the Quds Force will come from Israel. The Iranian project in Syria includes permanent basing of Quds Force–led forces in the country, plans to establish facilities in Syria to upgrade Hezbollah's rockets, and continuation of arms flow to Hezbollah, which are all considered red lines by the Israelis. Iran and Israel are on a collision course in Syria.

Chapter Seven

The Iraqi Campaign

The day 21 March 2003 was not an ordinary Friday Sabbath in Tehran. At 6:30 in the morning the spring equinox came, and with it the start of the Persian New Year. While Iranian citizens were gathering around traditional *Sofrehs* in their homes to mark the occasion, General Qasem Soleimani was at the Quds Force headquarters in Tehran. On that day, the U.S. and British militaries had launched an incursion into Basra, located on the Shatt al-Arab and only thirty miles from the Iranian city of Khoramshahr. Khatami's government in Tehran was concerned that the Bush administration's invasion of Iraq, with forces so close to the Iranian border, was a precursor to an invasion of Iran. The Iranian emissaries assured the Americans that they shared the same goal in Iraq: the overthrow of Saddam Hussein, the Iraqi leader who had invaded Iran and occupied Khoramshahr soon after the victory of the Islamic Revolution. The Iranians were ready to start negotiations with the West to resolve thorny issues in their relationship, including Iran's nuclear program. Within three months, the Iranians began talks with the EU-3 (Britain, France, and Germany) to address their nuclear program. The Bush administration refused to be involved directly with the Iranians, although the EU-3 was understood to be a cover for the Americans.

Soleimani, however, was not afraid. He told his senior staff that the U.S. invasion of Iraq was a golden opportunity for them, opening the gates of Iraq to the Quds Force–led Iraqi militants who had continued fighting Saddam from their base on the Iranian side of the border. They were the same militants who had fought on the side of the IRGC against Saddam's army in the 1980s. Soon after the collapse of Saddam's government and in the chaos that followed in the country, Soleimani, along with his senior officers and the leaders of the Iraqi militants living in exile in Iran, crossed the border near Basra and began recruiting Shia youths to rise up against the Americans and

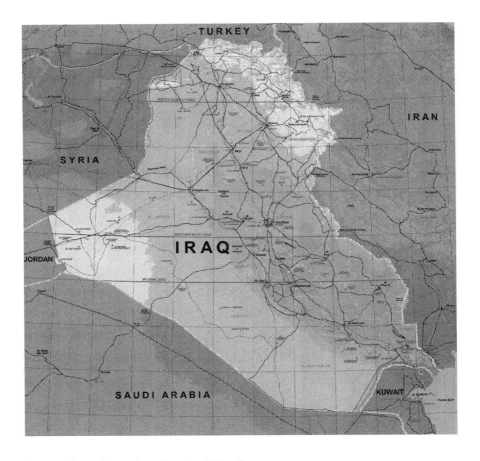

Iran and Iraq share a long border: 906 miles.

form a government representing the Shia majority in the country. In eight years of war against the Americans, the Iraqi Shia militants fighting on their home turf established themselves as committed warriors, and along with their Shia brethren in Lebanon, Hezbollah, formed the nucleus of the Quds Force's Foreign Legion, or SLA, a designation first used by a senior Iranian general. The militias would act as the Quds Force's ground force in the battles that followed the U.S. withdrawal from Iraq in 2011, including the war against ISIS.

On 4 June 2014, ISIS fighters crossed the Syrian border and marched toward Mosul, Iraq's second-largest city. In six days, ISIS defeated the Iraqi Army (IA) 3rd Armored Division defending Nineveh province. The division was almost totally destroyed, with its soldiers abandoning the battlefield or killed in the fighting. On 10 June, Mosul fell. The ISIS victory over the 3rd

Armored Division, which had fought hard against the IRGC and Artesh during the Iran-Iraq War, sent shockwaves through the Quds Force headquarters. In the biggest intelligence fiasco in Quds Force history, its intelligence operatives in Syria and Iraq, its fusion cells along with Hezbollah and Syrian intelligence units set up across Syria after the start of the civil war, did not detect the movement of thousands of ISIS fighters and hundreds of their technical pickup trucks with mounted machine guns and other weaponry crossing the border from Syria into Iraq and heading toward Mosul from their Fallujah stronghold inside Iraq. And the force had defeated one of the IA's storied divisions within days, albeit a division that was dissolved but later reactivated after the U.S. invasion. Left unchecked, Soleimani feared, Daesh could overrun Iraq and invade Iran.

As the summer progressed, Soleimani's fears quickly started to look like a reality. On 11 August, ISIS captured Jalula, a town only twenty-two miles from the city of Khanaqin on the Iranian border. The irony was Jalula itself, the place where an Islamic Caliphate of an earlier era, the Rashedin under the leadership of Caliph Omar, had defeated Persia's Sassanid Empire, reportedly killing so many Persians that the dead bodies had *jellat* (covered the ground) and so the area became known as "Jalula."

"Today [11 August 2014], the terrorist and *takfiri* forces are near our border," said a message from the general staff headquarters of the Iranian armed forces sent to subordinate units.[1] The commander of the Iranian army ground forces recalled those fateful August days, saying, "Daesh had recruited local supporters and had planned a series of [suicide] bombings inside Iran as a prelude to Daesh forces reaching the borders."[2]

Artesh, Iran's regular army charged with protecting the country's borders, sent five army brigades (roughly thirty thousand troops), including artillery and special forces, to the Iraqi side of the border to stop ISIS from crossing into Iranian territory.[3] ISIS, countering the swift response by Artesh, changed its plan to attack Iran and instead fortified its forces in towns near the border, including Jalula. The task of pushing ISIS out of those towns, which had mixed Shia-Sunni populations, belonged to General Soleimani and his Quds Force.

The Quds Force had already deployed hundreds of its officers into Iraq to advise and assist Iraqi Shia militias in the wake of ISIS's lightning advance toward Baghdad. It had shipped thousands of tons of weapons and equipment and millions of dollars in cash to sustain this force. Soleimani sought to establish a support network for the Iraqis, fortify their forces, and help keep Baghdad from collapsing. The offensive phase against ISIS had to wait a while.

In late August, Soleimani began to assemble a larger force, spearheaded by the Iraqi Shia militias acting as its ground forces. In the preparation phase for the offensive, senior Quds Force officers and Iraqi Shia militia leaders gathered to plan the military operation, drafting battle plans, addressing personnel issues, and arranging logistics. Gathering forces was the next stage. Shia militants, including members of the Badr Organization and the AAH, massed near Jalula weeks in advance of the battle. The militias used Iranian military hardware, including AM-50 anti-materiel rifles, Safir Jeeps mounted with 107mm multiple rocket launchers (MRLs), and 120mm HM-20 MRLs.[4] The IRGC deployed UAV, artillery, and armor units in support of the offensive.[5] Due to Jalula's proximity to the Iranian border, Soleimani asked the Islamic Republic of Iran Air Force (Artesh's air component) to provide air support.[6] Special forces from the IA and the Ministry of the Interior participated in the operation in support of the Quds Force.[7] The Kurdish Peshmerga linked to the Patriotic Union of Kurdistan (PUK), the Kurdish faction loyal to Iran, deployed large forces to the battlefield. On 23 November 2014, Soleimani-led forces and the Kurdish Peshmerga pushed ISIS out of Jalula and the neighboring town of Saadiya.[8]

By year's end, ISIS had also been driven out of Amirili, Jurf al-Sakhr, Balad, and Miqdadiyah. The Quds Force and the IRGC units on temporary duty in Iraq in support of its operations were based in Baghdad, Najaf, Karbala, the Samarra-Balad corridor, Camp Ashraf, Taji, and Khanaqin. The Iranians also operated out of the airports in Baghdad, Kirkuk, Sulaymaniyah, and Erbil. Iran was back in control.

THE PMF

The major Iraqi Shia militant groups have their origins in the Iran-Iraq War of 1980s. The Badr Brigade was organized, funded, and trained by the IRGC in 1982 as the military wing of the Iran-based Shia Islamist party, SCIRI. Badr members were mainly Shia defectors from the IA and included some Iraqi POWs who had changed sides. They fought alongside the IRGC, wearing its uniform, against their own country's military during the eight-year war. After the war, Badr members participated in operations against Saddam Hussein's regime, targeting Baath officials and installations in southern Iraq from their base on the Iranian side of the border. The organization was deployed to Najaf and Karbala to participate in the 1991 Shia uprising against Saddam, then was deployed back to Iran when the movement was crushed.

During the Iran-Iraq War, the IRGC organized a second Iraqi militia group, the armed wing of the Dawa Party, an old and predominantly Shia Iraqi party that had reconstituted itself in exile in Iran to escape Saddam's persecution. The military wing was led by Abu Mahdi Al-Muhandis, who directed the group's attacks against the U.S. and French embassies in Kuwait City and an assassination attempt against the Kuwaiti ruler in 1983 at the height of the eight-year war. Muhandis and his cohorts had to flee back to Iran. The Dawa militants eventually joined the Badr Brigade. For his bravery in Kuwait, the IRGC put Muhandis in command of the organization. The Badr Brigade, along with Hezbollah, became the first full-fledged Shia militia group organized and led by the IRGC.

When the U.S. invaded Iraq in 2003 and overthrew the regime of Saddam Hussein, the Iraqi militant groups in exile in Iran joined General Soleimani and his senior aides in crossing the border into a chaotic Iraq. Now on their home turf, the Iraqis reorganized and launched efforts to recruit Shia youths, especially in southern Iraq. The Badr Brigade changed its name to the Badr Organization. Many of its members were instructed to join the reconstituted Federal Police (FedPol) of the Ministry of Interior, which had come under SCIRI's control, and they formed paramilitary units within the ministry, which were later accused of acting as death squads at the height of the Shia-Sunni sectarian conflicts during the occupation years.

Controlling the Ministry of Interior and its armed component, FedPol, was a strategic objective of the Quds Force in the new Iraq. It gave the Iranians not only control of a major Iraqi security institution but also allowed its oldest proxy group to be funded by Iraqi oil revenues. The arrangement had its own costs: Badr's members could not continue drawing salaries from a government under U.S. occupation and attack the Americans at the same time. Soleimani needed to establish a new militia group to engage the U.S. forces without political limitations. His top man in Iraq, Abu Mahdi al-Muhandis, left Badr in 2007 and started a new militia group, the KH.[9] His chief of staff at Badr, Hadi Al-Amiri, replaced Muhandis as the commander of the Badr Organization.

The KH rose to prominence in February 2008 for attacking a U.S. military base in Baghdad using an IRAM, killing one American and wounding many more. The group also ran a smuggling network between Iran and Iraq in concert with the Quds Force, which enabled it to import deadly weapons, such as IRAMs and IEDs. Unlike Badr, the KH focused its operations on a deadly anti-U.S. campaign from its founding in 2007 until the Americans left Iraq in 2011.

Early in the occupation period, another Shia militant, the cleric Muqtada al-Sadr, organized an anti-American militia group, Jaysh al-Mahdi (the Mahdi Army) to oppose the U.S. occupation of Iraq. All Shia militia groups shared the strategic objective of raising costs for the occupation of the country, assuming that the Americans and their allies were not willing to pay heavy sacrifices. In 2004, the Mahdi army launched simultaneous attacks in Baghdad, Najaf, Karbala, and Kufa targeting U.S. and coalition forces. Although the Quds Force assisted Sadr in his campaign against U.S. forces, ideologically, the Iraqi cleric presented a challenge to the Iranian Shia orthodoxy. Sadr positioned his movement as a distinctly Iraqi phenomenon and did not accept the supremacy of Iran's Ayatollah Khamenei as *velayat-e faghih*. Soleimani's principal operative within the Mahdi Army, Qais Khaza-li, and his followers split from the Sadrists in 2006 and formed their own militia group under the command of the Quds Force: the AAH. The organization became notorious during the 2006–2007 sectarian violence in the country, conducting assassinations, kidnappings, and attacks on U.S. forces.

The three Quds Force–led militant organizations—the Badr Organization, the KH, and the AAH—formed the nucleus of the PMF after ISIS invaded Mosul in 2014 and began its thunderous march toward Baghdad and the Shia-majority south. The PMF's mission was to stop ISIS's advance. The KH's Muhandis became operations commander of the PMF. Badr's Amiri, an experienced commander who fought for Iran during the Iran-Iraq war, became the de facto field commander of PMF militias during combat operations. The trio of Soleimani, Muhandis, and Amiri became the power behind the PMF.

Fast forward two years later, in November 2016 the Iraqi Parliament formalized the PMF as a state security force. The law codified the PMF as a component of the ISF independent of the Ministries of the Interior and Defense, and with a budget of its own. The PMF could now access and retain weapons and equipment held by the Defense Ministry. The Quds Force–controlled PMF, fielding some eighty thousand Shia fighters[10] and receiving state funds and materiel, had cemented Iranian influence over Iraqi security policy.

Hezbollah has also been active in its support of the PMF. According to the KH's Muhandis, Hezbollah sent advisers from the beginning of the PMF's existence and helped with training, battle plans, and equipment acquisition.[11] Soleimani went a step further, saying that the PMF was moving toward becoming a "Hezbollah-like" army.[12]

PMF Leading Commanders

Prominent Iraqi Shia militia leaders emerged during the U.S. occupation of the country and still hold senior positions within the PMF.

Abu Mahdi al-Muhandis (Jamal Jafaar Mohammed Ali Ebrahimi). Former commander of the Badr organization and commander of the KH. Operations chief of the PMF. Along with Amiri, the most senior Quds Force operative in Iraq.

Hadi al-Amiri. Commander of the Badr Organization. Former minister of transportation. Commander of Badr Organization members at the Iraqi Ministry of the Interior and FedPol. Coordinator of Iraqi Shia militia groups on battlefields. Along with Muhandis, he is the most senior Quds Force operative in Iraq.

Qays al-Khazali. A former Muqtada al-Sadr lieutenant, he founded the AAH in 2006.[13] He has longtime personal and professional ties to the Quds Force. He was detained by the coalition forces from 2006 to 2009 but was freed by Prime Minister Nouri al-Maliki.

Abdal Aziz al-Muhammadawi. A former Badr member who participated in anti-Saddam operations, he also has longtime ties to the IRGC and the Quds Force. Operations chief of the KH.

Akram al-Kabi. A former Sadrist who co-founded the AAH along with Khazali.[14] He split from the AAH after the U.S. troop withdrawal from Iraq and founded a new militia group, Harakat al-Nujaba. He has long-standing ties to the Quds Force. He is an experienced militia leader, serving as acting commander of the AAH during Khazali's detention.

Shibl Muhsin Faraj al-Zaidi. A former Sadr lieutenant, he joined Khazali to found the AAH. He was also detained by the coalition forces from 2006 to 2009 and freed by Maliki. He later split from the AAH and with the approval of the Quds Force founded a new militia group after the ISIS invasion, Kata'ib Imam Ali.[15] He also has longtime personal and professional ties to the Quds Force.

Abu Mustafa al-Sheibani. A former Badr member along with Muhandis during the Iranian exile years. He directed the Sheibani network, smuggling IEDs into Iraq from Iran during the occupation years and supplied IEDs to the AAH and the KH. He is believed to be a commander of the militia group Kata'ib Sayyid al-Shuhada.[16] He has long-standing personal and professional ties to the Quds Force.

This list of leading commanders reflects the extent of the Quds Force's influence and its degree of control of the PMF. The Badr Organization, the KH, the AAH, Harakat al-Nujaba, Kata'ib Sayyid al-Shuhada, and Kata'ib Imam Ali are the most prominent Iraqi militia groups within the PMF, and all their founders and current commanders have strong personal and professional ties to the Quds Force and its commander, General Soleimani, and report directly to him.

The PMF, ostensibly formed to fight ISIS, has maintained an enduring presence on the scene in post-ISIS Iraq, becoming a legal, institutional, and permanent fixture in the Iraqi government. By reaching the status of an Iraqi security institution, the PMF reflects the extent to which the Iranians are in control of post-Daesh Iraq.

THE QUDS FORCE AND THE ISF

The Quds Force–led Iraqi Shia militia groups have gained varying degrees of influence in the ISF. FedPol and its relations with the Badr Organization is the most obvious case. Since the fall of Saddam in 2003, thousands of Badr members have been integrated into all echelons of the Ministry of Interior, and by 2006 after a series of purges against Sunni members, Badr had achieved a dominant position within the ministry. Badr militants in turn took up a large portion of FedPol ranks. Badr leaders fill much of the officer corps; indeed, the interior minister himself is a longtime Badr member and Amiri's lieutenant, the commander of the Badr Organization. FedPol has some fifty thousand personnel, and approximately 95 percent of them are Shia.

In battlefields in predominantly Sunni regions, Shia fighters who are not part of FedPol or the Badr Organization wear its uniform to hide their true affiliation and allow them to participate in battles that would be otherwise denied to them to prevent sectarian violence, especially in clearing operations. The practice also gives the Iraqi government a degree of deniability in the participation of Shia militias in clearing operations on Sunni lands.

The PMF, another branch of the ISF, is nominally under Iraqi government control, but the core of the organization is beholden to Iran, the Quds Force, and General Soleimani. PMF-affiliated militias generally have affiliated political parties in parliament led by Shia political leaders aligned with Iran. Their political positions are typically Shia sectarian, pro-Iran, and anti-U.S., and using their influence in the legislative branch, they seek to shape the PMF into a powerful, if not the most powerful, branch of the ISF. The PMF has already established a dozen military camps and operations bases inside Iraq.

The IA is a much more diverse organization. But starting with Maliki's premiership, friendly Shia officers assumed senior command posts in the army, potentially giving the Quds Force a degree of influence within the armed forces. Counter Terrorism Service (CTS) remains arguably the only apolitical branch of the ISF, although it increasingly cooperated with the Shia militias during its anti-ISIS campaign, giving the PMF some degree of influence over the CTS. A change in CTS leadership if a new government comes to power could further increase the Shia militant and PMF influence in the service.

SHIA MILITIAS IN ACTION

By the end of 2014, the Quds Force and Shia militias' counter-Daesh operations in Iraq were proving very effective. Jalula was cleared of ISIS, ending the immediate threat on the Iranian border. So were the towns of Amirili, Jurf al-Sakhr, Balad, and Miqdadiyah. Concurrently, the U.S.-led coalition of Iraqi and Kurdish security forces and Sunni tribal elements supported by the U.S. and allied airstrikes recaptured towns and oil facilities near Kirkuk, the strategic Mosul Dam, and the towns of Yusufyah, Hadithah, and Zummar.

Moving to ISIS–controlled Sunni areas was Soleimani's next phase of the campaign. But 2015 brought its own challenges. The Syrian front was deteriorating rapidly for the Quds Force and its militia army. The opposition against Assad proved more resilient than expected. Territory fully controlled by the regime shrank by 18 percent between January and August 2015. By mid-August, the government no longer controlled 83 percent of the country.[17] Soleimani personally went to Moscow to plead for Russian direct military involvement in Syria to turn back the opposition's gains and save Assad.[18] The pact reached in Moscow would change the trajectory of the war in favor of the pro-regime forces. The Quds Force would significantly increase its ground forces, while the IRGC and Artesh would provide artillery, armor, special forces, and UAVs. The Russians would provide air power to support Soleimani's forces. The Syrian military was to be used to fill in the gaps.

Implementing the Moscow agreement meant the deployment of significant numbers of Iraqi militants in Syria and away from the counter-Daesh battles in Iraq. The tactic was necessary because the Syrian army was facing serious recruiting problems and the latest victories by the opposition had exacerbated the low morale of its troops. But it was also a risky one. ISIS could use the lower numbers of the Quds Force–led militia army to its advantage. After all, just beyond Basra and the Shatt al-Arab waterway lies Iran. But saving the Assad regime had been a strategic goal of Iran since the country's civil war started in 2011, and Soleimani was not going to witness the collapse of the regime. He was ready to accept a lull in the fighting and indeed a stalemate inside Iraq to undertake major military operations in Syria. The Russians were in full agreement. They were ready to directly intervene in Syria if Soleimani would provide the bulk of the land forces. The conditions were set to retake Aleppo, Syria's largest city and its commercial center before the war.

But the strategy meant shrinking the ranks of the Quds Force–led army inside Iraq. Even prior to the Moscow agreement, Soleimani needed to deploy fighters to Syria who otherwise would have strengthened his forces in the counter-ISIS campaign. In March 2015, he committed around 25,000 Shia militants to the battle of Tikrit. They were supported by some three thousand members of the ISF, including special forces and armor and artillery units, all of whom were led by Quds Force and IRGC general officers. They were to surround the city and move into Tikrit. The siege lasted more than three weeks, with ISIS fighters, numbering only in the hundreds, putting up a robust defense of the city center—with IEDs covering all roads into the city—and pushing back Soleimani's superior forces. Instead of reinforcing the land forces, Soleimani deployed five thousand fighters into Syria to stabilize the deteriorating situation in the country. Prime Minister Haider al-Abadi, frustrated by the slow pace of the campaign, decided to ask for U.S.-led coalition airstrikes to soften ISIS's defenses. Soleimani was livid. He ordered the withdrawal of Quds Force officers and the militants under his direct command from the battlefield in protest of U.S. involvement, which left only three thousand fighters in the battlefield who were under his control. It is now clear that Soleimani's withdrawal of forces from the battle of Tikrit, messaged as an anti-U.S. move, was the beginning of the redeployment into Syria.

The intensive airstrikes by the U.S. and allied forces for three consecutive days softened ISIS positions, and the Iraqi security forces, accompanied by three thousand PMF militia fighters, liberated the city in April.

The battle of Tikrit, and the battle of Jurf al-Sakhr in late 2014, also exposed sectarian and ethnic fault lines in the conflict. In Jurf al-Sakhr, the victorious PMF fighters clearing the city soon began attacking Sunni civilians, burning or occupying their homes, expelling them from the city, and preventing the return of refugees who had fled ISIS.[19] In Tikrit, thousands of Sunni residents who had fled ISIS brutality were afraid to return home to face the PMF militias that controlled the city. The makeup of the majority of the PMF, being ideologically committed sectarian Shias, remained a major obstacle in the counter-Daesh campaign throughout the war, slowing down the preparations and implementation of major operations in Sunni-dominated areas, including Fallujah, Ramadi, and Mosul.

Taking advantage of perceived pandemonium within the ranks of pro-government forces prompted by Soleimani's withdrawal from the battle of Tikrit, ISIS planned its biggest surprise since capturing Mosul the previous year. On 17 May 2015, they forced their way into Ramadi and captured the capital of the country's Sunni heartland, Anbar province, after seven months of fighting on the city's peripheries. The insurgents used a wave of vehicle borne IEDs (VBIEDs)—in this case, large military trucks captured from the Iraqi forces laden with tons of explosives—and the cover of a sandstorm to enter the city. They proved their ability to launch a complex military campaign after withstanding intense airstrikes for months, while still being able to provide logistics support to sustain their forces. In July 2015, the U.S.-led coalition began a sustained and intensive air campaign against ISIS forces in Ramadi, which took nearly eight months and more than eight hundred airstrikes to soften the enemy defenses before the Iraqi security forces could recapture the town in February 2016. Conspicuously absent from the battle to liberate Ramadi was Soleimani and his Iraqi militia forces, many of whom had been deployed to Syria after the July Moscow agreement.

The militias that remained in Iraq that year saw action at Baiji and its major refinery. In October 2015, a combined force of ISF and Shia militias began an offensive to retake Baiji. Daesh, as expected, attempted to slow the operations with IEDs and by withdrawing its fighters when facing superior numbers, with some 20,000 pro-government forces against some 1,500 ISIS fighters. By mid-October, several PMF brigades, supported by a FedPol brigade led by Badr militants and an ISF brigade, moved on several axes toward their main targets. A PMF and ISF column seized the refinery perimeter and advanced toward Al Fatah Bridge. From south of the city, forces moved to retake the airfield. Forces west of the Tigris seized the refinery, with forces east of the river approaching the city. On 19 October, Baiji was liberated.

The battle of Baiji prevented the depleted PMF and ISF forces from focusing on Fallujah and other targets. In Fallujah, where the campaign to retake the city had begun in May, the fighting was at a stalemate for most of 2015. It was not until May 2016 that pro-government forces launched their major offensive against Daesh. The IA deployed two divisions, some ten thousand soldiers, in the operation, supported by its special forces and storied CTS commandos. FedPol under the leadership of Hadi al-Amiri deployed another division. Soleimani and his top lieutenant, Abu Mahdi al-Muhandis, the operations chief of the PMF, with the bulk of their forces still in the Syrian theater, mustered some 3,500 militants. The Iranians also deployed artillery and armor units. Quds Force and IRGC officers were deployed to guide the Shia militias as well as ISF forces, among them many high-ranking Iranian officers. The IRGC Aerospace Force also conducted ISR missions using UAVs. As in Tikrit and Ramadi, the U.S.-led coalition provided intense airstrikes against Daesh positions in and around the city. This time, however, Soleimani did not object to coalition involvement. Fallujah was cleared of ISIS more quickly than expected. The offensive began on 22 May 2016, and less than a week later, pro-government forces captured the city outskirts. By 30 May, pro-government forces had begun entering the city. On 28 June 2016, Fallujah was liberated. Compared to Ramadi, which took six months to be retaken, Fallujah was recaptured in less than a month.

The surge in pro-government forces, supported by U.S.-led coalition airstrikes, enabled them to mass and maneuver more effectively than in Ramadi. The rapid collapse of ISIS defenses was also a result of low morale in the rank-and-file of the Daesh fighting force. There were reports of fighters prioritizing safety of their families over fighting, which contributed to a breakdown of the group's command-and-control structure. Their haphazard evacuation from the city, unprecedented at the time, was a sign that Daesh was becoming increasingly unable to mount prolonged static defenses of urban areas when faced with a large number of land forces that attacked on multiple axes and were backed by sustained airstrikes. This strategy thus became the model that was to be used in the remaining battlespaces, including Mosul in Iraq and Raqqa in Syria.

Daesh's tactic in Ramadi and Fallujah, repeated again in Mosul and Raqqa, was to concentrate fighters, suicide bombers, and defensive barriers on the city's outskirts to channel and delay opposing forces, leaving minimal defenses within the city centers, where fighters' families lived. In almost all battles, Daesh was outnumbered by an average of 25 to 1. Ultimately, its undoing came from Daesh's inability to provide enough fighters to defend every avenue of approach to the cities when it was faced with coordinated assault on multiple axes.

THE BATTLES OF MOSUL AND TAL AFAR

Mosul was the last major Iraqi city to be cleared of ISIS. The city was liberated on 20 July 2017. Some 100,000 anti-ISIS forces supported by sustained U.S.-led coalition airstrikes participated in the battle. The ISF deployed 50,000 troops. The Kurdish security forces (KSF) contributed 40,000 fighters. The Quds Force–led Shia militia forces had some 10,000 troops in the battlespace, with many of these fighters embedded in the ISF and FedPol, whose 6th Division was practically created for the battle of Mosul while its Emergency Response Division was led by Soleimani's top aide, Badr secretary general Hadi al-Amiri. ISIS was believed to have some 6,000 fighters in the city.

The offensive began in October 2016. The IA 75th Infantry Brigade retook Al Qayyarah on the first day of the battle, facing small-arms and indirect fire from ISIS fighters. FedPol and PMF forces were deployed south of the city. The PMF forces were to advance toward Tal Afar. The IA 73rd and 76th brigades began isolating Talkayf against strong ISIS resistance using suicide bombers, shock troops, and anti-tank weapons. In the second week of the battle, the IA 3rd Infantry and 36th Armor brigades retook Al Hamdaniyah after stiff ISIS resistance. Iraqi Special Operations Forces (ISOF) cleared villages east of Mosul, while the ISF and KSF continued slow and steady clearing operations toward Mosul amid ISIS harassing attacks. On 1 November, ISOF units advanced to the eastern edge of Mosul and conducted clearing operations in the city's last suburban areas while preparing to enter the city. Meanwhile, CTS units forced their way into the eastern edge of Mosul City, with the IA 9th Infantry Division on their right flank. On 3 November, they entered the eastern Mosul neighborhood of Al Intisar, starting a protracted process to clear all the eastern neighborhoods, a process that would take more than two months. Other IA units advanced to east Mosul from other axes to join the forces on the ground.

On 25 December, the pro-government forces began their offensive operations to capture west Mosul. Soleimani's militants also advanced from their positions southwest of Mosul. The multi-axis assault, enabled by U.S.-led coalition airstrikes, weakened ISIS defenses. Then units of the Iraqi forces began advancing toward west Mosul from their position northeast of the city, crossing the Tigris on rafts from east Mosul. By year's end, the first phase of the Battle of Mosul, the preparation for capturing the entire city, had been accomplished. The CTS had taken control of Al Intisar, while other units had captured most of the Karma district. The pro-government forces now controlled over 60 percent of east Mosul.

On 13 February, ISIS fighters launched an attack on Quds Force–led militias in three villages west of Tal Afar with tanks and VBIEDs to regain a line of communications between west Mosul and their stronghold of Raqqa in Syria. PMF and FedPol forces eventually retook the villages in heavy fighting and continued capturing more villages west of Mosul.

Meanwhile, the Iraqi forces continued their advance in west Mosul. By April, the operations required a slow, block-by-block advance against Daesh defenses. PMF units embedded with FedPol and the Rapid Response Division of the Ministry of Interior engaged ISIS on southern and western fronts at the edge of the old city. The battle for central Mosul began in June and lasted more than a month. On 10 July 2017, Iraqi prime minister Haydar Al Abadi declared victory over ISIS. Mosul was liberated at a heavy human cost and with over $1 billion in damage to the city infrastructure.

The Quds Force–led forces continued the fight alongside the ISF to retake Tal Afar, engaging ISIS fighters in heavy fighting for two weeks, from 20 August to 2 September 2017. Soleimani deployed nearly 20,000 Shia fighters alongside FedPol forces. The Iraqis deployed nearly 40,000 troops from the IA 7th Infantry Division, 9th Armor Division, and elements of the 15th and 16th divisions. The ISOF deployed its 1st and 3rd divisions.

On 2 December, PMF captured Tal Afar Airfield and turned it into a permanent military base and operations headquarters for northern Iraq and the Iraqi-Syrian border area. The militias soon repaired damage to the airfield's infrastructure. The IRGC relocated its artillery elements and UAV force to the airfield. On 20 August, Prime Minister Abadi announced the beginning of the Tal Afar offensive, telling insurgents, "Either die or surrender." PMF units advanced toward the city from the south. The U.S.-led coalition conducted intensive airstrikes against ISIS defenses on the outskirts of the city. FedPol forces advanced from the west. CTS forces approached the city from the southwest. Within two days of the start of the offensive, IA units entered the city from the southwest and northwest. By 25 August, pro-government forces had captured the city center and more than 90 percent of the town. Two days later, Tal Afar was liberated entirely, and cleanup operations started. On 2 September, Tal Afar was cleared of ISIS fighters. The counter-ISIS struggle was rapidly coming to an end. And the Quds Force–led forces had positioned themselves to control the Iraq-Syria border, a key Iranian strategic goal in building a land bridge connecting Iran to Syria through Iraqi territory and controlled by the Quds Force.

KURDISTAN

When Tikrit fell to ISIS in June 2014, the ISF fled their positions in Kirkuk, only seventy-one miles from Tikrit. The KSF filled the gap, ostensibly defending Kirkuk from advancing ISIS fighters but also fulfilling the Kurdish dream of returning the city to Kurdistan. The new Kurdish front, replacing the Green Line, began at Sinjar, just bordering Mosul, and contained Kirkuk. That city and its oilfields were vital for an economically viable, independent Kurdistan. Under Saddam's regime, Baath officials had forced the Arabization of the predominantly Kurdish town, driving out Kurds and Turkmen. In the post-Saddam era, the new Iraqi constitution declared Kirkuk a disputed territory, with its final status to be determined by referendum. The Shia government that replaced Saddam, however, did not want to have an independent Kurdistan and were in no hurry to hold a referendum on the status of Kirkuk, being certain that the locals would opt to join the Erbil-based Kurdish Regional Government (KRG). The result of such a referendum would also facilitate a declaration of independence by the Kurds. The Iranians also were dead set against Kurdish independence or return of Kirkuk to Kurdish rule under the KRG. Soleimani, during his many visits to Erbil, had made no secret of the fact that his forces would oppose any unilateral declaration of independence by the KRG, especially if it contained Kirkuk.

On 25 September 2017, the KRG, under the leadership of Masoud Barzani, held its own referendum in territories under its control, including Kirkuk. The Americans had warned Barzani of the negative consequences of holding a unilateral referendum, which could lead to the independence of Kurdistan without any agreement with other stakeholders in Iraq. Barzani, whose forces, the KSF, had fought bravely against Daesh and were a major actor in pushing ISIS out of Iraq, believed the Kurds had paid their dues and should be allowed to hold the referendum in the face of a government in Baghdad that had consistently and provocatively ignored the country's constitution when it came to Kurdish rights, oil revenue sharing, and the holding of an eventual referendum to determine the final status of disputed territories like Kirkuk. Barzani also believed that Soleimani was in Iraq to fight ISIS and not to interfere in the country's internal affairs, including the holding of any referendum.

The Abadi government and the Quds Force–led Shia militias used the KRG referendum as an excuse and moved their forces toward Kirkuk three weeks after the Kurds had voted overwhelmingly for Kurdish independence. In a well-publicized trip, Soleimani visited Suleymaniyah, the stronghold of the PUK, and clinched a deal with the Talibani family who ran the PUK. The PUK would withdraw its Peshmerga forces from Kirkuk, which was under its protection, allowing the ISF and PMF militias to enter the town unopposed. In return, the Quds Force would apparently allow the PUK to continue exporting some $1 million a day worth of oil through its pipeline into Iran and on to Iranian export facilities in the Persian Gulf. The Democratic Party of Kurdistan (DPK), led by the Barzani clan, called the PUK's decision to withdraw its Peshmerga forces from Kirkuk a traitorous act against the Kurdish nation. On 16 October 2017, ISF and PMF militias entered Kirkuk City. Badr's Hadi al-Amiri and PMF's Abu Mahdi al-Muhandis were photographed with the militants in Kirkuk lowering the Kurdish flag and raising the Iraqi flag over the government building.[20]

When the PUK ordered the Peshmerga to raise the Kurdish flag on the oil-pumping station in Kirkuk in March 2017, the regional government was exporting more than 600,000 barrels of crude oil per day, 17 percent of Iraq's total. The only major oil pipeline runs from Kirkuk through KRG territory through Turkey to a Turkish oil export terminal. Barzani believed that the pipeline was his leverage with Turkey. But the theory did not hold, and Ankara joined Baghdad and Tehran in vehemently opposing the referendum. Barzani believed with even greater confidence that after fighting ISIS side-by-side with the U.S. military, and especially considering the Kurds' significant participation in the battle of Mosul and the years of cooperation between their two militaries, Washington would not stand by as the Kurds were forced to retreat in the face of advancing Iraqi- and Iranian-led forces. Barzani especially believed that direct weapons shipments to the KRG were a key sign of Washington's commitment to Erbil. But on this issue too he erred. The Trump administration's decision not to defend the Kurds likely raised serious questions in Kurdistan and across the region, including, "Is America's word any good? How could America abandon the Kurds?"

The Quds Force–Kurdistan conflict will remain a major destabilizing factor in post-Daesh Iraq, which could fracture the country if only military force is used to resolve the status of disputed territories and the future of the KRG and its leadership.

THE QUDS FORCE MOVES BEYOND MOSUL AND KIRKUK

In November 2017, Quds Force–led PMF militias, supported by IA units, entered Al Qaim, an Iraqi town on the border with Syria. A week later, Quds Force–led Shia militias on the Syrian side of the border, supported by Syrian army units, entered Abu Kamal, the town on the Syrian side of the border opposite Iraq's Al Qaem. Through these offensive operations, Soleimani achieved arguably the most important strategic goal of the Islamic Republic: building a land bridge connecting Iran through Iraq to Syria and Lebanon and reaching the northern border of Israel. It is true that Iran already has an air bridge connecting a number of Iranian airports to Damascus International Airport. However, in times of conflict, Iranian airports could be taken out in the first days or hours, leaving a land corridor as a necessity to transfer troops and materiel to fronts beyond Iranian borders, including Syria. Now with the control of significant parts of Iraqi territory all the way to the Syrian border, the Quds Force had a land corridor to supply and reinforce its militia force inside Syria and up to the Israeli border.

When the Americans left Iraq at the end of 2011, the Quds Force and its Iraqi militia forces began establishing themselves as the main military power in the country. By 2012–2013, Soleimani had full control of Iraq. Then Daesh began its advance inside Iraq. In December 2013, ISIS engaged Iraqi security forces in Anbar province. By January 2014, they had captured Fallujah and parts of Ramadi. And in June 2014, they overtook Mosul and began a thunderous advance south toward Baghdad and the Iranian borders. Soleimani had to redeploy Shia militias fighting in Syria to Iraq and deploy IRGC and Artesh specialized units into the new battlespace against ISIS to stop its momentum. The next three years became the years of counter-Daesh operations in Iraq. As a result, Soleimani enlarged his militia forces inside Iraq and after Mosul exercised unopposed power in the country, first recapturing Kirkuk from the Kurdish Peshmerga forces and then marching to the border towns of Al Qaim on the Iraqi side and Abu Kamal on the Syrian side to establish his land bridge. By the end of 2017, the forces under his command controlled contiguous territories from the western borders of Iran through Iraq and Syria to Lebanon and the Israeli border. In post-Daesh Iraq, the Quds Force had reached an even stronger position than in the post–U.S. withdrawal period. Soleimani had become viceroy of Iraq in all but name. On 21 November, the newspaper *Afkar* even went so far as to print a cover story with the title "Kingdom of Soleimani."[21]

But Soleimani probably overplayed his hand. As long as Daesh posed a credible threat to Iraq and its Shia community, all Shias were united under the leadership of Soleimani to fight Daesh. What Soleimani probably did not account for was that the unity in the community could quickly evaporate in post-Daesh Iraq. And it did. In the first post-Daesh parliamentary elections, held in May 2018, the predominantly Shia parties presented four competing blocks. Hadi al-Amiri led a coalition of PMF militia groups, which were solidly pro-Iran. Muqtada al-Sadr organized a coalition that included the Left and opposed Iran's continued military presence in Iraq. The sitting prime minister Haider al-Abadi and former prime minister Nouri al-Maliki formed two Shia-led blocks, the former offering a centrist platform on working with Iran and the U.S. in the post-Daesh period, the latter solidly in support of Iran. The anti-Iran, Sadr-backed bloc finished with the most votes, followed by pro-Iran Amiri, and then Abadi and Maliki.

The elections results were only a manifestation of the political divide within the Shia community. But it was a wake-up call of sorts for the Quds Force. The country's citizens, including its Shia majority, are Iraqis. Most see themselves as Iraqis first. This was something that the Iranians missed altogether. Heavy-handed tactics to influence the country's security and other government institutions by Soleimani and his men in Baghdad had come back to haunt them. It would be painful for the Iraqis, Shia or not, to see a foreign power practically controlling their country.

The Quds Force is now being forced to make a decision on their Iraq strategy. Should they withdraw the Quds Force officers and other foreign personnel under their control in Iraq and try a softer approach to maintain their influence in the country? Their heavy-handed approach could cause them to lose their influence in the country at a time they can afford it the least. Isolation seems to be the trend when it comes to the Islamic Republic's relations with the outside word.

Chapter Eight

Sanaa Calling

In September 2014, General Soleimani was in Baghdad planning Operation Ashura to retake Jurf as-Sakhr when news reached him that Houthi rebels had captured the Yemeni capital of Sanaa. This was a "golden opportunity," the general was quoted as saying.[1] A Zaydi-Shia Houthi–led government was now in control of the capital of a country bordering Saudi Arabia, the nemesis of the Islamic Republic. A week earlier, Alireza Zakani, a member of the Iranian Majlis and the secretary general of Rahpouyan, a militant Shia organization calling for the spread of the Islamic Revolution in the region, had predicted the event: "Iran now controls three capitals [in the region]: Baghdad, Damascus, and Beirut. In future, Sanaa will also join the list of Iranian capitals. We are after unification of all [Shia] Islamic territories."[2]

The Houthis' new position in Yemen opened an avenue for the Quds Force to extend its influence on the Arabian Peninsula and counter Saudi influence in the region at the same time. Soleimani could now launch a Shia expeditionary force in the Saudis' backyard. He wasted no time doing just that; within days of the Houthi takeover of Sanaa, the IRGC–linked Iranian airline Mahan Air began fourteen weekly direct flights from Tehran to Sanaa.[3] Mahan was establishing an air bridge linking the two countries. The Quds Force used the daily flights to deploy senior officers to Yemen. Commanders and specialists from the Quds Force–led Shia militia forces were also deployed to Sanaa to offer military advice and technical assistance to the Houthis. They included members of Hezbollah and militia advisers from the Iraqi Shia groups KH, AAH, Harakat al-Nujaba, and Kata'ib Imam Ali.

The Quds Force used Mahan Air and its cargo aircraft to ship a significant volume of advanced weaponry to the Houthis. In October 2014, the Houthis also captured the major seaport of Hudaydah, enabling the Quds Force to send them cargo ships loaded with ASCMs, theater ballistic missiles,

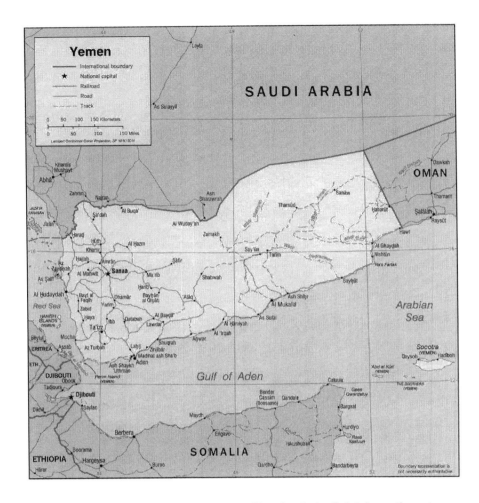

Four Yemeni cities tell the story of the conflict: Saada (or Sa'a), in northwest Yemen; Sanaa, Yemen's capital; Hudaydah, Yemen's major Red Sea port; and Aden, a port city on the Gulf of Aden.

ATGMs, explosive boats, parts, ammunition, and equipment. The Quds Force could handle such heavy lifting by air and sea because a friendly government was controlling an international airport and a major seaport in the country, advantages that would disappear when a Saudi-led coalition blockaded Yemeni airspace and seaports six months after the fall of Sanaa.

The blockade highlighted the Quds Force's limits in operating in hostile environments, especially in places without a land bridge linking them to Iran. That experience would prompt the Quds Force to build a land bridge to Syria in case the country's airports were to be taken out in hostile actions. But during the period of its free rein in Yemen, the Quds Force deployed advisers to the Houthis and delivered advanced weapons they needed not just for fighting the government but for launching attacks against Saudi Arabia and coalition forces in Yemen.

THE ISLAMIC REPUBLIC AND THE HOUTHIS

The Houthis are followers of the Zaydi branch of Shia Islam and have kept a close relationship with the IRGC and Quds Force for many years. The leaders of their movement visited Iran during the first days of the Islamic Revolution.[4] Housein al-Houthi and his brother Abdulmalek even spent a year in Iran in the early 1980s, receiving religious, political, and security briefings in Qom and Tehran, and they have regularly visited Iran since then.[5] [6] After their stay in revolutionary Iran, they brought home a militant interpretation of Shia Islam. An attack in 1990 by militant Sunnis, reportedly under Salafi influence, against a Zaydi mosque in the Houthis' stronghold of Saada, the capital of the northwestern Yemeni governorate of the same name, which borders Saudi Arabia, made the Houthis more radical and sectarian.[7] In 1997, with the IRGC's backing, Housein al-Houthi founded a militant Shia group using Hezbollah as its model.[8] The group was eventually named Ansarallah (Partisans of God), but was popularly known as "the Houthis" as the Houthi clan dominated the organization and its leadership.

In 2004, the Houthis rebelled against the government of Ali Abdullah Saleh. Housein al-Houthi was executed by the government that year.[9] The episode began a complex relationship between the Houthis and Saleh. They rebelled against him when he was president. Then an Arab Spring–inspired uprising engulfed the country, which led to Saleh's ouster and exile. Then the Houthis and Saleh became allies, planning to capture Sanaa, and they succeeded in 2014. Three years after the fall of Sanaa, however, Saleh turned against the Houthis. The Houthis assassinated Saleh on 4 December 2017, claiming the assassination was revenge for Housein's execution thirteen years earlier.

When Abdulmalek succeeded his fallen brother as Houthi leader, the Quds Force kept close relations with him. Abdulmalek and several senior Houthi leaders visited Iran on a number of occasions, and the Quds Force provided an advanced training program inside Iran for Houthi fighters. Beginning in 2004 until Saleh's government fell in 2012, the Houthis fought five short wars against the government. The Quds Force shipped weapons to the Houthis during that period, and Houthi fighters traveled to Iran for training. Saleh repeatedly accused Iran of interfering in the internal affairs of the country and siding with the Houthis in their uprising against the government.[10] A UN Security Council report identified a pattern of Iranian arms shipments by sea destined for the Houthis starting in 2009, with the possibility of earlier shipments.[11] In February 2011, an Iranian fishing vessel carrying nine hundred Iranian-made anti-tank and anti-helicopter rockets was seized by Yemeni authorities. Smugglers, using dhows and organized by the Quds Force, continued transferring significant volumes of weapons, including AK-47s, rocket-propelled grenades, and other arms to replace older weapons used by the Houthi rebels. Shipments of EFPs via freighters were also delivered to the Houthis during this period.[12]

When the Saleh government fell, the Quds Force–backed Houthis were battle tested, well armed, and trained in advanced weaponry and had practically established a proto-state in the Saada governorate. Their capture of Sanaa and subsequent move to capture Aden deepened the instability in Yemen and invited the military intervention of Saudi Arabia and the UAE to save the Yemeni government and stop Iranian military expansion on the Arabian Peninsula. The IRGC and the Quds Force had propped up Houthi forces for four decades, beginning in the first days of the Islamic Revolution. Capturing Sanaa only raised their profile, making them a prized member of the Quds Force–led SLA. For Soleimani, the prize, the "golden opportunity," was to have the Houthis challenging the Saudis and Emiratis in their own backyards.

BAB AL-MANDEB

Bab al-Mandeb, or the Mandeb Strait, is a strait between Yemen and the Horn of Africa, connecting the Red Sea to the Gulf of Aden and ultimately the Indian Ocean. The strait is a key strategic channel for global trade and commerce, especially oil, with some twenty tankers transiting it each day. And like the Persian Gulf's Strait of Hormuz, Bab al-Mandeb is a major maritime chokepoint. The closure of Bab al-Mandeb would lead to a significant disruption in the global oil supply, preventing tankers originating in the Persian Gulf from reaching the Suez Canal and ultimately Europe. The Quds Force has delivered ASCMs, unmanned explosive boats, radar systems, and mining equipment to the Houthis, giving them the ability to attack U.S. ships and those of its allies transiting Bab al-Mandeb and the southern Red Sea.

The Houthis conducted their first successful strike on 5 October 2016 against an Emirati high-speed vessel.[13] They used an ASCM and a Bavar unmanned explosive boat and then conducted follow-on attacks from land and sea, using small arms and Katyusha rockets against the Emirati ship. Four days later, the Houthis launched ASCMs at a U.S. ship off the coast of Hudaydah. The USS *Mason*, the intended target, fired a counterbattery at the inbound missiles, stopping the strike. The U.S. Navy retaliated three days later and destroyed the Houthis' coastal surveillance radars used to target the ship.[14] The attacks on the UAE and U.S. ships showed that the maritime capabilities of the Quds Force–backed Houthi forces pose a significant and imminent threat to U.S. and allied ships transiting the area.[15]

BALLISTIC MISSILES

After the Houthis captured Sanaa, they took control of the Yemeni army's missile force. Days after the takeover, the Quds Force provided technical help to modify the army's older ballistic missiles, extending their range to four hundred miles, enabling them to target Jeddah, Saudi Arabia. Within a year, the Houthis unveiled a new SCUD-class missile, the Bukran-1. On 9 October 2016, the Houthis fired a Bukran-1 at King Fahd Airbase, outside the Saudi city of al-Taif.[16] On 27 October, they hit King Abdulaziz International Airport in Jeddah, 390 miles from the Yemeni border.[17] The Quds Force technicians continued their work to further enhance the capabilities of the Houthi missile force. By early 2017, the Houthis unveiled their new SCUD-class Bukran-2, with a smaller warhead contained in a separating and more stable reentry vehicle. On 6 February 2017, a Bukran-2 hit al-Muzahimiyah, a Saudi military base twenty-five miles southwest of Riyadh.[18] The Quds Force technicians also repurposed the Yemeni army's SA-2 surface-to-air missiles (SAMs) into Qahir-1, a surface-to-surface firing mode using mobile launchers. The emergence of the Qahir-1, Bukran-1, and Bukran-2 missiles was the clearest indication of the successful Iranian work in modifying SCUD-class missiles for the Houthis as Yemen had no history of producing or modifying ballistic missiles. The Houthis, under the supervision of the Iranian advisers, used the technology and parts sent to them by the Quds Force to upgrade legacy missiles that had come under their control. The Quds Force also directly transferred Qiam-1, a more advanced SCUD-class missile, to the Houthis.

On 6 November 2017, Saudi Arabia charged Iran with an "act of war" after the Houthis fired a ballistic missile at Riyadh International Airport.[19] The missile hit an airport parking lot. On 19 December, the Houthis and the Iranians, undeterred by the Saudi warning, fired a ballistic missile at the royal palace in Riyadh.[20] The Saudi Patriot surface-to-air missile system intercepted the incoming missile.

UNMANNED EXPLOSIVE BOATS

Beginning with the arrival of Quds Force advisers and technicians at Sanaa in 2015, the Iranians transferred technology, equipment, and expertise to the Houthis to develop explosive boat capabilities. These remote-controlled, unmanned speed boats are laden with bombs and equipped with cameras and antennas. They can fuse and detonate anti-ship warheads for use against opposing vessels. By mid-2016, the Houthis were converting small boats into remote-controlled unmanned explosive boats modeled after Iran's Bavar explosive boats.

On 30 January 2017, the Houthis used an unmanned and guided boat against the Royal Saudi Navy frigate *Al Madinah*, killing two Saudi sailors.[21] The Houthis expanded the use of explosive boats to include attacks on the strategic infrastructure of their opposing forces. In April 2017, they launched a boat to attack the Saudi Aramco oil distribution terminal in the Red Sea on the Saudi coast. The boat was one mile from the terminal's off-loading buoys when it was stopped by security forces' gunfire.[22]

These unmanned and guided explosive boats, and other versions of unmanned surface vessels, built under the Quds Force's guidance, have given the Houthis an asymmetric warfare advantage in their fight against the Saudi-led coalition forces and have increased their maritime threat in the Red Sea and Bab al-Mandeb.

UAVS

As part of arming the Houthis with more advanced military equipment, the IRGC began delivering lethal one-way (kamikaze) UAVs and ISR UAVs to them.[23] The Quds Force also helped the Houthis set up limited production facilities to produce UAVs in country, including the Abatil-T drone (named Qasef-1 in Yemen).[24] There were no reports, however, of Iran delivering its most advanced UAV, Shahed-129, to the Houthis.

THE CHALLENGE OF SUPPLYING LETHAL AID TO THE HOUTHIS

In March 2015, a coalition led by Saudi Arabia and the UAE intervened militarily in Yemen to prop up its government, which had been under siege since the Houthis captured Sanaa six months earlier, and to stop a rapid Houthi advance. But the coalition's strategic goal was to stop the Iranian project on the Arabian Peninsula. The capture of the capital by Houthi rebels, who increasingly acted as an Iranian client and relied on its assistance, sounded alarm bells in Riyadh and Abu Dhabi. The Quds Force was practically unopposed in its operations in Iraq and Syria and now was turning Sanaa into another base where it could place advisers and advanced weaponry and use a local militant Shia organization as its proxy to advance its regional project. The ascension to the Saudi throne of King Salman in January 2015 and the rise of his son and eventual crown prince, Mohammad bin-

Salman, showed the new face of a country fed up with the growing influence of the Islamic Republic and ready to take the lead in stopping the Quds Force and its commander. The resulting coalition declared Yemeni airspace a restricted area and later blockaded Yemeni seaports to stop Iranian arms shipments to the Houthis.

In April 2015, Iran attempted to challenge the Saudi-Emirati blockade by openly sending a flotilla of vessels, including crew boats, support ships, and missile boats to deliver lethal aid to the Houthis. On 20 April, the convoy rendezvoused with the IRGC Navy's 34th Deployed Naval Group: *Alborz*, a Vosper MK5-class frigate, and *Bushehr*, a Bandar Abbas–class oiler.[25] In response, the United States sent the aircraft carrier USS *Theodore Roosevelt* to the Gulf of Aden, ready to intercept the Iranian military convoy.[26] Challenged by U.S. naval power, the Iranian convoy reversed course and headed home.[27] Five days later, the Iranians sent a Mahan Air aircraft to deliver humanitarian aid to Yemen, effectively to test the Saudi-declared restricted airspace. Saudi jets bombed the Sanaa airport runways to stop the Iranian plane from landing. The Mahan flight had to reverse course and head home.[28] The two episodes, on sea and in the air, manifested the Quds Force's serious limits when operating in hostile environments.

After the setbacks in the Gulf of Aden and over Sanaa airspace to overtly deliver cargo to the Houthis, the Iranians went back to covert arms shipments of smaller volumes, including using the old smuggling routes, to deliver lethal weaponry. A number of these shipments have been interdicted since. On 24 September 2015, for example, the Australian Royal Navy seized 19 Tosan and 56 Toophan ATGMs, Iranian versions of Russian Konkurs-M and U.S. TOW missiles, and associated launchers, from an unflagged dhow in the Arabian Sea. Saudi authorities who announced the interdiction said the debriefing of the Iranian crew and analysis of a GPS device onboard the dhow indicated the dhow loaded at the Iranian port of Sirik and departed on 19 September en route to the coast of Somalia for an at-sea transfer of cargo to other vessels that would deliver the weapons to Yemen.[29]

The Iranians also use dhows to deliver cargo to an Omani port for transfer overland to Yemen. They have also used Oman Air on occasion to send shipments to Muscat for eventual overland transit to Yemen. As the conflict in Yemen drags on, the Houthis need additional arms to replace weapons used or destroyed in the conflict, and Iran has ramped up its arms smuggling to Yemen.[30]

THE SAUDIS IN YEMEN

Saudi Arabia laid out its objectives at the onset of its military campaign in Yemen in March 2015. It demanded that the Houthis withdraw from major cities and return to their stronghold of Saada, sever military ties with Iran and the Quds Force, and surrender heavy weapons taken from the Yemeni military after the fall of Sanaa. It also called for reinstating the Saudi-backed and internationally recognized Yemeni government. They, alongside the Emiratis, succeeded in rolling back the Houthi advances to the south of the country, including the capture of Aden, and stopped the Iranians from overt delivery of military aids to the Houthis. But the Saudi-led coalition struggled to achieve most of its objectives, especially in driving the Houthis out of Sanaa and some other cities. The Saudis also struggled to defend their border with Yemen, with the Houthis launching incursions deep into the border regions of Saudi Arabia.

Saudi underachievement in Yemen can partly be explained by their reliance on anti-Houthi tribes and their foreign proxies, including the Sudanese, who act as the major part of their land forces in the war. Anti-Houthi military units known for their capabilities are mostly stationed in former South Yemen and are generally not involved in battles in former North Yemen. Reliance on tribesmen and foreign proxies has shown its limits. Their inexperience in urban warfare, lack of combat initiative, and subpar command-and-control systems have given the battle-tested Houthis a marked advantage.

The Houthis' ability to mass ideologically driven forces and hold defensive lines has placed them in a favorable position to defend territories under their control. However, in a protracted war, as the trajectory of the current conflict indicates, these advantages could disappear as losses of fighters and weapons in the face of Saudi-Emirati air superiority, and their special operations forces combined with the Houthis' own limited resources could significantly weaken Houthi combat readiness and the morale of their forces. This is especially true if the Saudi-Emirati coalition should continue their success in denying the Quds Force access to Yemeni airspace and seaports. The Houthi army needs to replenish its weapons and equipment lost through major arms deliveries by the Quds Force, which requires use of the Sanaa airport and Hudaydah port. The Saudi-Emirati blockade denies such access and limits the Quds Force efforts to smuggling ever fewer advanced arms. Notwithstanding these limits, the Houthis are expected to defend the territory under their control, defend their Red Sea routes, and increase attacks across the Saudi border. The Saudis will be forced to react by continuing their airstrikes and working with their local and foreign partners to increase the cost of operation for the Houthis and their Iranian backers.

THE IRAN-SAUDI CONFLICT

From the very beginning of the conflict, Iran made an effort to raise the cost to the Saudi-Emirati coalition by covertly supporting Houthi rebel training and assisting their forces. The Saudis in turn limited Iranian access to Yemeni territory and used their financial and diplomatic powers to unite Arab countries and isolate Iran. The diametrically opposed objectives of the two superpowers of the Islamic world, and the proximity of their forces and those of their allies in the Yemeni theater, could at any time create a cycle of retaliation that, given the current tense geopolitical landscape, might lead to direct military confrontation between the two countries. The conflict has devastated Yemen and its people, with thousands dead or driven out of their homes and generally left with no support, facing famine and hunger. On top of these tragic factors, an Iranian-Saudi military confrontation arising from the conflict in Yemen could devastate the entire region.

THE EMIRATIS IN YEMEN

Since their arrival in Yemen in 2015, UAE Special Operations Forces have enhanced the effectiveness of the coalition and led counterterrorism efforts in the country. In July 2015, the UAE-led southern Yemeni forces recaptured Aden from the Houthis, striking a fatal blow to the Houthi claim that they represent Yemen as a whole. The control of Aden also enables the UAE to better patrol the eastern approach to the Red Sea and Bab el-Mandeb, countering the Iranian-Houthi strategy to control the strategic strait.

In addition, the UAE Special Operations Forces have organized and trained a force of southern soldiers and tribesmen to control the former territories of South Yemen. In 2016, the UAE-led forces captured Mukalla from Al-Qaeda in the Arabian Peninsula (AQAP).[31] This strategically located city lies on the Gulf of Aden, on the shores of the Arabian Sea. In 2017, the UAE-led forces recaptured the town of Mahfad, an al-Qaeda stronghold in the southern province of Abyan.[32]

By 2018, the UAE-led southern forces were in total control of ports and military installations throughout southern Yemen.[33] The UAE navy is also active in the Red Sea, positioning UAE forces for an assault on the Houthi-controlled port of Hudaydah, the major Yemeni port on the Red Sea. By capturing Hudaydah, the coalition forces not only could stop any flow of Iranian arms to the Houthis through the port but could allow humanitarian aid to flow freely.

The Houthis will defend the port with weaponry they have received from the Quds Force, including coastal defense cruise missiles, long-range rockets, unmanned explosive boats, and small-crew boats armed with RPG and Katyusha rockets, and they will put up stiff resistance on the port grounds. A Houthi defeat in Hudaydah, however, would change the trajectory of the war in favor of the Saudi and Emirati–led coalition forces.

THE YEMEN BATTLESPACE

Yemen's civil war entered a new phase in 2018. Former president Ali Abdullah Saleh, the Houthis' main ally in capturing Sanaa, broke with them and was assassinated by the Houthis in December 2017. The Southern Transitional Council (STC), headed by former Aden governor Aidarus al-Zoubaydi, broke with the Yemeni government-in-exile in January 2018, taking control of Aden and most of the former South Yemen territories, but he did not declare independence for the south after Saudi mediation to maintain a united anti-Houthi front. The two back-to-back developments made the situation on the ground even more complicated, as both sides saw breaks in their alliances. What follows is a look at the individual battlespaces in the country.

Hudaydah. Hudaydah is a priority for both sides. It remains under a coalition blockade that allows only humanitarian aid to reach the country. The UAE-led forces are positioned for an offensive to capture the port. The Houthis will need to control the port to smuggle in arms and supplies as the conflict continues. The Quds Force regards Hudaydah as a strategic port and will give its full support to the Houthis to fiercely counter a UAE-led offensive if and when it comes.

The Highlands/Western Yemen. This area includes Houthi-controlled Sanaa, Hudaydah, and the stronghold of Saada. The Quds Force regards the area as vital to the Houthi project on the Red Sea and Saudi border and as an autonomous or independent proto-state if or when Yemen fractures. For those reasons, for the anti-Houthi coalition, recapturing Hudaydah is the first step to push the Houthis north to their Saada homeland. Taiz, in the southern part of the highlands and the second-largest population center, remains a stalemate. Saudi-backed Islah has the upper hand, and in case the country fractures, Taiz could go with the south.

Marib/Northeast Sanaa/Al Jawf. The Saudi-led forces have the upper hand in the battlefield here. The moderate Islamist party Islah, along with anti-Houthi tribal groups, are the key players in the area. The coalition forces have been unable to advance on Sanaa due to limited resources. But the forces have restricted the Houthi supply route running from Saada to Al Jawf.

The Saudi Arabia–Yemen Border. Houthi-affiliated forces, including the Republican Guard and tribal militia guard on the Yemeni side of the border, have increased their incursions into Saudi territory here. U.S. Special Operations Forces advisers assist the large Saudi forces, including the Saudi special forces, deployed to the border area. The Saudi-backed anti-Houthi fighters conduct border operations in Saada and Hajjah, which are under Houthi control. The Quds Force and the Houthis regard military operations against the Saudis on Saudi soil as vital for keeping Saudi forces from advancing into Yemen.

Aden/The Tribal South/ Coastal Hadramawt (Mukalla). This is under the control of the UAE-backed STC and their loyal tribal groups, a force of some five thousand tribal fighters trained and armed by the UAE. The area forms the nucleus of an independent South Yemen. The city of Mukalla was cleared of AQAP in a major victory over the terror group. U.S. advisory teams work with UAE Special Operations Forces to deny AQAP egress routes in the area.

Northern Hadramawt/Al Mahre. Saudi-backed tribal groups and Islah-affiliated military units have the upper hand in this area. In the Mahre governorate, Saudi-backed tribal and Islah-affiliated groups, along with UAE-backed forces and Oman-backed groups, are the major players.

YEMEN FRACTURING

In 1967, South Yemen, led by the National Liberation Front (NLF), rebelled against British colonial rule—what was then known as the Aden Protectorate—and became independent from Britain. In its two decades of independence, South Yemen instituted reforms and brought a degree of social liberalism to the country never seen on the Arabian Peninsula.[34] Reforms for women were particularly striking. Women were encouraged to work, and family laws treating women equally were passed. Women were also free to dress as they liked, with or without hijab. Girls were sent to mixed schools with boys.

In 1990, after the collapse of the Soviet Union and the end of its economic aid to South Yemen, the two Yemeni states, South and North, agreed to unite to form a single country. But sentiments for independence remained alive in the south, and for a brief period in 1994 South Yemen seceded from North Yemen. The north quelled the rebellion militarily and occupied the south.

It is against this background that in 2007, southern secessionists formed the STC to regain independence. The movement accelerated when the Islamist Houthis captured Sanaa in 2014. The STC, backed by the UAE, took control of Aden and most of the former South Yemen territories in January 2018. With the mediation of Saudi Arabia, the STC did not declare independence and kept South Yemen nominally under the Yemeni government-in-exile of Abdrabbuh Mansour Hadi, who lives in Riyadh. The arrangement maintains a veneer of alliance among anti-Houthi factions during the current conflict, but the rebirth of an independent South Yemen is now only a matter of time.

The Quds Force and their Houthi allies consider the South Yemeni movement a threat to their project in the country. Aden would be a counterbalance to Sanaa, delegitimizing the Houthi claim that they are more than a provincial player and represent all of Yemen. Establishment of a progressive South Yemen would also be an enduring challenge to the anti-progressive, Islamist-led Houthi movement, whether still occupying Sanaa or defeated and relocated to their stronghold of Saada. When Yemen fractures, the Quds Force will support an autonomous, if not independent, Zaydi-Shia Houthiland in northwest Yemen, bordering Saudi Arabia.

CHALLENGES FACING THE HOUTHIS

The Houthi forces have demonstrated their skill in conducting battles against the Yemeni government and Saudi and UAE–led coalition forces in platoon-size elements, skills they developed and improved during their wars with the central government between 2004 and 2010. Their long history of anti-government struggle has won them the support of the population and tribal groups in the regions under their control. However, the informal nature of their organization, based on the leadership of influential personalities, has created serious command-and-control issues for their forces. Their alliance with former Saleh-affiliated forces, including elements of the Republican Guards and tribal groups, crumbled across the country after the former president disagreed with their strategy and was assassinated by them.

Among other challenges is a shortage of personnel. The Houthis, after so many years of fighting and losing many of their fighters, are increasingly relying on recruiting less-disciplined and inexperienced tribal fighters, who are not committed to their core ideology and doctrine. The Saudi-UAE air and sea blockade has also made it impossible for the Quds Force to deploy large numbers of senior officers and battalions of foreign Shia militants to the Houthi-controlled territories, the way Soleimani conducted his war in Syria. A prolonged conflict will challenge the Houthis to organize, train, and arm enough fighters for their cause if they want to hold on to the territories captured in 2014. The lack of ability of the Quds Force to replenish the ammunition used by the Houthis in this long war will hamper a Houthi force that depends on Iranian aid to sustain its operations.

Prolonged airstrikes by the Saudi-led coalition and the growing humanitarian crisis, fueled by airstrikes and a mismanaged and weak economy, will alienate civilians in the Houthi territories and will add to the Houthi challenge of holding and effectively managing Houthiland.

CHALLENGES FACING THE QUDS FORCE

Without a shared border, and with Yemen's airport and seaports closed, Soleimani's efforts to build a full expeditionary force in Yemen akin to those in Iraq and Syria became logistically challenging for the Quds Force. Soleimani did not have freedom of movement to deploy battalions of Shia fighters and IRGC ground force personnel and equipment to Yemen. The expeditionary model of the Quds Force's way of war developed in Iraq and Syria was showing its limits. Without shared borders and facing a hostile environment, and without the logistic ability to deploy as many officers, operatives, and militia members as necessary into a foreign land farther than its immediate surroundings, the Quds Force has been forced to limit its involvement to deploying only dozens of officers and trainers and smuggling weapons to its local allies. Soleimani has had to redefine the term *near abroad* in Iran's case. He can operate unimpeded in the very near abroad with friendly governments, as in Iraq and Syria; operate more limitedly in the very near abroad without the consent of the local government, as in Afghanistan; and operate only with extreme difficulty in the not very near abroad, and especially in a hostile environment, as in Yemen.

The Quds Force command-and-control structure in Yemen is also a major issue for the Iranians as the Houthis, unlike Hezbollah and other Shia militias, do not take tactical advice from the Iranians often and do not always follow Iranian strategic guidance. There are no indications that Iran has established a formal, combined command-and-control structure with the Houthis. Soleimani must rely on direct communications with Houthi leader Abdulmalik Badreddin al-Houthi and on the relationships of a few senior Quds Force officers with their counterparts in the Houthi ranks.

As in Syria and Iraq, long-term Iranian involvement in Yemen will create serious issues for their Quds Force. If the Houthis retaliate against the Emirati-led forces advancing toward Hudaydah and fire more ballistic missiles against targets in Saudi Arabia and succeed in hitting a major target, Iran could find itself in a direct military conflict with the coalition forces. Miscalculations by the Quds Force and the Houthis in disrupting the transit of a ship at Bab el-Mandeb or in targeting Saudi, Emirati, or U.S. vessels off the Yemeni coast could likewise escalate into a wider regional conflict.

THE HUMANITARIAN CRISIS IN YEMEN

Three years of intense conflict in Yemen have resulted in a widespread humanitarian crisis. The United Nations estimates that 22.2 million people in Yemen, out of the country's population of 29 million, need some kind of humanitarian assistance or protection, including 11.3 million who are in acute need.[35] There are 2 million internally displaced persons (IDPs) and 500,000 refugees. At least 17.8 million people are food insecure; 16 million need assistance to establish or maintain access to safe water, basic sanitation, and hygiene facilities; 16 million need assistance to ensure access to adequate healthcare; and 4 million school-age children require assistance to continue their education. The country's economy has lost $32.5 billion in cumulative real GDP from 2014 to 2017, a staggering number for a country that was already among the poorest in the world before the current crisis.[36] The humanitarian crisis puts that much more pressure on Iran, the Quds Force, and the Saudi and Emirati–led coalition to negotiate an early cease-fire and to bring lasting peace to the country.

THE WAY AHEAD IN YEMEN

The situation at a national level is chaotic. There is no functioning central government. The Iranian-backed Houthi government in Sanaa controls the highland regions in the north and west. The coalition-backed Hadi government is in exile, having the support of tribal groups and military units in northern Yemeni territories not affiliated with the Houthis. The UAE-backed and Aden-based STC, under the leadership of former Aden governor Zubaydi, is the functional government of the de facto independent state of South Yemen. Non-state actors, like AQAP and Daesh, as well as some tribal groups, control their own zones of influence outside the control of the three major groups headed by the Houthi, Hadi, and Zubaydi.

A likely end to the current conflict would involve the fracture of Yemen and the re-creation of an independent South Yemen, with Aden as its capital, together with a Sanaa-based North Yemen where the Zaydi-Shia Houthis and Hadi-led forces of the internationally recognized Yemeni government-in-exile will need to negotiate a settlement to their dispute and form a coalition government. Soleimani could also be planning the creation of an autonomous Houthi sub-state controlling the northwestern highlands, with Saada as its capital, if the Houthis are unable to come to terms with Hadi-led forces and the Saudi-Emirati coalition on how to govern North Yemen.

The success or failure of the Quds Force in influencing the end state in the Yemeni conflict will be a critical test of how the Quds Force–led SLA will be involved in future regional conflicts, especially in areas outside Iran's traditional land-linked, near-abroad zone.

Chapter Nine

Unfinished Business in Afghanistan

Iran and Afghanistan share a border nearly five hundred miles long. Western Afghanistan shares an especially close connection with Iran through a shared history, common language, and close economic ties. A significant segment of the population follows Shia Islam, not just in the west, but also in the central Bamiyan region, the home of the Hazaras—a large ethnic group who speak a variant of Dari, itself the eastern version of Persian.

In 1978, political turmoil engulfed both countries. In Iran, the growing anti-shah movement was transforming into a full-fledged revolution. The Islamists were nostalgic for the Golden Age of Islam and craved the establishment of an Islamic state to replace the monarchy, which had begun to modernize Iran at the turn of the century. Lacking a coherent doctrine of revolution, they substituted Islamic phraseology for Marxist language: *imperialism* became *estekbar*, and *proletariat* became *mostazafan*. They wanted to beat the Left at its own game. Meanwhile, in Afghanistan, the socialists had come to power and begun a massive drive to modernize the traditional Islamic society through women's rights, land reform, and universal education. The Islamists opposed the initiatives and started a movement to overthrow the socialist government.

When the Islamic Revolution triumphed in Iran in February 1979, the new government immediately began siding with the Islamists in Afghanistan, and the newly established IRGC began recruiting Afghan refugees and migrant workers in Iran and training them to take up arms against the socialist government. This was the very first time the IRGC deployed foreign militias, comprised of mostly Afghan Shia Hazaras, to battlefields in the near abroad. The Afghan militants were named the Abouzar Brigade and were put under the command of the IRGC Office of the Liberation Movements (Daftar-e

The Quds Force conducts covert operations along the long Iran-Afghanistan border, from Herat to Farah to Zaranj, to maintain its arc of influence in western Afghanistan.

Nehzatha-ye Rahaei-Bakhsh), a precursor to the Quds Force tasked with handling extraterritorial operations.[1]

The growing revolt against the government in Kabul forced the Soviet Union to invade Afghanistan in December 1979. During the ten-year occupation of Afghanistan by the Red Army, the Islamist movement, operating under the moniker "the Mujahedeen," became an all-out anti-Soviet revolt, with significant support from the United States and its allies, the Soviet's Cold War–era enemies.

The new Islamist government in Tehran also supported the Mujahedeen. Iran's principal ally within the Mujahedeen movement was the Wahdat (Unity) party, whose area of influence was the Shia Hazara-dominated Bamiyan. The party was led by Abdul Aziz Mazari, a Hazara and longtime associate of the IRGC and the Quds Force and their principal man in Afghanistan until his death in 1995 in Mazar-e Sharif. Iran was also close to other members of the movement, including Jamiat-e Islami (Islamic Association), active in Herat, Baqdis, and Fariab. Other principal members of the Mujahedeen were Harakat Enghelab Islami (Movement of Islamic Revolution), active in Farah, Zabol, Paktia, Helmand, and Kandahar; Hezb-e Islami (Islamic

Party) of Younis Khalis, active in Nangarhar and Paktia; Hezb-e Islami (Islamic Party) of Gulbodin, active in Parvan and Ghazni; and Shoura-ye Enghelabi Etefaq-e Islami (Revolutionary Council for Islamic Unity), active in Vardak.

The heavy fighting between the Mujahedeen and the government and its Soviet backers forced hundreds of thousands of Afghans to flee to Iran. The IRGC's extraterritorial branch continued its recruitment from the growing refugee community. The new recruits were trained and armed and deployed back to Afghanistan to fight on the Mujahedeen's side.

In 1980, Iraq invaded Iran and an eight-year-long bloody war ensued. As the IRGC began diverting its focus from Afghanistan to Iraq, it began deploying the Afghan militants to the Iraqi front. The Afghans had proved their loyalty to the Islamic Revolution, and more than three thousand of them died in the fighting from 1980 to 1989.

The end of the Iran-Iraq War coincided with the withdrawal of the Soviet troops from Afghanistan. The Mujahedeen finally defeated the socialist government, significantly weakened after the Soviet departure, and in 1992 took power in Kabul. From the very beginning, the new order was marred by bitter and bloody infighting, with ethnic, linguistic, religious, and tribal loyalties splitting the Mujahedeen movement. Compounding the problems were the endemic crime and corruption that engulfed the country. The situation finally opened the path for the Taliban, a predominantly Pashtun group of Sunni fundamentalists from Kandahar, to start a law-and-order and anti-corruption campaign and take power in 1996. Another wave of refugees fled the Taliban and settled in Iran.

The anti-Taliban factions inside Afghanistan, predominantly Tajik, Uzbek, and Hazara Mujahedeen in the west and the north, and a Pashtun-dominated faction in the east, formed the United Islamic Front, popularly known as the Northern Alliance. They stopped the Taliban from gaining control of the entirety of Afghanistan, holding nearly 10 percent of the country's land mass centered on Panjshir, the home of their legendary commander, Ahmad Shah Massoud. When the U.S. and allied forces invaded Afghanistan in 2001 following the 11 September attacks by Taliban partner al Qaeda, the Northern Alliance joined forces with the U.S.-led coalition to oust the Taliban. The Iranians sided with the Northern Alliance and the U.S. forces in Afghanistan.

For the liberation of Herat, the Northern Alliance forces, under the command of Ismail Khan, nicknamed the Lion of Herat for his bravery and leadership during the anti-Soviet war, joined forces with Afghan Shia militias, under the command of Quds Force officers, to fight alongside U.S. and British special forces. Ismail Khan's and the Quds Force operatives inside the city coordinated an insurrection against the Taliban in October 2001, and Herat was liberated within one month.

I was a guest at Ismail Khan's grand compound in Herat in 2010, nine years after the liberation of the city. He was serving as minister of water and energy in the Karzai cabinet at the time and still as proud of his leading role in the fight against the Soviets, as the Lion of Herat, and then against the Taliban. His biggest regret was that the U.S. military had abandoned him and the forces loyal to him two years after the liberation of Afghanistan, apparently wanting to sever ties with the regional strongmen. Ismail Khan believed that his forces could have played a major role in stopping the Taliban resurrection in the country, a decade after their defeat with the help of Ismail Khan and other regional leaders. The U.S. had opted to support and only work through the central government in Kabul, ignoring that historically Kabul exerted little influence over the provinces and their powerful figures. That debate continues to this day.

THE QUDS FORCE AND THE TALIBAN
IN THE POST–11 SEPTEMBER PERIOD

The Taliban were defeated but not destroyed, nearly eighteen years after 11 September. The Quds Force faced a quandary. Iran was an ally of the anti-Taliban forces that brought the current government to power. But the Taliban were also the most powerful anti-American force in the country, and the Quds Force could through them raise the cost of the U.S. presence in Afghanistan, both in blood and treasure, bleeding the Americans to leave the country. So beginning at least in 2007, the Quds Force began supplying the Taliban with arms such as IEDs and EFPs, mortars, machine guns, and rifles and assisting them with logistics. The Quds Force also operates four training camps for the Taliban, in Tehran, Mashhad, Kerman, and Zahedan.[2]

The Taliban has also kept offices in Mashhad and Zahedan. The Mashhad office houses senior political operatives, a type of "Mashhad Shura." The office in Zahedan, in Iranian Baluchistan, conducts liaison work with the Quds Force regional headquarters in the same city. The Iranian ambassador to Afghanistan said in 2016 that Iran's contacts with the Taliban were for intelligence purposes.[3]

The depth of Iran's ties to the Taliban came into full view in 2016 when a U.S. drone struck a car on a desert road in Pakistani Baluchistan, near the border with Iran. Dead inside the car was Mullah Akhtar Muhammad Mansur, then the leader of the Taliban, returning to Pakistan from a trip to Iran, where he had been meeting with senior Iranian security officials.[4] Mansur had been close to the Iranians since the days of the Taliban government in the 1990s. The main purpose of Mansur's visit was tactical coordination with the Iranians for their operations during their upcoming offensive season.

The bold offensive began in October 2016 when scores of Taliban fighters seized the western riverbank of the city of Farah in western Afghanistan and began a three-week siege of the city. It took U.S. airstrikes to clear the Taliban from Farah. Afghan intelligence officials told the *New York Times* that four Quds Force personnel were among the scores of dead after the airstrikes and that many of the Taliban dead and wounded were taken back across the nearby border with Iran. Funerals were held in Iran for the Quds Force personnel killed in the bombing.[5]

The 2016 death of the supreme leader of the Taliban in a U.S. drone strike as he was returning to Pakistan from a week-long trip to Iran, and the death of four Quds Force officers a few months later in an American airstrike against Taliban positions in Farah, manifested the magnitude of the Quds Force support for the Taliban. Incidents like these open a window on the covert operations of the Quds Force, in this case in Afghanistan.

The Quds Force involvement with the Taliban was something of a marriage of convenience, despite clashing religious beliefs. As the U.S. and NATO missions in Afghanistan expanded, the Iranian commanders saw an already trained, fierce, militia-style force that could counter the threat they saw in American and NATO forces.

The IRGC further stood to economically benefit from an alliance with the Taliban and its overlapping interest in opium. Afghanistan is the world's largest source of the drug, and the Afghan traffickers needed to use Iran as the main conduit to get their shipments to Turkey and Iraq, where they could deliver the opium to the drug cartel for transfer to Europe. The Taliban and the IRGC both benefited from the illicit trade, exacting payments from the traffickers. Quds Force brigadier general Gholamreza Baghbani, who headed the Quds Force headquarters in Zahedan, the capital of Iranian Baluchistan, and oversaw the Iranian part of the illicit operation, was tasked by the U.S. Treasury in 2012 with overseeing Afghan drug trafficking. He became the first Iranian general officer to be designated under the Kingpin Act.[6]

The Fatemiyoun

When the Arab Spring reached Syria in 2011, the Quds Force, fearing the imminent collapse of the Assad regime, rushed senior advisers and Shia militia forces into Syria to save the regime. The IRGC and the Quds Force had a long history of affiliation with Afghan Shia militants going back to the first days of the IRGC. The Afghan militias fought against the socialist government of Afghanistan and its Soviet backers at the behest of the IRGC in the early days of the Islamic Republic. They joined the IRGC under the banner of the Abuzar Brigade to fight against the Iraqis during the eight-year Iran-Iraq War in the 1980s and suffered heavy casualties during the war. And they fought the Taliban as members of Sipah-e-Muhammad (Muhammad

Corps) under the command of the Quds Force during the 2001 Afghan war.[7] And now they were being deployed to Syria to fight under the command of the Quds Force against the opposition and save Assad.

The veterans of the Abuzar Brigade and Sipah-e-Muhammad formed the nucleus of the group of Afghan militants deployed to Syria in the first days of the civil war. The Quds Force also began a concerted and successful drive to recruit many more Afghans to fight in Syria. The new recruits were initially comprised of settled Shia Hazara Afghan refugees in Iran but expanded with the recruitment of undocumented Afghans and soon spread to Afghanistan itself, where the Quds Force recruiters sought to enlist persons interested in both the ideological fight and the financial incentives that came with it. By 2013, the growing number of Afghans deployed to Syria reached a point that allowed the Quds Force to establish an independent unit, the Fatemiyoun Brigade, of all Afghan Shia militants in Syria. The Fatemiyoun were deployed to all major battlefields and suffered heavy casualties in the war. A senior Quds Force general officer serving in Afghanistan called them the "vanguards" of Iranian-led forces in the country.[8]

How the Quds Force Recruits Afghans

In modern times, Afghan migrant workers, pilgrims, and merchants have settled in Iran since the nineteenth century, when significant numbers of Shia Hazaras formed their communities in Torbat-e-Jam and other Iranian cities near the border of Afghanistan. Revolution, war, and poverty in the years after produced refugees who fled their country to reside in Iran, Pakistan, and the Persian Gulf nations. Today, the number of Afghans living in Iran, political refugees as well as migrant workers, is estimated at 2.5–3 million people. They have settled mainly in the outskirts of Mashhad, Tehran, Zabol, and smaller communities near the border. But only one-third of them are registered as refugees, with the rest lacking formal residency status. Joining the Quds Force and receiving a monthly salary and Iranian residency offers the quickest path for Afghan youths to a steady income and Iranian residency.

When the civil war in Syria started, the Quds Force needed to recruit tens of thousands of fighters to save Assad. And the Quds Force began exploiting the situation of undocumented Afghans in the country to recruit them for the fight in Syria.

The recruiters emphasized religious duty in recruitment, seeking young Afghans to "defend the shrine" of Sayyidah Zaynab, the daughter of Ali, the first Shia imam, in Damascus, even though the shrine was located hundreds of miles away from the main battlefields where the Afghan recruits would fight. Once in training, Fatemiyoun recruits were indoctrinated in a militant interpretation of Shia Islam, as espoused by Khomeini, and the doctrine of *velayat-e faghih*.[9]

The Afghan recruits were paid a salary of $500 a month, with a promise of Iranian permanent residency and citizenship for those already settled as refugees. The Quds Force also promised them that in case they were killed in action, their family would also get residency. The recruiters focused not only on the Afghan refugee community inside Iran but also on the 6 million Hazaras living inside Afghanistan, mainly in Bamiyan.

There were reports, including a 2017 report by Human Rights Watch, that in their zeal to recruit as many Afghan volunteers as possible to fight in Syria, the Quds Force recruited young men, some as young as fourteen, violating international covenants. [10]

Onward to Syria

The Quds Force maintained several military training camps for the Afghan recruits in northeastern Iran. [11] Typically, the new recruits were sent to boot camp for one month to be trained in weapons and tactical movement. The best prospects were then sent for advanced training, including sniper courses and tank warfare. Upon completion of the training courses, they were flown to Damascus to join Quds Force–led forces on the battlefields.

The Fatemiyoun Brigade was deployed to the front lines in Aleppo, Daara, Damascus, Hama, Homs, Latakia, Palmyra, and Deir El-Zour. The Afghan fighters fought the tough fights in the most casualty-heavy battles—like Aleppo, Daraa, and Palmyra. [12] A Fatemiyoun official reported in 2018 that about two thousand Afghans had died over the course of the conflict in Syria. [13]

By 2015, the Fatemiyoun Brigade was the second-largest foreign military contingent fighting in Syria, second only to Hezbollah. The late deputy commander of the brigade, Sayyed Hassan Husseini, claimed that his forces numbered as many as fourteen thousand fighters, organized around three divisions in Damascus, Hama, and Aleppo, and were equipped with their own artillery, armor, and intelligence units. [14]

How the Fatemiyoun See Themselves

For their part, the Fatemiyoun see themselves not just as a fighting force in Syria but as a permanent member of the Quds Force–led SLA and ready to fight until the "annihilation" of Israel. The Fatemiyoun Brigade sent a letter to the Quds Force commander declaring the unit's readiness to fight to the end.

> [The Fatemiyoun] would continue to fight alongside the "axis of resistance" to annihilate Israel. . . . Thanks to the leadership of the Leader of the Islamic World [Khamenei] and [General Soleimani's] supreme command and prudence, a group of men have now emerged from Afghanistan and joined the

axis of resistance. With their respected commander, they have sworn that they will not sit down until the elimination of the international Zionism.[15]

General Ismail Ghani, deputy commander of the Quds Force, reiterated the Fatemiyoun's declaration, saying the Afghan fighters "do not recognize borders" to defend Islam and that their mission is not confined to Syria.[16] Tellingly, the Fatemiyoun have also reportedly been deployed to fight in Yemen alongside Houthi forces.[17]

And as the conflict winds down in Syria, the Quds Force could use the Fatemiyoun to guard the land corridor it has built to link its forces remaining in Syria through Iraq to its supply base in Iran.[18] Securing the corridor will require securing the Syria-Iraq border for the Quds Force, which would be resisted by the Kurdish Rojava forces and the Sunni opposition.

More importantly, the Quds Force has the capability now to send these ideologically committed and battle-tested forces back to Afghanistan to challenge the power dynamics there. The fighters, along with Pakistani militants who also fought in Syria under the command of the Quds Force, can blend in with Afghan and Pakistani citizens and be used in any future conflict in the country or elsewhere in South Asia.[19]

THE WAY AHEAD IN AFGHANISTAN

The Quds Force has a covert military presence in Afghanistan. It is supporting the Taliban financially and logistically, and it has been providing the Taliban with arms and artillery. It is providing local Taliban commanders with sanctuary and local insurgents with weapons, money, and training.[20] Its immediate goal in Afghanistan is raising the cost of military involvement for the U.S. and allied forces deployed to the country, bleeding them with help from the Taliban until they exit Afghanistan.

The Quds Force can always deploy its Afghan Fatemiyoun Brigade, now stationed in Syria under its command, back to Afghanistan. The move would be certainly opposed by Ghani's government. But Iran has established enough connections in the western provinces of the country, Herat, Farah, and Nimruz, that moving Afghan militants across the border to those provinces, and mixing them with the local population would not be that difficult a task.

At the height of the war against the opposition in Syria, the Fatemiyoun had over fourteen thousand fighters, who are now battle tested and experienced in fighting in a gray zone. Because of their ideological commitment to the Quds Force, their acceptance of Iran's supreme leader as their *marja'*—the highest level of Shia authority—and their dependence on the monthly salaries paid by the Iranians, most of these militants would likely accept deployment to Afghanistan to be part of the expansion of Iranian influence in that country. The issue would be if the Iranians overplay their hand and create a fissure in the Shia community in Afghanistan for interfering in the internal affairs of their country, similar to what they did in Iraq.

Soft Power

The Quds Force has created a network of its own associates inside Afghanistan who covertly engage in operations at its behest. It uses IRGC–controlled economic foundations and charities, including the Imam Khomeini Charity Committee, to funnel money to its local operatives and spies. It is involved in vast information operations in the country through broadcasting channels and other media. And in one of the most corrupt environments in the region, its bags full of cash buy favor at national, provincial, and local levels, including the officials and strongmen of Afghanistan.

The Afghans, especially the Shias, have a long history of living, working, and studying in Iran. Mashhad, the capital of Iranian Khorasan and one of the holiest cities for the Shias, has always been a hub for Afghan pilgrims and tourists. A major highway connects Herat to Mashhad, which are only 230 miles apart. Many Afghans make the five-hour trip by car. Iran has built a railway connecting Mashhad and Herat, supposed to be operational in 2019. Afghans also study at the university in Mashhad, and many have families living or working in Iran.

The personal ties between Afghans and Iranians are priceless for the Quds Force to take advantage of, from recruiting militants for the Fatemiyoun to expanding its network of associates in Afghanistan. These personal and family ties are an important component of Iran's soft power in Afghanistan.

Cultural ties also play an important role in Afghan-Iranian relations. The two peoples speak a common language, although in different dialects. The Heratis and other Afghans living in the western provinces speak Dari with an accent similar to the Farsi spoken in Mashhad and especially the border towns of Iranian Khorasan. Iranian singers are also among the most popular artists in Afghanistan. The closeness of the two peoples is such that visitors to Herat, for example, soon recognize that the city has the feel more of an eastern Iranian city than of an Afghan city.

Iran also remains one of Afghanistan's largest trading partners. Iran exported about $1.8 billion worth of goods—including food, medicine, and oil—to Afghanistan in 2016. The Iranian government seeks to establish an economic sphere of influence, especially in southwest Afghanistan, in order to create a security buffer zone. In 2002, Iran committed $560 million to Afghan reconstruction, and it pledged an additional $100 million four years later.

The extent of these personal and cultural ties, as well as the high volume of trade between the countries, provides the Iranians with priceless soft power in Afghanistan, especially in the western region of the country.

The Great Game—Part 2

Afghanistan and neighboring territories were the scene of intense political and diplomatic confrontation for most of the nineteenth century between the British Empire and the Russian Empire in what became known as the "Great Game." Today as the country vies for stability and reintegration into the global economic system after decades of war and insurgency, global as well as regional powers will be competing against each other to gain influence in the country. The U.S. is expected to play an important role in the security institutions of Afghanistan even after the major drawdown of its forces in the country.

China is already positioned to exploit the mineral resources of the country in the next several decades, and its long-term One-Belt, One Road project passes through Afghanistan. Chinese firms have already begun investing in the Afghan mining sector. The country's vast mineral resources are valued at over $1 trillion.[21] In 2007, the Metallurgical Corporation of China and Jiangxi Copper Corporation won a $4.4 billion bid to develop the vast copper deposits at Aynak, twenty-two miles southeast of Kabul.[22] China is buying into Afghanistan.

Russia is rethinking its strategy thirty years after it unceremoniously withdrew its troops and left the country. Russia is interested in checking the spread of the Islamist fundamentalist movement in Central Asia and within Russia itself. At the same time, it has begun cooperating with the Taliban to increase pressure on the U.S., not unlike Iran's strategy of bleeding the Americans with help from the Taliban.[23]

Afghanistan is also on the path to becoming a battleground for proxy warfare between Iran and other regional powers, including Pakistan and Saudi Arabia. India and Turkey are expected to join China as major foreign investors in post-Taliban Afghanistan.

The continued readiness of the Fatemiyoun Brigade, with its more than fourteen thousand religiously and ideologically aligned, battle-hardened fighters, will give an advantage to Iran in any proxy war. The return of the Fatemiyoun fighters to Afghanistan will enable the Quds Force to extend its influence within the country's government and security institutions, similar to the role the PMF plays in Iraq. Added to this advantage is the considerable soft power Iran has in Afghanistan.

Chapter Ten

Resourcing the Quds Force Regional Campaigns

Military and Financial Support Network

The Quds Force draws its fighting forces from the SLA, the IRGC, and Artesh. Its functional directorates include personnel, intelligence, operations, logistics, training, and the secretive Department 400, responsible for sensitive covert operations that include terrorist attacks, assassinations, kidnappings, and sabotage. Its regional directorates, or "the Corps," cover Iraq; the Levant (Syria, Lebanon, Israel, Palestine, and Jordan); the Arabian Peninsula; Afghanistan, Pakistan, and India; North Africa; Central Asia; and Europe and the Americas. The Corps manages relations and provides command of local Shia militia groups. The Quds Force also runs training camps inside Iran for its foreign Shia fighters, including Imam Ali Base near Tehran and Wali Asr Base near Shiraz. Quds Force University in Qom covers ideological and theological courses for foreign recruits. It operates recruiting centers in the region, generally near Shia holy sites or in Shia-dominated areas. Those centers are usually housed within religious or cultural foundations to mask their mission. The size of the Quds Force headquarters staff is estimated at about fifteen thousand. To run a complex organization active globally, the Quds Force needs support from the Iranian military and financial support from Iran's government and revolutionary institutions.

IRGC MILITARY SUPPORT

The Quds Force is part of the larger IRGC support network and can use the IRGC's vast ballistic and cruise missile capabilities and its highly trained ground forces in support of its offensive operations in the region. The IRGC also provides multifunction UAVs and other advanced military systems in support of Quds Force operations. The IRGC's capabilities also serve as a deterrent against foreign militaries if they challenge Quds Force operations in Syria, Iraq, or Yemen.

The IRGC Missile Force

The IRGC has the largest ballistic missile force in the Middle East, its primary means of applying conventional military force in a theater conflict. More importantly, all of Iran's missiles are domestically produced. In early March 2018, Brigadier General Amir Ali Hajizadeh, chief commander of the IRGC Air Force, said that missile production "has increased three-fold compared to the past." He also said that there was a consensus among all government officials to resist Western pressure and increase Iran's missile production capacity.[1]

IRGC missile garrisons are spread across Iran. The primary units of operations are missile battalions. Al Ghadir Missile Command (AGMC) is the headquarters of the IRGC ballistic missile force and is located northwest of Tehran. The command's force disposition includes a dozen regional commands and independent groups across Iran. In a time of conflict, the AGMC becomes subordinate only to Khatam ol-Anbia Headquarters, the central command of war operations, whose commander then reports directly to the country's supreme leader.

SRBMs and MRBMs make up the bulk of the IRGC's ballistic missile inventory, although it also deploys space launch vehicles (SLVs), which could be converted into intercontinental ballistic missiles (ICBMs). It is believed the IRGC possesses about three thousand ballistic missiles.[2]

IRGC's MRBMs have a range of 1,240 miles, enabling them to reach targets across the Middle East, including Israel and U.S. military bases in the region. Khoramshahr is the IRGC's newest generation of MRBM, based on North Korea's BM-25. It carries a unitary, high-explosive warhead, significantly increasing the mass of the MRBM payload. The reentry vehicle (RV) also has a payload option designed to thwart the ballistic missile defenses of an opposing force. Khoramshahr, with its range of 1,240 miles and multipayload options, is not only the IRGC's primary deterrence weapon, it is designed to be used in preemptive offensive strikes as well, including operations led by the Quds Force.

Fateh-110 variants are the workhorse of the IRGC's SRBMs and have been used in support of Quds Force–led operations in current conflicts. The latest extended-range variant of Fateh-110 has a range of 310 miles and may have an accuracy within 30 yards. The IRGC deploys an anti-ship ballistic missile, Khalij-e Fars, which is based on the Fateh-110.

The IRGC also deploys highly accurate cruise missiles, both as ASCMs and as land-attack missiles (LACMs). Meshkat LACMs complement the ballistic arsenal and are one of the most potent offensive elements of the missile force. The ASCM inventory includes Noor, an advanced, domestically produced version of the Chinese C-802, and Qader, which is to date the most precise ASCM deployed by Iran.

Iran denies that it has worked on building ICBMs, but its domestically produced SLVs, like the Simorgh and Safir, are orbital carrier rockets that are technically capable of ICBM booster capacity. This technology could be used to develop ICBM variants of SLVs. The IRGC's MRBMs already use RVs, whose technology would allow Iran to produce multiple independently targetable reentry vehicles (MIRVs), part of the modern design of ICBMs, allowing a single missile to carry several warheads, each of which can strike a different target. However, it is not clear if the current RVs could survive the stress of ICBM range, making the research and development phase in building fully functional ICBMs a priority for the IRGC.

Domestically produced ballistic and cruise missiles are cornerstones of Iran's overall strategic deterrence and offensive capabilities. Most U.S. and GCC military bases in the region are within 310 miles of the Iranian border, and Israel is less than 1,240 miles away, making them vulnerable to the IRGC's SRBMs and MRBMs. The force's doctrine has always included salvo options against large-area targets but is rapidly evolving to point target engagement. The IRGC has deployed Fateh-110 and Zelzal SRBMs against targets in Pakistan—hitting Iranian Baluch separatist fighters in 2013—and in Syria against opposition targets during the current conflict. Use of seeker technology has significantly improved the accuracy of the missiles.

In short, the offensive component of Iran's missile strategy relies on an ability to overwhelm enemy missile defenses. On the defensive side, the IRGC follows its doctrine of Deter, Survive, Retaliate. A newly acquired Russian air defense system, SA-20, aka S-300, will be a major component of the air defense systems protecting core strategic sites.

Use of Missiles in Current Conflicts

The Quds Force has deployed IRGC units in charge of missile operations on temporary duty to battlefields in Syria and Iraq. The missile battalions are set up in country in support of the Quds Force's operations, especially during major battles. The deterrent effect of the IRGC's most advanced MRBMs against enemy forces in battles in Syria and Iraq has been a significant factor in these battlespaces, even with a myriad of different actors actively participating.

The Quds Force also supplies the IRGC's missiles to select Shia militia groups. SRBMs and MRBMs have been supplied to the Houthis, which they used to target Riyadh's international airport and royal palace. Those specific missiles were intercepted by the Saudi anti-missile defense force. A direct hit could have caused a direct military confrontation between Saudi Arabia and Iran.

Since late 2017, the Quds Force has begun a comprehensive, long-term project, the Precision Project, to upgrade hundreds of thousands of Hezbollah rockets by increasing their accuracy and range, making them significantly more lethal against Israeli targets. The upgrading efforts take place at plants in Lebanon and Syria. These installations in Syria have been hit, sometimes repeatedly, by the Israelis, who consider the project a direct and significant threat to the security of their country. The plants in Lebanon are also under threat of Israeli airstrikes.

The Quds Force has expanded its Precision Project into Yemen to upgrade older SCUD missiles of the Yemeni military that came under Houthi control after they captured Sanaa in 2014. Upgraded variants of those missiles, with extended range and significantly more accuracy, have been used by the Houthis against targets in the southern provinces of Saudi Arabia near the border with Yemen. The missiles used against targets in Riyadh, however, were Iranian-supplied missiles, most notably Qaim-1s.

The Quds Force has also supplied the Houthis with ASCMs, which they used against Saudi and Emirati vessels off the coast of Yemen. These missiles pose a particular danger to the freedom of shipping through the Bab el-Mandeb, which along with the Strait of Hormuz in the Persian Gulf is a major chokepoint of international commerce. More than 30 percent of all seaborne-traded crude oil and other liquids passes through the Strait of Hormuz daily, which at its most narrow is just twenty-one miles wide. The Bab el-Mandeb can be as narrow as eighteen miles, with an estimated 4.8 million barrels per day of crude oil and refined petroleum products passing through this waterway.[3] If the Quds Force and its proxies were to gain any degree of control over either strait, it would present a serious threat to U.S. and allied forces in the region.

Drones

The IRGC employs a number of advanced electronic warfare systems, including GPS jammers.[4] It also deploys a large fleet of multipurpose UAVs used as attack aircraft or on ISR missions. Lightweight engines, a crucial ingredient of UAVs, are produced domestically in Iran. The IRGC's UAV fleet generally features smaller, shorter-range tactical models. Iran has also manufactured drones based on captured U.S. drones, including RQ-170 Sentinel stealth UAVs and two versions of the ScanEagle.[5] In 2018, Israel shot down an Iranian drone, Saeqeh, that entered Israeli airspace. The drone was based on an RQ-170 intercepted over Iranian airspace six years earlier.[6]

Among other IRGC drones are Karrar, a drone bomber, and Shahid-129, an attack drone used in Syria in support of Quds Force–led operations. Iran has also displayed attack UAVs with guided munitions.

Other Advanced Military Systems

Aside from its ballistic and cruise missiles, Iran has developed advanced radar systems, including systems for surveillance. Its development of electro-optic systems has significantly increased its missile accuracy. The IRGC Navy also uses guided explosive boats, which have been used against GCC vessels off the Yemeni coast, usually along with ASCMs, during the conflict in Yemen.

Cyber Capabilities

The Quds Force has an active and growing cyber warfare component as well. It manages dozens of cyber actors inside Iran, including local hacking contractors, and maintains a close relationship with the cyber departments of Hezbollah and the Houthis.

The Stuxnet cyber-attack on Iran's uranium enrichment units at Natanz by a U.S. and Israeli task force in 2009 and 2010 pushed the IRGC and the Quds Force to develop defensive and offensive cyber capabilities. The Quds Force is now capable of launching sophisticated distributed denial of service attacks on online services by overwhelming them with traffic from multiple sources. It targeted a number of U.S. banks in September 2011 by commandeering massive computing power from data centers used to host services in the Cloud to launch attacks against bank websites, displaying substantial scale, scope, and effectiveness. Since then the Iranians have breached Saudi ARAMCO's network, disrupting Saudi oil operations, and targeted the U.S. military's Internet service.[7]

Ground Forces

The IRGC maintains some forty infantry brigades, and a dozen armor and mechanized brigades, as well as artillery, commando, and airborne brigades that together make up the IRGC ground force (IRGC-GF). At least one IRGC brigade is deployed to each of Iran's thirty-one provinces. The force disposition includes ten regional commands.

The IRGC-GF maintains a commando force, Saberin. This elite unit is comprised of five commando and airborne brigades and a special forces unit. Specially designated Saberin commando battalions are dispersed throughout Iran's regional provinces.

The Basij Force, the IRGC's principally volunteer force, also allocates a dozen Ashura battalions to each IRGC brigade at the provincial level. Those battalions are fully integrated into the IRGC-GF. The strength of the IRGC-GF is estimated to be around 130,000 troops with an additional 100,000 Basij elements.

The IRGC-GF adheres to an asymmetric doctrine that stresses mobility, dispersion, and concealment of its task forces in open spaces. Its brigades are the force's basic maneuver elements, but a recent reorganization of the force, based on its asymmetric doctrine, has made battalion- and company-size elements operational commands.

The primary mission of the IRGC-GF is to protect the Islamic Republic against foreign and domestic enemies. But elements of the IRGC ground forces are regularly deployed to major battlefields on temporary duty in support of Quds Force operations.

Iran's regular army, Artesh, is tasked with defending the Iranian borders, but it also contributes elements of its ground forces, especially its elite special forces units, namely elements of its 65th Airborne Special Forces Brigades, to major battlefields under the temporary command of the Quds Force. The extent of Artesh's participation became especially apparent during the Quds Force–led Battle of Aleppo in Syria.

Elements of Artesh's premier 92nd Armored Division, tasked with defending the southern portion of the Iran-Iraq border and protecting Iran's oil fields, crossed the border into Iraq during the initial Daesh drive south in 2014 and played a major role in pushing the insurgents out of towns near the Iranian border.

The IRGC-GF faces serious deficiencies in logistics and equipment, including tanks, armored personnel carriers, and infantry fighting vehicles. An emphasis on missile strikes and asymmetric warfare has in effect stalled Iran's development of advanced conventional weapons, including tanks, jet fighters, and warships. Sanctions imposed on arms trade with Iran could be just one reason. Notwithstanding these sanctions, Iran has developed an advanced missile industry. The lack of focus on advanced conventional weapons, especially for a non-nuclear actor, will significantly limit Iran's ability to advance their offensive and deterrent strategies.

New Military Strategy

Iran has had a long-standing strategy of deterrence and a focus on outlasting enemies in a conventional conflict. It has routinely emphasized preserving forces during an initial attack by a superior foe, allowing sufficient forces to survive for retaliation. Since Iran's involvement in regional conflicts in the post–Arab Awakening period, beginning in 2011 in Syria and followed in 2014 in Iraq and Yemen, the military strategy appears to have changed to preemption. The IRGC ballistic missile force and the Quds Force's SLA are the major elements of Iran's new offensive strategy. These capabilities are also believed to advance deterrence, especially against regional adversaries.

It is unclear if building nuclear weapons still remains part of Iran's military strategy. In 2003, after the U.S. invasion of Iraq and the overthrow of Saddam Hussein's regime, the Iranians shelved their nuclear weapons program. But an Israeli raid of the IRGC's nuclear archive in Tehran in 2018 showed that the country still has weaponization files, including simulation results, that could be strongly interpreted as Iran's willingness to restart a weapons program at a future date if circumstances allow it.

THE FINANCIAL SUPPORT NETWORK

The Quds Force funds its operations through multiple budgetary sources, including the official budget, off-budget funding, and extra-budget resources. The government's official budget does not have a specific line item for the Quds Force, but it is generally estimated that around $3 billion annually is allocated to Quds Force headquarters operations. That amount is hardly enough to maintain military involvement in Syria, Iraq, and Yemen and the Quds Force's other programs elsewhere in the region, hence the importance of funding beyond the official budget. The Quds Force is believed to receive additional funding from the government that is not disclosed—so-called off-the-book or off-budget funding—making exact calculations for the Quds Force budget nearly impossible. In addition to off-budget funding, the Quds Force also receives funding through extra-budget resources, which is not disclosed publicly, and includes funding from the Office of the Supreme Leader; revenues from the business enterprises controlled by the IRGC; and revenues generated by the Quds Force's own business activities outside Iran. The extra-budget funding actually supports the bulk of Quds Force–led military operations in Syria, Iraq, Yemen, and Lebanon.

Considering the difficulties in obtaining the organization's extra-budget funding, we can start with estimating the costs of those wars, which will give a rough estimate of the funding required to have the Quds Force lead those projects. Syria is the single most costly project. The estimates include the cost of forces deployed in the country, including the Quds Force–led Shia militias and Iranian military units deployed on temporary duty to specific battlefields. Added is the cost of training, weapons, and equipment used in the theater by SLA units and Iran's own battalions deployed to Syria. The logistics costs are also an important part of the total expenditure, including the maintenance of air and land bridges connecting Syria to the supply base in Iran to move personnel and materiel to the battlespace.

The Iranian government also provides Syria with goods and services required for the country to maintain its ability to continue waging war against the opposition, including some sixty thousand barrels of crude oil per day, lines of credit, and military assistance.

A 2015 report by the UN Special Envoy to Syria estimated Iran's expenditure to prop up Assad's regime at $6 billion annually.[8] Tufts University research showed that Iranian spending in Syria in 2012–2013 exceeded $14 billion.[9]

Iran's military involvement in Syria began in 2011, and the cost to wage war in the country during this long period is in the tens of billions of dollars.

The Quds Force also requires funding for its significant military efforts in Iraq, including financing operations and military equipment for some of the largest Shia militia groups in the country. In Yemen, the Quds Force provides advanced weaponry to the Houthis, including cruise and ballistic missiles and explosive boats. In Lebanon, as the chief of Hezbollah has said, Iran provides nearly all his organization's budget, which is estimated to be close to $1 billion annually. The Quds Force operates in central and western Afghanistan as well. It also maintains a large Afghan Shia militia force, the Fatemiyoun, estimated to be fifteen thousand strong. The cost of these operations are all shouldered by the Quds Force.

Outside these five major theaters, Syria, Iraq, Yemen, Lebanon, and Afghanistan, the Quds Force supports a myriad of Shia militant organizations in countries like Bahrain, Kuwait, and eastern Saudi Arabia. And it maintains a vast network of associates across the globe.

Iran not only finances these projects, it has to pay for the majority of these expenses in hard currency. The Syria project alone costs between $7 billion and $14 billion annually. The annual cost of all these projects together could approach $20 billion, or nearly 5 percent of the country's GDP, a major expenditure for a country facing an economic crisis of its own.

It is not entirely clear how Iran finances its Quds Force–led projects, but the bulk of its military involvement in the region could be funded by the business empire run by the IRGC and the Office of the Supreme Leader. Between the two, they control a dozen major foundations, which in turn control more than five hundred companies and enterprises.

A 2017 report by the Iranian opposition has revealed the extensive business empire behind the extra-budgetary funding. An understanding of the extent to which the country's leader and its main military branch, the IRGC, control the Iranian economy is key to understanding the funding of Quds Force–led projects. The information on the foundations and their companies that follows is based on a book published in 2017 by the National Council of Resistance of Iran and is used in the following tables with its permission.[10]

* * *

FOUNDATIONS AND BUSINESS ENTITIES UNDER THE CONTROL OF THE IRGC

I. Khatam al-Anbiya Construction Headquarters (KACHQ)

The KACHQ is an official part of the IRGC's organizational structure. It is Iran's largest government contractor and employs 5,000 subcontractors, while 135,000 people work on KACHQ projects. The state-run news agency reported in 2011 that the organization's contracts in the oil, gas, and petrochemical sector exceeded \$25 billion.[11] The following are some of the KACHQ's affiliated companies.

- Oil and gas: Oriental Oil; Sepanir Oil and Gas Engineering
- Dam construction and infrastructure development: Sepasad
- Tunnel construction and drilling: Imensazan Consulting Engineering Institute; Fater Engineering Institute; Rahab Institute
- Naval structures: Makin Institute
- Railroad: Sahel Construction
- Land and real estate: Nour Institution; Sama Institution

The Ghadir Investment Company

Oil and Gas Development

Persian Oil and Gas Development Group

Oil Refineries

- Tabriz Oil Refinery
- Shiraz Oil Refinery

Petrochemicals

- Zagros Petrochemical (one of the world's largest producers of methanol)
- Pardis Petrochemical (one of the largest producers of urea fertilizer in the Middle East)
- Kermanshah Petrochemical
- Tabriz Petrochemical
- Shiraz Petrochemical
- Khorasan Petrochemical
- Kian Petrochemical
- Pars Petrochemical
- International Petrochemicals Commerce Company

The International Construction Development Company

- ASP
- Royay-e Zendegi Kish
- Tisa Kish
- Ghadir Engineering Consulting
- Pars Structures
- Fars Shelter
- Narenjestan Gostar
- Behestan Pars
- Ghadir Khuzestan
- Azerbaijan Construction
- Ghadir Mehr Iranian Engineering Research

The Ghadir Capital and Industry Development Company

Cement factories:

- Sharq Cement
- Sepahan Cement
- Kurdistan Cement
- Dashtestan Cement
- Sarouj Bushehr Cement

Investment companies: Mehr and Azar

Ghadir International Mining Companies

- Zarshouran (Iran's largest gold mine—West Azerbaijan)
- Kerman (titanium)
- Semnan (zinc)
- Sang Ahan Iron Ore

Metals and industrials:

- Ghadir Caspian Steel
- Iranian Iron and Steel
- South Aluminum Industries Complex
- Alloy Steel
- Shahid Bahonar Wood
- Shahid Qazi Pharmaceutical

Ghadir commerce and service sector: Ghadir Management and Commercial Services and other companies

Power and energy:

- Gilan Masir Electricity
- Gilan Power Generation
- Khuzestan Power Generation
- Lamerd Power Generation
- Hamoun Abu Musa Energy

Sea transport:

- Iran Marine Shipping Services
- Kish South Iran Daryaban
- Ghadir Sepehr Transportation

The IRGC Cooperative Foundation

The IRGC Cooperative Foundation, Bonyad Taavon Sepah, is one of Iran's largest institutions. Its holdings span major sectors of the country's economy, including the automotive industry. Its financial holdings make it the country's largest investment institution. It is also involved in telecommunications, construction, and commerce.

Automobile manufacturing (Bahman Holding)

- SAIPA (automobile manufacturing): Joint ownership and management control of Pars Khodro (manufacturer of SUVs) and twenty-one SAIPA subsidiaries
- National Iranian Investment Company
- Bahman Investment Company
- Bahman Leasing Company
- Bahman Diesel (assembler of Isuzu trucks)
- Iran Chassis Production

Financial holdings

- Thamen Al-Ameh Financial and Credit Union (with five hundred branches nationwide): Saman Majd Investment
- Ansar Bank (with six hundred branches across Iran): Ansar Currency Exchange and twenty Ansar Bank subsidiaries
- Iranian Negin Khatam Investment
- Ayak Investments
- Behshar Industrial Investment (shareholder)

- Iran Credit

Industry

- Kermanshah Petrochemical
- Kerman Petrochemical (shareholder)
- Zagros Steel
- Shahab Sang Mining
- Esfahan Zinc Smelter
- Iran Welding
- Baharizad Wool Weaving
- Sina Pharmaceutical (shareholder)

Telecommunication

- Iran Electronic Industries in a joint venture (51 percent) with South Africa MTN (49 percent)
- Mobin (shareholder)
- Talia (shareholder)
- Sayyar Communications (providing service for the Mobile Telecommunications Company of Iran; shareholder)

Construction

- Prefab Light Structure Engineering
- Jihad Residential Builders, operating in twenty provinces
- Sepah Residential Complex Builders
- Razmandeh Residential Complex Builders

Food and Agriculture

- Shadan Khorasan Industries: Shadab Khorasan Agro Business
- Maedeh Food Industries

Commerce and Services

- Pars Air: Pars Air Travel
- South Pars Oil Field (contractor)
- Bahrestan Kish
- Twelve other companies

The Pasargad Group

The IRGC Cooperative is a major shareholder through its Thamen al-Aameh Credit Union (see above):

- Pasargad Bank
- Pasargad Leasing
- Middle East Mining
- Pasargad Arian Information and Communications
- Pasargad Insurance and Re-insurance Companies
- Pasargad's thirty-one other subsidiaries

Khatam al-Osia Construction Headquarters

Oil and gas development projects and pipelines (the IRGC and the Department of Defense)

Development of South Pars (World's Largest Gas Field, Shares with Qatar)

- Phase 15 and 16
- Phase 22 and 24

Development of Gas and Oil Pipelines

- Phase 3 of a cross-country gas pipeline
- Peace Pipeline: Iran-Pakistan gas pipeline
- Nekah-Jusk oil pipeline
- Oil pipelines in Khorasan, Kerman, and Hormozgan
- Construction of methane, ethylene, and LNG pipelines

There are six other projects, including LNG production and railway electrification projects.

The Cooperative Foundation of the Basij Force

- Iranian Mehr Economic Investment
- Iran Tractor Manufacturing—Tabriz
- Parsian Bank
- Zinc Mining Development Holding Company
- Iranian Aluminum Industries
- Esfahan Mobarakeh Steel Company
- Tabriz Tractor Soccer Club
- Eleven other enterprises

The Cooperative Foundation of the State Security Forces (NAJA)

- Qavamin Bank
- Bimeh Omid—NAJA Hope Insurance
- Pardis Hotel Group
- Fourteen other enterprises

FOUNDATIONS UNDER THE CONTROL OF
THE OFFICE OF THE SUPREME LEADER

The Headquarters for Executing the Order of the Imam (SETAD)

- Tadbir Energy Development Group: Tadbir Energy Development Holding Group (oil and gas, refineries, petrochemicals), including Pars Oil and ten other companies
- Mobin Iran Electronics (telecommunications and mobile phones), including Mobile Communications and five other holdings
- Barkat Pharmaceutical Holding Company, including Alborz Pharmaceutical, the country's second-largest pharmaceutical company, and thirteen other companies
- Tadbir Construction (residential, commercial, and tourist projects) with four companies under its control
- Tadbir Investment (active in financial markets and in securities) with six companies under its control
- Barkat Foundation, registered as a charity but reportedly also the holder of SETAD's significant cash revenues
- Banks and insurance, including shares in Parsian Bank, Kar-Afarin Bank, and Mellat Insurance
- Other investments, including shares in Iran Khorro and three other companies

Mostazafan Foundation

The Mostazafan Foundation owns hundreds of commercial companies, producing 28 percent of the textiles in the country, 22 percent of the cement, 45 percent of the non-alcoholic beverages, 28 percent of the tires, and 25 percent of the sugar. Some of its holdings are listed below.

- Alavi Foundation: Alavi Urban Engineering
- Sina Bank (270 branches)
- Payvand Ferdous Pars Agriculture (fourteen major agro-industrial and livestock enterprises)

- Pars Milk and Beef (sixteen major farms and agro-businesses across the country)
- Sina Food Industries (eight major meat producers, dairies, and a manufacturer of non-alcoholic beverages like Abe Ali)
- Parsian Tourism and Recreation
- Zamzam
- Tehran Cement
- Tehran Shomal Freeway (construction)
- Saba Power and Energy

Astan-e Quds Razavi

Astan-e Quds Razavi owns 58 major enterprises, with shares in 31 other companies as well as large swaths of farmland. It is the largest employer in eastern Iran and reportedly provides 20 percent of the IRGC budget. Some of the companies are listed below.

- Quds Razavi (construction holdings, including concrete, residential, and water and soil companies)
- Manufacturing enterprises, including Shahbad Auto and Combine Manufacturing
- Razavi food industry enterprises, including Razavi Food, Razavi Dairy, Razavi Bread, Abkoush Sugar, Torbat Heydarieh Sugar, and Chenaran Sugar
- Razavi Agribusiness enterprises, including the Chenaran, Esfarayen, Anabed, Sarakhs, and Nemouneh companies
- Carpet and textile companies, including Astan-e Quds Razavi Carpet and Khorasani Weaving and Textile
- Pharmaceutical companies, including Thamen Pharmaceuticals
- Financial companies, including Razavi Credit Union and Razavi Brokerage
- Other enterprises, including Razavi Oil, Astan-e Quds Razavi Wood, Quds Razavi Mining, Quds Razavi Livestock (with over 130,000 cows), and Imam Reza University and Razavi Islamic Sciences University

The Shahid Foundation

The Shahid Foundation funnels funds to Quds Force–led Shia militant organizations, including Hezbollah and Quds Force–affiliated militant organizations, including Hamas and Palestinian Islamic Jihad. The foundation has branches in Lebanon to facilitate the transfer of funds. Inside Iran, the Shahid Foundation owns some thirty major companies and banks.

Dey Bank

The bank has forty-seven branches and owns thirteen other companies, including Dey Electronic Commerce, Dey Currency Exchange, Dey Brokerage, and Day Insurance.

The Kowsar Organization

- Sobhan Investments
- Tehran Electric
- Zakhireh Shahed Investments and its own ten companies
- Shahed University

The Emdad Committee

The Emdad Committee has offices in Iraq, Syria, Lebanon, and Afghanistan and distributes aide reportedly to the families of Quds Force–led Shia militias. Following are some of its holdings in Iran.

- Gostar Basir, Tehran, Emdad, and Nassim construction companies
- Bahar-e Rafsanjan Agro-Business, Sabzdasht-e Fars Agriculture, and ten other companies
- Qom Mining, Emdad Faravar, and three other companies
- Approximately 1,200 charity boxes across the country
- Significant land acreage in the Fars, Khozestan, Gilan, Golestan, Mazandaran, Homozgan, Kerman, Yazd, and Markazi provinces

* * *

ECONOMIC OPPORTUNITIES AND CONSTRAINTS

The IRGC and the Office of the Supreme Leader are estimated to control about 50 percent of the Iranian economy through the mega-foundations outlined above. Such massive economic control creates both opportunities and constraints for the Quds Force.

The IRGC's business empire provides the Quds Force with a secure source of funding even if the government budget is cut due to competing priorities at home. The foundations controlled by the IRGC and the Office of the Supreme Leader are both exempt from taxes and are off official records, making them especially suitable as emergency funding for Quds Force war efforts without any scrutiny by the Majlis, the parliament, or the public. The Quds Force also has established its own businesses in the region, partly through the IRGC-controlled foundations operating in the near abroad. Access to those funds, coupled with its vast network of Shia militant groups and associates and its arms caches across the region, would enable the Quds Force to continue its operations as the headquarters of the Shia militancy in the Middle East, albeit at a diminished level, in case of an emergency in Tehran.

The disadvantage of relying so heavily on businesses, however, is the uncertainties they face at times of economic slowdown. Iran is currently facing a myriad of economic challenges that affect all major businesses, including those controlled by the IRGC. The current state of the economy is characterized by deep economic stagnation, loss in the value of the national currency, and a banking crisis unparalleled in recent times. The economic stagnation has resulted in a slowdown of the activities of many factories and business enterprises, including those controlled by the IRGC. The currency issues have significantly raised the cost of wars in the region, which are funded in hard currency. Furthermore, the banking crisis, caused by major banks being significantly undercapitalized and customers losing confidence because their deposits are not insured, affects IRGC-controlled banks and the availability of capital for their businesses in general.

The ownership of major businesses by the IRGC and the Quds Force also has a corrupting effect on both organizations. IRGC and Quds Force generals are not supposed to consider the business ramifications of their military decisions and advice. Doing so dilutes discipline and the military doctrine. The generals' decisions should be based solely on military grounds and not business considerations. The business environment surrounding the IRGC also spreads corruption within the organization. The mixture of guns and money gives generals an opportunity to circumvent laws and regulations not just to help their businesses but also to enrich themselves. Importing goods into the country without going through customs and distributing them outside regulated distribution channels, for instance, makes military personnel, including general officers, effectively smugglers and black marketers.

Some in the IRGC and the Quds Force leadership might realize that mixing business with military affairs has negatively affected the morale and military discipline of their fighting force. But the profits made by their foundations are much too great, and so many officers are involved in corrupt practices that getting out of the world of business is not on the agenda. And the longer they stay, the deeper the problems get. Corruption has become the Achilles' heel of the IRGC.

HIGH COSTS OF THE EXPEDITIONARY FORCE

Quds Force operations require major investments in personnel and materiel. The SLA supports some 100,000 active militia fighters, most of whom are deployed to battle zones. It also supports the training and arming of another 100,000 militants who make up the SLA's reserve forces. Maintaining such a large force is a costly endeavor.

Personnel

The expenses begin with recruiting costs, including sign-on bonuses, salaries and benefits, and payments to the families of fighters killed in action. Training is the next major item. New recruits are generally deployed to Iran to undergo basic training in one of the Quds Force's military camps inside the country. Some fighters are sent back to Iran for advanced training multiple times. The Quds Force also finances the training camps run by Hezbollah, major Iraqi Shia militia groups, and the Houthis.

The Quds Force relies on influence operations to maintain and expand its worldwide network of associates to conduct influence and intelligence activities on its behalf. The program is costly, including setting up and running cultural and religious centers in the region and globally. The Quds Force, through a web of IRGC-controlled foundations and so-called charity organizations, sponsors academic centers and endowed chairs in universities and research institutions in the West and in Shiite Islamic universities across the Islamic world, especially in Africa. Iran runs vast information operations outside its borders, including Arabic-, English-, and Spanish-language radio and TV networks, and it spends significantly to influence both Arab and Western media.

Intelligence

The Quds Force maintains robust and costly intelligence operations on and outside the battlefield. In Lebanon, Syria, Iraq, and Yemen, it maintains joint intelligence cells and fusion centers with major groups within the SLA. Its external-operations unit directs highly trained operators, chosen from among the ranks of the Quds Force and the SLA, to conduct terrorist operations, including kidnappings, assassinations, and bombings. It also maintains a large network of intelligence operatives both within Iranian diplomatic missions and outside of them in many countries of the world.

The Quds Force maintains intelligence training centers in Iran for Shia militants who volunteer to work as intelligence agents or covert operators. Imam Ali University in Qom and garrisons inside Iran—Shahid, Kazemi, Beheshti, and Vali-e Asr—serve as Quds Force training centers. [12]

Operations

The Quds Force provides weapons, military equipment, and materiel to SLA units, which constitutes another costly line item in its budget. Some of the known materiel used by Quds Force–led forces in Iraq and Syria are listed below.

- Fateh-110 and Zelzal CRBMs
- Tanks, ATGMs, anti-tank rockets
- Howitzers, artillery, mortars, and Quds Force improvised rocket-assisted munitions
- UAVs, Su-25 Frogfoots, and F-4 Phantoms in the Iraqi theater
- Man-portable air defense systems
- IEDs, EFPs, mines, hand grenades, detonators, and fuses
- AK-series rifles, sniper rifles, and ammunition
- Communications gear, night-vision goggles, cameras, and scopes

In Yemen, the Quds Force has delivered advanced weaponry to the Houthis to be used against Saudi and Emirati ships off the coast of Yemen and against targets inside Saudi Arabia. Known weapons delivered include:

- ASCMs
- Qaim-1 SRBMs
- Explosive boats, speedboats, and mines
- Ammunition

Outside the battlespaces of Syria, Iraq, and Yemen, the Quds Force provides high levels of military aid to Hezbollah.

Shia militant groups in Bahrain, Kuwait, and other countries in the gulf also receive military aid from the Quds Force, including advanced explosive devices and small arms.

Outside the SLA, the Quds Force provides military support to selected Sunni militant organizations for their anti-U.S. and anti-Israel campaigns. These groups include Palestinian Islamic Jihad and Hamas, as well as the Taliban in Afghanistan.

Logistics

The vast and ever-expanding Quds Force logistics network supports its forward operations centers in the region and the operations of the SLA. The Quds Force has built and will continue maintaining at high cost land and air bridges connecting Iran through Iraq and Syria to Lebanon and the Mediterranean. It maintains logistics centers near Damascus International Airport, Baghdad International Airport, and other airports in Syria and Iraq to handle the transfer of personnel and materiel.

The Damascus airport center, manned by Hezbollah fighters, has been a frequent target of the IAF, which wishes to disrupt regular supplies of weapons from Iran that are sent by commercial and military cargo planes. [13]

The Quds Force and its affiliated business enterprises run air operations for transporting personnel and cargo to Iraq and Syria; shipping lines—vessels and dhows—for transfer of weapons to Yemen; land transport lines to transfer personnel and materiel to Afghanistan; and logistics operations in other parts of the region.

Command and Control

The Quds Force provides command, control, communication, and computer support to all its assigned forces, both asymmetric and symmetric.

The deployment of regular forces is coordinated between the Quds Force and Khatam-ol-Anbia Central Headquarters, the senior wartime operations command in Tehran. The deployment of foreign Shia militia units is coordinated with parent groups like Hezbollah.

The Quds Force has established a long-term headquarters and communications infrastructure in Iraq, Syria, and Yemen in support of its military operations. In Iraq and Syria, the Quds Force runs joint command-and-control centers with military and Shia militia groups. It uses joint communications networks to coordinate operations and facilitate communications with SLA units. These communications networks built by the Quds Force provide it with long-term, secure communications capabilities in those countries.

The Force Structure

The Quds Force is commanded by a general officer (nominally a two-star but operationally the equivalent of a four-star general). The operational chain-of-command runs from Iran's supreme leader directly to the Quds Force commander.

The Quds Force is divided into regional and functional directorates. Its regional commands cover Iraq, the Levant, the Arabian Peninsula, North Africa, Afghanistan, Pakistan, Turkey and Central Asia, Russia and the Far East, the Balkans, and the Americas.

Quds Force operations in Iraq are under its Ramazan Corps. This unit oversees Shia militia groups inside Iraq and maintains military training camps for Iraqi militants inside Iran. The officers of the Ramazan Corps operate almost overtly in the permissive environment of Baghdad.

The Quds Force Levant Corps is responsible for operations in Syria, Lebanon, Jordan, and Israel. Its commander, Brigadier Javad Ghaffari, is considered the most powerful of General Soleimani's commanders and possibly his successor. The officers of the Levant Corps operate almost as overtly in the similarly permissive environment of Damascus.

The Rasulallah Corps is responsible for operations on the Arabian Peninsula, including the war in Yemen and Quds Force activities in Bahrain, eastern Saudi Arabia, and other Arab states of the gulf.

The Ansar Corps is responsible for operations in Afghanistan.

Quds Force functional directorates cover R&D, which is responsible for explosives like EFPs and battlefield rockets; special external operations, which is responsible for bombings and assassinations; rockets and missiles; special forces; and electronic warfare.

The Office of the Commander also oversees command directorates: Personnel; Intelligence; Operations; Logistics; Plan and Policy; Command, Control, Communication, and Computers (C4); and Training and Force Structure.

The Quds Force's headquarters is located on Farahabad Military Base in eastern Tehran. The Quds Force also maintains a forward headquarters near the border with Iraq, its Zafar headquarters in the town of Mehran.

Quds Force headquarters personnel are estimated at around six thousand.

SUSTAINING WAR EFFORTS

Military efforts are always bound by resource limitations. Iran most likely will struggle to fully resource its war efforts in the midst of economic hardship and competing priorities. Iran's official armed forces budget, which includes funding for the IRGC, the Quds Force, Artesh, the Ministry of Defense, law enforcement (NAJA), as well as the pension funds of all services, is around $23 billion annually, or nearly 6 percent of Iran's GDP. There are also the undeclared costs of the IRGC's ballistic missile and nuclear programs. And then there is the cost of wars and other Quds Force–led operations outside Iran. Total military-related expenditures could be over 10 percent of GDP. This situation is not sustainable for the country, especially at current oil prices and production levels, and the full funding of Quds force–led operations will be a challenge long term.

POLITICAL CONSTRAINTS

During nationwide protests in late December 2017, among popular chants was a call to end military involvement in the region, and specifically in Syria. The protesters demanded that the government allocate funds spent in the near abroad on improving the economy at home. Such sentiments at times of economic hardship, high unemployment, and rising costs for basic goods like food could undermine the Quds Force's expectation of public support for its projects abroad.

Regimes in Iran have always been vulnerable to economic downturns, especially if the problems persist for a long period. Many of the economic problems facing the country are structural, and corruption has become systemic. Reforms are needed, but the regime is unable or unwilling to undertake the reforms, a vicious circle that undermines the legitimacy of the regime, which does not bode well for the IRGC and the Quds Force.

Chapter Eleven

Long Road, Uncertain Future

In the first days of the Islamic Revolution, the IRGC's extraterritorial branch began training dozens of Afghans and Iraqis in makeshift camps outside Tehran and deployed most of them to battlefields inside Afghanistan and on the Iran-Iraq border. Since then, the expeditionary arm of the Islamic Republic has come a long way. It has perfected the doctrine of proxy warfare in which foreign militias, supported by specialized elements of Iran's armed forces, compete militarily against opposing forces without triggering an all-out war that would require the Iranian military's involvement. Quds Force–led forces' victory in the Battle of Aleppo marked the execution of this doctrine to the fullest extent possible. In that battle, tens of thousands of highly trained, armed, and committed Shia fighters from different countries in the region formed the Quds Force's infantry force. Supported by IRGC and Artesh artillery, armor, UAV, and special forces elements and Russian air power, they defeated one of the largest forces the Syrian opposition had assembled during the civil war. The battlefield successes of the Quds Force–led forces cemented Assad's hold on power.

The victory in Aleppo, however, was only the beginning of a period of challenges to the Quds Force's involvement in the Syrian conflict. Following that battle, Iran could have declared victory over the opposition—the original goal of its military involvement in the civil war—and pulled its foreign Shia militias out of Syria. Instead, Iran opted to keep its forces in the country for the long haul and to build a land corridor connecting them to a supply base in Iran. At this juncture, Iran fundamentally redefined its mission; its goals changed from defeating the Syrian opposition to maintaining a permanent presence in Syria in order to challenge Israel along its borders. The Quds Force began leasing space in more than twenty Syrian military bases to house its command-and-control centers, its personnel and equipment, and tens of thousands of foreign fighters. The IRGC's UAVs and surface-to-air and land-attack missiles were deployed in these Quds Force installations. This change in strategy invited attacks by Israel Defense Forces (IDF), which saw permanent Iranian basing in Syria near its northern front lines as a threat to Israel's security.

The Quds Force's recent moves in Syria of basing proxy forces in fixed installations in order to challenge a superior military meant deploying and exposing its forces in a manner that could eventually lead to a full-fledged war with Israel—even though the Quds Force's doctrine called for avoiding such an outcome, which could only signify a major change in Iran's proxy war doctrine.

In February 2018, an IRGC drone took off from the Syrian T4 Airbase that housed the Quds Force's UAV command-and-control center for the country. The unmanned aircraft was on an ISR mission to survey Israeli military positions in the vicinity of Quds Force–led forces stationed in southern Syria. The drone entered Israeli airspace and was shot down by an Israeli attack helicopter. Israeli jets then launched an air attack against the Quds Force UAV command center at T4 Airbase and destroyed the facility. Syria's air defense shot down an Israeli jet, and the Israelis retaliated by destroying half of Syria's air defense capability. Three months later, the Quds Force launched a rocket attack on Israeli positions on the Golan Heights, firing Fajr 3 and Fajr 5 rockets operated by the IRGC missile unit deployed to Syria. In retaliation, Israel launched its biggest air operation in more than four decades and simultaneously attacked sixteen Syrian Quds Force military bases, which housed almost all of Iran's command-and-control centers and militia based in the country. This attack killed Quds Force senior officers and scores of foreign militants. These incidents exemplify how conflicts intended to be limited can quickly spiral out of the initiator's control.

Thus Iran and Israel have started on a trajectory toward war on Syrian soil in the span of a few short months. The U.S. will not sit on the sidelines if a war breaks out. The Quds Force could find itself countering combined Israel–U.S. forces in the country. This prospect is not favorable to Iran.

Syria is not the only theater of war in which the Quds Force's presence could precipitate a full-fledged war. The situations in Yemen and Iraq also pose serious challenges for Iran.

In Yemen, the Quds Force decided to arm the Houthis to fight as militants in Iran's proxy war with the Saudis and Emiratis. The arms delivered included ballistic and cruise missiles and explosive boats. The Houthis then used the cruise missiles and the explosive boats against Saudi and Emirati vessels off the coast of Yemen and fired the ballistic missiles at Saudi and Emirati cities. If those ballistic missiles had hit their intended targets, which included the international airport and the royal palace in Riyadh, the Saudis and Emiratis would have retaliated against Iranian targets, with U.S. support.

Decisions like these on the Quds Force's part could start a major war on the Arabian Peninsula.

THE THREAT TO THE U.S. IN THE POST-ISIS PERIOD

In Iraq, the situation is different—but just as precarious. The Quds Force mobilized all available Iraqi Shia militant forces to fight ISIS. Now that ISIS has been defeated, Iraq has no national security needs that call for the continued existence of a large militia force under the command of a foreign military in parallel to Iraq's own national military. The Iraqi government, supported by the U.S. and the coalition, could demand that the militias be disarmed. Since Iran has no justification for maintaining militia forces in a post-ISIS Iraq, such a request would put the Quds Force under heavy pressure to either fully integrate the militias into the Iraqi military or disarm them altogether.

The major Iraqi Shia militias under the command of the Quds Force fought the U.S. and U.S.-led coalition forces during the 2003–2011 Iraq War. Nearly five hundred U.S. servicemen were killed in action during Operation Iraqi Freedom. During those years, the Quds Force flooded Iraq with EFPs. Many Americans were killed by EFPs planted by the Shia militants. Those militia groups are still the leading Quds Force–led irregular forces in Iraq and pose a serious threat to thousands of U.S. personnel in the country. Rogue elements of these groups could also independently take action against Americans, such as organizing rocket attacks on U.S. military bases and diplomatic installations in the country. The risk is tremendous and could potentially provoke a direct military confrontation between the Quds Force and U.S. forces on Iraqi soil.

THE QUDS FORCE MISSION

The Quds Force's own mission statement defines its mission as exporting the principles of the revolution and performing special operations. The IRGC/Quds Force's insignia displays part of a *surah* (chapter) from the Quran, "Against them make ready your strength to the utmost of your power," setting the tone for Iran's us-against-them attitude toward social and political forces, foreign and domestic, that do not subscribe to the ideals of the Islamic Revolution and its militant interpretation of Shia Islam.

The Quds Force was given a wide and continuing mandate to organize, train, equip, and finance militant—mostly Shia—groups in the region. Iran's supreme leader Ayatollah Ali Khamenei reiterated the organization's mission by tasking the Quds Force with establishing Hezbollah cells all over the world.

The growing, region-wide Shia militancy under the command of the Quds Force, supported by the ideologically driven wing of the Islamic Republic and led by its supreme leader, is bent on ending the U.S. presence in the Middle East and upending the political order in Sunni powerhouses. Four decades after the Islamic Revolution, the Quds Force has become a clear and present danger to U.S. personnel and interests in the region and those of its allies, Israel and the GCC.

THE WAY AHEAD

I began this book by saying that the founders of the Islamic Republic intended to create a revolutionary movement that was not about just Iran but the entire region. Four decades later, the Quds Force has become the embodiment of that doctrine, recruiting and arming Shia militants across the region to unite Shias under the militant ideology of the Islamic Republic and its supreme leader. The ultimate goal is to create a Shia nation, albeit noncontiguous, and what alternatively is referred to as a "Shia crescent." By establishing a land corridor connecting Tehran through Iraq and Syria to Lebanon and Israel's northern fronts, the Quds Force has indeed succeeded in creating a Shia arc of influence across the Middle East.

The founders of the revolution also wanted to establish a strong government in Tehran to be in charge of the day-to-day management of the country and put its full resources behind the revolutionary movement in the region inspired by the Islamic Revolution in Iran. But things did not go as planned. The Islamic Republic government is now the weakest it has been in four decades of existence. The national currency has dropped in value from 70 rials to the dollar at the time of the victory of the Islamic Revolution to 42,000 rials to the dollar today. Corruption has become endemic, and unemployment is precariously high. A banking crisis, stemming from severe undercapitalization of major banks, has become a drag on the economy. Development of light industries, once a promising aspect of the country's non-oil industry, has come to a screeching halt. Major foreign investment has all but disappeared. The state of human rights and basic freedoms in the country is at an all-time low. For all these reasons, various groups of people are protesting government policies and calling for a regime change.

U.S. sanctions against the Islamic Republic have exacerbated the country's economic problems, and Iranians are also questioning the wisdom of spending billions of dollars annually in other parts of the region, such as Syria, at a time of severe economic hardship at home.

The Islamic Republic came to power through a regime change in 1979, upending 2,500 years of monarchy. Four decades later, the youths of Iran might regard another regime change as necessary to reverse the country's economic and political downturn. The worsening domestic situation has been exacerbated by serious foreign policy setbacks, including the U.S. exit from the 2015 Iran nuclear deal and the results of the 2018 Iraqi elections. The specter of a full-fledged war with Israel in Syria or with the Saudi-Emirati–led coalition in Yemen, with the U.S. becoming involved in support of its allies, has unsettled internal markets and foreign investment prospects. On the fortieth anniversary of its founding, the Islamic Republic may be facing its demise in the not-too-distant future.

Can the Quds Force Outlast the Islamic Republic?

Over the years, the Quds Force has created a strong support network for the SLA. Through foreign branches of the IRGC-controlled economic foundations, the Quds Force has created a web of companies in the Middle East that includes banks, currency-exchange outlets, and transportation services that have contracts with established air and shipping lines in the region. These enterprises will meet the logistics needs of the Quds Force and its major Shia militia groups in any future battlefield. They will also provide external financial revenues for the Quds Force.

The Quds Force also runs a vast network of non-combatant associates throughout the world. These are used to recruit young refugees settling abroad, especially in Europe. They run the Quds Force business network outside Iran. They provide information operations in support of the Quds Force, a propaganda-type network through cultural and religious centers. The academics among them provide intellectual justification for Quds Force operations.

To prepare for any eventuality, including the disruption of supplies from Iran or the fall of the Islamic Republic, the Quds Force has stored caches of arms in areas of its operation, mostly in association with major Shia militant groups.

The Quds Force's future plans call for an enduring existence as the headquarters of militant Shias across the Middle East. These structures, as well as the Quds Force's caches of weapons, represent the ways in which the Quds Force is organized in such a way as to outlast the Islamic Republic should the government in Tehran fall.

An Interconnected Region

For better or worse, the Middle East is interconnected. The modern-day Islamist movement that began with the establishment of an Islamic government in Tehran soon spread across the region. The Taliban's Islamic emirate and Daesh's Islamic state were Sunni attempts to create a governance based on Quranic teachings and idealized Islamic caliphates that enjoyed the height of their power during the Islamic Golden Age, which began with Harun al-Rashid in the eighth century and ended at the hands of the invading Mongols and the collapse of the Abbasid caliphate five centuries later.

A more moderate version of political Islam, advanced by the Muslim Brotherhood and its affiliates, also came to power during this period in Turkey and temporarily in Egypt. A lack of respect for the rule of law, disregard of basic freedoms and human rights, and mismanagement of national territories were common attributes that defined Islamic governments in Tehran, Kabul, Raqqa and Mosul, Cairo, and Ankara.

The extremely violent nature of Daesh and its eventual defeat may be a turning point in the history of political Islam as it generally ended youths' romanticizing of the distant past and hoping to replicate a Golden Age Islamic state in the twenty-first century. The remaining Islamic governments in Tehran and Ankara will be under heavy pressure to change their ways or face across-the-board protests similar to the continued nationwide demonstration in Iran.

The defeat of Islamist organizations and ideologies is producing cascading effects across the region. Conservative Arab governments have taken note of the political landscape transforming around them. The Saudis and Emiratis lead the charge against political Islam by cutting funding to the extremists and diminishing their power and influence in their societies. Many other regional governments are following their lead.

The loss of Islamist influence in the region could pose serious problems for the Quds Force, with fewer youths who commit their lives to serve the interest of the supreme leader in Tehran in the name of creating a militant Shia nation.

THE NEW GREAT GAME

External state actors have become particularly active in the region of late, making Syria and Yemen the region's current flashpoints.

Russia deployed a robust military element to the Syrian conflict in 2015, which was its largest military expedition since the end of the Cold War. From the beginning of its involvement, Russia picked Assad's side and entered into a partnership with Iran. Iran and Syria shared Russia's anti-U.S. strategy in Syria and elsewhere in the region.

Russia also reactivated its old naval base in the Mediterranean at the seaport of Tatrus in western Syria. It has in addition taken over the Bassel al-Assad airfield, also in western Syria and not far from Tatrus. Russia intends to keep both bases open permanently.

But Russia was not ready for the sudden shift of Iranian focus toward Israel shortly after Assad's opposition was largely defeated. Russia does not share the anti-Israeli ideology of the Iranians. This difference, especially if it ends in a direct military conflict between Iran and Israel in Syria, could be a blow to the Iran-Russia partnership.

Turkey was the last state actor to enter Syria and did so mainly because of its concerns about the growing power and influence of the Kurds in northern Syria. The Turks deployed a proxy force of Syrian Sunni Arabs as their land force, supported by Turkish military units, and succeeded in occupying the predominantly Kurdish enclave of Afrin. The continued movement of the Turkish military into Kurdish-majority regions in Syria could result in a continuation of military conflict between the Turks and the Kurdish YPG and the Kurdish-Arab alliance of SDF east of the Euphrates where the U.S. forces have backed the Kurdish fighters in their war against ISIS. Such a conflict would test the limits of the U.S.-Turkish friendship and alliance. Iran will also be hard pressed to take a side in the conflict as its fear of Kurdish nationalism matches its distaste for Erdogan's brand of Islamism.

The American involvement in Syria has been limited to the war against ISIS. In the Syrian civil war, however, the U.S. has generally not been a participant—unlike Russia, Iran, and Turkey. The exceptions were its opposition to chemical attacks by the Assad regime and its punishment of the regime for such attacks. Also, the U.S. took limited military action against Quds Force–led militia forces and Russia-led mercenary forces approaching the small American base in al-Tanf in the Syrian desert, near the Iraq border and on the major road connecting Damascus and Baghdad.

The fast pace of events after the defeat of Daesh and major setbacks of the opposition in Aleppo and Damascus might force the U.S. to enter the Syrian conflict more forcefully. Direct military conflict between Iran and Israel is also likely to trigger direct U.S. involvement.

Yemen and the Bab el-Mandeb are two other flashpoints. A Sunni alliance of regional powers is lined up against the Zaydi-Shia Houthis backed by Iran and the Quds Force. Saudi Arabia and the UAE are the key Sunni players.

The UAE has fielded a small but highly cohesive military package and has demonstrated skills rarely seen in the region, including a high proficiency in conducting special operations, airstrikes, and amphibious operations. The Emiratis have also displayed their skill in small-unit combat maneuvers. They have deployed advanced military systems to the battlespace, including aircraft, attack helicopters, and artillery rocket systems.

The Emiratis' joint effort with the Saudis in Yemen is stopping Iran from turning the Houthis into another Hezbollah and establishing a permanent military presence in the heart of the Arabian Peninsula.

It is important to note that a new flashpoint in the region could develop as a result of this Emirati and Saudi desire to roll back Iran's influence in the region. The UAE's claim over the three islands of Abu Musa and Greater and

Lesser Tunbs in the Persian Gulf, which have been occupied by Iran since the British withdrawal from the Persian Gulf in 1971, could result in the occupation of any of the three islands by Emirati and Saudi forces, which could lead to a direct military conflict with Iran. The UAE might believe that a war with Iran is inevitable and that in a coalition with Saudi Arabia and other GCC countries, supported by Israel and the U.S., it can help stop Iranian expansion in the region.

Under its new leadership, Saudi Arabia is challenging Iran militarily and ideologically. The latter is best seen in the Saudi drive to diminish the influence of political Islam in its own country and in the region, reversing nearly four decades of efforts by previous Saudi leaders to appease Islamist groups. Militarily, the Saudi-led coalition in Yemen stopped the Iranian advance there after the Quds Force had operated unopposed in other parts of the region for many years. The continued use of Iranian-made ballistic missiles by the Houthis to hit targets in Riyadh could well lead to a regional conflict, pitting the Saudis and Emiratis and their backers against the Iranians.

The Bab el-Mandeb could present the biggest flashpoint in the region. The Houthis have used Iranian ASCMs and explosive boats, supplied by the Quds Force, to hit Saudi and Emirati vessels off the coast of Yemen. Those weapons, and well as advanced Iranian naval mines supplied to the Houthis, could be used to disrupt or attempt to control the flow of commerce through the Mandeb Strait, which would lead to a major conflict involving regional and Western powers.

China is also involved in the Great Game. It has recently established its first military base in the greater region, a naval base in Djibouti on the Horn of Africa. The Chinese are putting their military behind their long-term economic and business plans for the region. China's Belt and Road Initiative is a twenty-first-century maritime silk road connecting China through South Asia to the Middle East and Africa.

The region as a whole, from Afghanistan to the Levant, has become a flashpoint and attracted global and regional powers to a new Great Game. A Saudi-Emirati-Israeli-American coalition could emerge as the most powerful alliance in the Middle East in recent years.

The Iranians have fewer cards to play in such a landscape. Ideologically, political Islam is under pressure, in the streets and by moderate governments. Militarily, it faces an array of regional and global competitors in conflicts that the Quds Force alone, relying on irregular proxy war, will not be able to overcome.

THE QUDS FORCE AND ORGANIZATION CHALLENGES

Meanwhile, the Quds Force will continue its operations in the Middle East with the full support of the government in Tehran. The operations in Syria against Assad's opposition were an unqualified success for the Quds Force and its commander, but the Quds Force's continued presence in the country has since been challenged by the Israelis. This Israeli opposition could potentially derail Iranian plans to extend the Shia arc of influence into the Levant and up to the Israeli border. The operations in Iraq against Daesh also marked a great success for the Quds Force and its commander. But maintaining a unity of purpose among the various political factions within the Shia community in the post-Daesh environment has become increasingly challenging, even for a capable leader like Soleimani. The situation in Yemen is far from settled; in fact, the Houthis have all but lost their earlier momentum. It seems that they will soon suffer major losses and be forced to withdraw from the capital toward their traditional stronghold in the northwestern part of the country, with Yemen fracturing into an independent South Yemen and a north comprising autonomous regions ruled by the Saudi-backed government and the Houthis. The Quds Force faces serious challenges in the region's political landscape.

Expeditionary Force

The Quds Force faces growing competition in the region in its efforts to establish a Shia arc of influence across the Middle East. The Saudis were the first actors to inhibit the growth of Iranian influence. With their risky military intervention in Yemen, the Saudis and Emiratis sent a clear signal that Iran would not have free rein in the Arabian Peninsula, as it did in Iraq and the Levant. They closed Yemeni airspace and seaports to the Iranians, stopping daily cargo flights from Tehran to Sanaa that had delivered advanced weapons to the Houthis and deployed Quds Force officers and Shia militias to assist the rebels in their efforts to seize control of Yemen. The Saudi-led resistance poses unique challenges to the Quds Force and its doctrine. The SLA can perform best in countries connected to Iran by land that have friendly governments, such as Iraq and Syria. In these types of places, it can facilitate the flow of Iran's weapons and personnel into battlegrounds. Launching similar operations in places like Yemen, on the other hand, requires the SLA to maneuver in a hostile environment without easy access to its supply base in Iran.

The experience in Yemen has exposed the limitations of reliance on proxy militia forces. Iran's military has rapid reaction capabilities, including armor, artillery, and airborne assets that are trained to deploy within a few hours. Countering the Saudis in Yemen and challenging their closure of airspace and seaports to the Quds Force requires the use of a hybrid model, with regular forces like the IRGC and Artesh rapid reaction forces to facilitate the movement of the SLA into a hostile environment. But launching such an operation would trigger direct military conflict with the Saudi-led coalition forces, making the landscape unfavorable to the Quds Force, which prefers to operate in gray zones, in a state between war and peace, achieving military advantage through aggression and use of force without going to war with a powerful adversary.

But solely relying on proxies to compete militarily against opposing forces without going to war has certain limits. The approach worked against the irregular forces of the Syrian opposition because the Quds Force was operating in a country with a friendly government. But victory under such conditions did not mean that the Quds Force was prepared to face Saudi-Emirati–led regular forces in a hostile environment.

Quds Means Jerusalem

The Quds Force's path forward is one of staunch opposition to Israel, as has always been a core tenet of the Islamic Revolution. Ever since its founding, the Islamic Republic has threatened Israel, repeatedly calling for its destruction. The Quds Force's name itself, *Quds* being the Arabic name for the city of Jerusalem, signifies the Islamic Republic's ultimate mission of "liberating" Jerusalem and dismantling the Jewish state.

Involvement in the Syrian civil war gave the Quds Force a pretext for deploying forces to Syria. Since then, Iran has engaged Israel in a low-intensity conflict on Syrian soil. The most contentious issue is the establishment of permanent basing in country by the Quds Force to house its command-and-control centers, missile and UAV facilities, weapons depots, and foreign Shia militias. Israel considers the bases, the majority of which are located near Israeli front positions on the Golan Heights, a clear danger to its security, and Israel has not hesitated to attack them as they are being constructed. In May 2018, Israel launched simultaneous aerial attacks against sixteen Quds Force installations within Syrian military bases and will undoubtedly launch similar attacks as those instillations are being rebuilt or as new ones are being constructed. The attacks came in direct response to the Quds Force's firing of some twenty Zelzal rockets at the Israeli front positions in the Golan.

There are two other Israeli red lines regarding Quds Force activities in Syria. One is the Quds Force's efforts to upgrade Hezbollah's rockets for better accuracy and longer range, the Precision Project. The IAF has repeatedly attacked Precision Project plants.

The other Israeli red line is delivery of advanced weaponry, especially ballistic missiles, by the Quds Force to Hezbollah using the Damascus airport and storage facilities in the area as the delivery hub. The Israelis have launched numerous aerial attacks against those facilities and the convoys transporting missiles and other weapons to Lebanon. This low-intensity conflict between the two countries is on a trajectory toward full-fledged war.

Chokepoints

The IRGC and the Quds Force can deploy ASCMs and naval mines to exert influence over the strategically important maritime transit routes at the Strait of Hormuz and the Bab el-Mandeb, two major chokepoints through which a significant percentage of global trade, including oil, transits. The Iranian navy has long been active in the Strait of Hormuz. Now the Quds Force is attempting to establish control over the Bab el-Mandeb through the Houthis. It has shipped ASCMs, explosive boats, and naval mines to its proxies in Yemen. The Houthis have fired the weapons against Saudi and Emirati vessels off the Yemeni coast. Their missiles have also hit a Turkish vessel bringing humanitarian aid to Yemen. These missiles and mines could also be used by the Houthis to disrupt the flow of commerce through the Bab el-Mandeb. With this new capability, Iran can now disrupt the flow of commerce through two major chokepoints, threatening international trade and stability regionally and globally as well as challenging the enduring U.S. and Western presence in the region.

The Challenges of Shia Militias

The Quds Force's successful organization of Shia youths across the region currently enables it to maintain a strong presence in key parts of the region. Hezbollah is present in Lebanon and Syria, and along the Israeli borders. Iraqi Shia militia groups cover Iraq. The Houthis are vying for power in Yemen and exerting influence over the Arabian Peninsula and the strategic waterway of Bab el-Mandeb. The Afghan and Pakistani militants have a strong presence in Syria. Shia militant organizations operate in Bahrain and other countries of the region. And Quds Force officers are embedded with major militant organizations, training and controlling their operations.

To maintain discipline and avoid rogue behavior, the Quds Force will need to maintain its militias on active status in the post-conflict period. Different components of the militia force could be redeployed to new theaters; for example, the Afghan Fatemiyoun Brigade could be deployed to Afghanistan after the drawdown or withdrawal of U.S. forces in the country.

But keeping the rest active will be a major challenge for the Quds Force. Unless some of the fighters can be used in development projects in Syria, Iraq, or even inside Iran, there will be a growing danger that these highly trained, ideologically motivated, and armed young fighters could form smaller rogue groups and launch terrorist attacks against their opponents, and against targets in the West.

Intra-Shia Rivalry

The final victory over Daesh by Iraqi and Kurdish security forces with the support of the U.S.-led coalition and the Quds Force–led Shia militias marked the beginning of the unraveling of Shia unity in Iraq. The fight against Daesh united the Shia community around the leadership of General Soleimani and his Quds Force–led Iraqi Shia militias; the Shia praised their heroism in saving Baghdad and the Shia south.

Beginning in August 2015, however, the Sadrists, followers of the Shia cleric Muqtada al-Sadr, staged ongoing street protests targeting corruption and advocating political reform. They even occupied the parliament building and the prime minister's office to air their grievances. The Quds Force had to deploy the PMF to fight these fellow Shias and help quell the protests.

The Sadrists broke from the Quds Force and ran under the banner of Iraqi nationalism during the country's first parliamentary elections in the post-Daesh period. Iraqis first, Shias second, they said. The Shia militias in turn formed a parliamentary alliance, which was inspired by Soleimani and led by Badr chairman Hadi al-Amiri and PMF operations director Mahdi al-Muhandis, Iran's men in Baghdad. Their alliance finished a distant second to Sadr's. The prime minister and his alliance came in third, ahead of former prime minister Maliki and his cohort.

The split of the Shia community into four blocks, with Sadr's alliance coming out on top, was a reality check for Soleimani and the supreme leader. They learned that politics based on sectarianism can unite people against a common enemy from another sect but that unity is often short lived. The factionalism among Shias in Iraq is now as strong as the Shia-Sunni split. And the new landscape ends aspirations of the Quds Force and its commander to act as the ultimate arbiter of Iraqi politics. The future of the Quds Force in Iraq hangs in the balance in this new political landscape with its intra-Shia rivalries.

War Casualties

The many hardships of the Quds force's battle experience eroded the Shia militias' moral legitimacy and command over their fighters.

The Quds Force suffered greatly on the battlefields to which it deployed Shia militias. In the Battle of Aleppo alone, the Quds Force, and elements of the IRGC, Basij, and Artesh, suffered more than 250 killed in action, including at least 10 general officers. The Iranians had not witnessed such casualty rates since the eight-year Iran-Iraq War. Quds Force efforts to employ proxy forces and operate in a gray zone encountered great obstacles in Syria, where the battlefields often required the deployment of regular forces against entrenched and determined opposition forces. Without armor, artillery, and air support—all elements of regular warfare—the Quds Force could not win the war. The Quds Force's lack of extensive experience in hybrid warfare, and command and communication problems with the Iranian regular forces, contributed to the high casualty rates. The much higher casualty rates of the militias, in thousands as opposed to hundreds for the Iranian forces, also raised political and moral issues among Shia militia groups.

Drawn-out wars in Syria, Yemen, and even Iraq have eroded the agility of the militia forces, which are trained for rapid response to conflicts with limited scope and duration. Hybrid warfare that lasts for a long time, as in Syria or Yemen, takes away the quickness of the militia force, their main attribute, and along with a sustained and heavy casualty rate can inflict heavy blows on morale.

Special External Operations

The Quds Force Special External Operations Department, which grew out of the IRGC Intelligence Organization, is responsible for clandestine operations, including assassinations, bombings, kidnappings, and covert influence campaigns.

The Office of the Supreme Leader must authorize these operations, and Quds Force officers and proxy leaders direct them. The operatives, including proxies, receive lethal aid, including rifles, rockets, and explosives, from the Quds Force. The Special External Operations Department's main targets are hostile foreign governments and Iranian dissidents living abroad. Its terrorist activities began soon after the formation of the IRGC in the first days of the revolution and will continue as part of the Quds Force's mission, even in post-conflict Iraq, Syria, and Yemen.

The rapid growth of the SLA has raised concerns that rogue elements within the highly trained and highly armed militia forces could form independent terrorist cells. Even without rogue elements, the sheer number of armed militants—200,000 armed Shia youths, according to an IRGC top commander—poses a formidable threat to Europe and the U.S. homeland. Maintaining control over the SLA following or between participation in regional conflicts is a herculean task that the IRGC and Quds Force clandestine departments are unlikely to succeed at. Those departments do not have enough manpower and command-and-control capability to exert tight control over all the militias, especially in post-conflict periods.

However, on the world stage Iran will be held responsible for Shia militias' actions; the Quds Force will likely come under extreme pressure globally for supporting the militias' acts of terror.

The Quds Force also works closely with Iran's Ministry of Intelligence and Security (MOIS) on external special operations, focusing on confronting threats to the Iranian regime. It particularly focuses on assassinating and killing Iranian oppositionists. In 1992, the Quds Force and MOIS operatives assassinated Iranian Kurdish leaders in a Berlin restaurant. The largest operations against the opposition outside Iranian borders, however, have targeted the Mujahedeen Khalq, or MeK, the largest Iranian opposition group. With the tacit support of Quds Force–backed Iraqi security units, a team of Quds Force officers and MOIS operatives organized Iraqi Shia militia operatives from the KH and the AAH to attack unarmed MeK members at Camp Ashraf in Iraq and Camp Victory in Baghdad. The operation killed dozens of MeK members.

The Quds Force and MOIS also cooperate in setting up front organizations in the West that connect Tehran to Shia communities abroad. The Quds Force actively supports more than twenty such organizations.[1] One of the most significant is Ahlul Bayt World Assembly, a religious-cultural group that promotes the ideology of the Islamic Republic overseas. These structures are intended not only to assist the Quds Force in rallying Shias to support its operations but could be particularly useful if the government in Tehran falls and the Quds Force is forced to survive as the headquarters of Shia militants in the region.

Quds Force Funding

The official budget of the Quds Force is around $3 billion annually. This figure does not include off-budget and extra-budgetary funding, which make up a huge portion of its revenues. The Syrian involvement alone costs upward of $7 billion annually. These figures show that the Quds Force draws a substantial portion of its revenues from sources other than the Iranian government.

The Quds Force receives off-budget revenues from the Office of the Supreme Leader, which in turn receives off-budget revenues from a business network under its control, including major foundations in the country and hundreds of their associated companies. The IRGC also provides the Quds Force with off-budget funding from the revenues of its own business enterprises inside Iran, which include companies in major economic sectors, including oil and gas, construction, telecommunications, transportation, and banking.

The Quds Force's own business network outside Iran provides extra-budgetary revenues; the income from these businesses is estimated to be around $3 billion annually.[2] The Quds Force money machine also includes illicit revenues from drugs. In 2012, the U.S. Treasury designated Quds Force brigadier general Qolamreza Baqeri a specially designated narcotics trafficker due to his involvement in smuggling opium from Afghanistan to Iran; he was the first Iranian general designated under the Kingpin Act. While Baqeri was the commander of Quds Force forces stationed in Zahedan, near the tristate border region linking Iran with Pakistan and Afghanistan, he facilitated the transport of opium from Afghanistan to Europe. His involvement in the drug trade allowed Afghan narcotic traffickers to smuggle opiates into Iran and gave them the protection necessary to carry the drugs through Iran to border areas in the Kurdish region, from which they were transported to Europe. Some of this opium was thought to have been distributed inside Iran as well.

These nongovernmental sources of funding, coupled with the decentralized financial structure of the off-budget and extra-budgetary funding of the Quds Force, reflect its mission to sustain activities even in a post–Islamic Republic era.

The current economic problems facing Iran, including sanctions inhibiting foreign investment in the country, negatively affect not only the government's budget but also the revenues of the foundations controlled by the supreme leader and the IRGC. The government provides the official budget of the Quds Force. The foundations are generally behind Quds Force–controlled economic enterprises outside the border. Drops in government revenues and the foundations' profits have immediate effects on Quds Force funding.

The resulting decrease in revenues could directly affect Quds Force operations in the region, including its ability to pay full salaries to the tens of thousands of Shia militants on its official payroll. Hezbollah alone maintains upward of seven thousand fighters in Syria, and financial aid from Iran amounts to close to $800 million annually. Any cut in this sum could adversely affect Hezbollah's ability to pay the salaries and overall costs of deployment. Likewise, other Shia militia groups would be affected. Iran pays the salaries and cost of operations for all its Afghan and Pakistani militias. It covers the budget of major Iraqi Shia militias and contributes significantly to the Houthi organization.

THE CHANGING ROLE OF IRAN IN THE REGION

The Iranian leadership holds a zero-sum view of the region; it believes that any gains by the U.S., Israel, or the Sunni Arab governments constitute a loss for Iran, and vice versa. Iran has invested tremendous resources and sacrificed many lives on operations in the Middle East in order to diminish American influence, destroy Israel, and topple Sunni governments allied with them. Iran's actions have precipitated the creation of a powerful coalition in the region composed of the U.S., Israel, and the Arab states of the gulf. While

Iran may have been able to maneuver out of this weak position a decade ago, the region's new political landscape is such that Iran now experiences much greater difficulty in rallying the support of Shia populations on which it relies. Political Islam is a spent ideology. By continuing to advance its hard-line ideology, the Islamic Republic may well erode Shias' sense of unity, as occurred in the 2018 Iraqi parliamentary elections. The worsening economic and political situation inside the Islamic Republic is diminishing the appeal of its hard-line anti-West doctrine and thus decreasing the strength of Iran's hand.

The Quds Force will attempt to continue to advance its doctrine by defending the land corridor connecting Iran to Syria, Lebanon, and Israel and bankrolling its diminishing Shia militia force, among other operations in the region. The Quds Force desires to and is capable of maintaining an enduring presence in the region, albeit with a smaller footprint, if the political situation deteriorates further. Despite the changing political landscape, the Quds Force continues to realize Khomeini's assertion that the Islamic Revolution must spread beyond Iran's borders and reshape the entire region. The Quds Force will continue fighting for that ideal even after the Islamic Republic's demise.

Conclusion

I started this book by telling a story about my meeting with Ayatollah Khomeini three months before the triumph of the Islamic Revolution in Iran. The future supreme leader of the Islamic Republic told me that the revolution was not about Iran but the whole region. Four decades later, if the ayatollah could see modern Iran, he would caution us against a literal interpretation of what he had said. Yes, the revolution was about the region, but an isolated Iran could not advance the cause. In fact, Khomeini offered an apology of a sort in the last year of his life. He had to end the war with Iraq before achieving the total victory that he had vowed, saying that the decision was more deadly that drinking a vial of poison.

The Quds Force has advanced the cause up to a point. It has established a land corridor linking Tehran through Iraq to Syria and Lebanon. But if the purpose was to connect a supply base in Iran to forces under its command in Syria, the continued presence of those forces so near the Israeli border is questionable. They have come under direct fire from the Israelis, but Iran cannot count on any regional power to come to its aid to launch a retaliatory response. The Shia militias, the proxies, as valuable as they are to supply manpower, cannot bring Iran out of its isolation. The land corridor becomes a bridge to nowhere if the Iranian-led forces on its other end cannot remain in Syria, which increasingly is the case with the Quds Force and its Shia militias in the country.

The Islamic Republic's isolation looks to be its hubris in its aspirations to drive its interpretation of Islam throughout the region. Pushing the U.S. out of the Middle East, destroying Israel, and defeating the gulf monarchies become empty promises, and may be nothing more than sloganeering. The Iranian government needs to explain to its citizens why it has spent so much in blood and treasure for goals that were not realistic. Ayatollah Khomeini would have probably pulled Iranian forces out of Syria by now, apologizing for not being able to "liberate" Jerusalem.

THE SHIA LIBERATION ARMY

The militants, mostly young, committed, and courageous, proved their worthiness in major battles like Aleppo, but that comes at a high risk. At best, the Quds Force can keep the core activists under tight control in post-conflict Syria, Yemen, and Iraq for use in future regional conflicts. But out of approximately 200,000 armed Shia youths across the region (as claimed by the IRGC), a significant number could go rogue in a post-conflict environment, building their violence-prone and ideologically motivated cells to attack Western targets in order to remain active and truthful to their militant ideology. The Quds Force, as well as the Islamic Republic in general, do not have the financial and manpower resources to keep all the militias they have created under tight control and will be held accountable for their misbehavior.

And what if the government in Tehran falls? I said earlier in the book that the Quds Force is organized to outlast the Islamic Republic. Its funding will be provided, albeit partially, by the business enterprises it has created in the region. It will probably have tens of thousands of the most committed militants still under its command. It will have access to arms caches it has stored across the region. At the same time, the danger of rogue elements establishing their own independent terrorist networks would significantly increase if Tehran fell, which would in turn invite major regional and global powers to unite against the Quds Force and its militias, rogue or genuine.

THREE FRONTS

Since the Arab Spring, Iran has gone to war in Syria, Iraq, and Yemen. The results have been mixed. In Iraq, it succeeded in stopping the advance by Daesh toward the Iranian border, helped save Baghdad and its Shia government, and established a long-term presence within the country's security institutions and other government agencies. But at the same time, the Shia unity under the leadership of the Quds Force in fighting Daesh disappeared in the post-conflict period, with a myriad of Shia groups competing for leadership of the sect and the country, offering different political as well as ideological platforms that were at times contradictory and often inadequate. And then there are significant differences between the Shias and the Sunnis and Kurds. The idea of a unified, Shia-led Iraq, under the influence of Iran, increasingly looks unattainable.

The situations in Syria and Yemen bode even worse for Iran. In Syria, the land bridge to Iran has been established, the Sunni opposition groups are largely defeated, and Assad is saved, at least for the time being. But the continued presence of Iranian-led forces, some fifty thousand or more Shia militants and a few thousand Quds Force officers, is constantly challenged by Israel, with Iran lacking allies and the ability to deploy its military to the country to defend its badly exposed forces. Pulling all its forces out of Syria, as demanded by Israel and pushed by Russia, is not an attractive alternative for Iran. After spending billions of dollars and having hundreds killed among the Quds Force officers, and thousands among the Shia fighters, a large literal and metaphoric cost has been sunk into Syria. However, keeping the forces in country might lead to a war with Israel, which is unattractive as an outcome. The Iranians have cornered themselves in Syria, like walking into an irresistible trap.

Yemen has turned out to be even more problematic. Quds Force General Soleimani saw a golden opportunity in the capture of Sanaa by the Houthis at the doorstep of Tehran's archenemy, Saudi Arabia. What he could not enter into his calculations then was a radical change in the leadership of the House of Saud, and the power and influence of Mohammad bin Salman, who was determined to stop the Iranian project in Yemen. Bin Salman led a coalition of Sunni Arab states to counter Iran in Yemen and lobby the U.S. for a more aggressive posture against Iran throughout the region. Until 2015, the Quds Force operated in the region, including Iraq and Syria, largely unopposed. Now Soleimani was challenged.

The coalition of the Saudis, Emiratis, and their allies closed the Yemeni waterways and airspace to the Iranians, halting the flow of personnel and materiel into Yemen. The Iranian navy and air force were not strong enough to counter the Saudi and Emirati–led blockade. The Quds Force was now forced to seek smuggling routes, which were inefficient and not designed for large-scale transfer of weapons and fighters. The Quds Force showed its operational limits in theaters where access was contested. Its near abroad is, practically speaking, countries with land access and friendly governments.

Yemen presented another important challenge. The use of advanced weapons by its proxies could trigger a direct military conflict with regional and global powers. Before the blockade, Iran had flown and shipped ballistic and cruise missiles and explosive boats to the Houthis. Those ballistic missiles were now being used by the Houthis to hit Saudi targets, including attempted attacks on Riyadh airport and the presidential palace. ASCMs and explosive boats were used to hit Saudi and Emirati vessels off the Yemeni coast and presented a serious threat to Bab el-Mandeb navigation. A direct hit on such a target or closure of the strait could well trigger a war on Iran. Proxy wars have their own limits.

THE LONG WAR

The Quds Force's covert involvement with the Taliban will create additional challenges for U.S. forces in Afghanistan and its current government, as intended. It also presents the risk of further isolating the Islamic Republic in the region. Thousands of Afghan militants present an even higher risk. If the Quds Force deploys them inside the country to counter the U.S. and allied forces, it might face a swift response and the prospect of a direct military conflict with the U.S. Unengaged in post-Syrian conflict, those Afghan militants could potentially be involved in terrorist operations at the behest of the highest bidder. Keeping them engaged in development projects in Syria and inside Iran could be the answer, notwithstanding its high financial costs.

COMPLEX POLITICAL SYSTEM

The complex political system that has developed in Iran in the past four decades, being the headquarters for the government as well as the Shia militant movement, has shown its strengths but also its limits. All presidents of the Islamic Republic have invariably come to an uneasy, even at times hostile, relationship with the supreme leader, even when the president was ideologically aligned to the supreme leader and his circle, like Mahmoud Ahmadinejad. Iran's resources are limited, and the way the resources are allocated between the two systems has continuously been a source of tension between the two parallel, but potentially contradictory, systems. The main political fissure might not be between the hard-liners and moderates but between the revolution and its government; that is, the Office of the Supreme Leader and the institutions under its supervision, including the IRGC and its economic foundations, versus the bureaucracy, which increasingly finds itself without power to drive the country's strategic and economic policies.

FINANCING THE REVOLUTION

The economic foundations under the control of the Office of the Supreme Leader and the IRGC ensure the continued power and influence of the revolutionary wing of the Islamic Republic and the long-term resilience of the Quds Force should the government collapse in Tehran. The involvement of armed forces in business management has had a corrupting effect on the forces. General officers should not have the economic consequences of their military decisions in mind, a dangerous departure from the military doctrine. IRGC personnel, including its leaders, have become agents of financial corruption to an extent unparalleled in the modern history of Iran. The expediency of running its own financial empire could very well be the undoing of the Islamic Revolution in Iran.

MILITARY SUPPORT NETWORK

The Quds Force has developed a policy of irregular proxy warfare for its expeditionary operations. Its parent organization, the IRGC, has controlled the development of weaponry for regular warfare, building potent missile and UAV forces, and engaging in nuclear R&D. Combining both regular and irregular warfare divisions has been problematic. The use of advanced weapons by the proxies is causing friction and raising the risk of wider regional conflicts. The stationing of proxies in Syria likewise is causing friction and risks a direct military conflict with Israel. These issues, probably unplanned and unexpected, call for sense-making and soul-searching for Iran's military strategists. The hybrid offensive strategy pursued by the Quds Force, mixing irregular land forces augmented with regular military elements like ballistic missile units, as effective as it was in the war against the Syrian opposition, creates serious challenges when applied to an anti-Israel policy, exposing tens of thousands of militants who now need to be based permanently in Syria.

THE WAY AHEAD

The Quds Force and its network of Shia militias and associates will remain a potent force in the Middle East and a driver of conflict for decades to come. But in its quest for primacy in the region, the Quds Force has hit several roadblocks. The most challenging is the use of hybrid war tactics against a powerful military, which runs contrary to the Quds Force proxy war doctrine itself and risks a war that it cannot win. Logistics limitations in hostile environments, like Yemen, present another challenge. The most urgent problem the Quds Force faces, however, is the management of tens of thousands of Shia militants in a post-conflict environment. If the Quds Force cannot create effective non-combatant roles for the militants, having such a large force under its command will become a serious liability, with the highly trained and armed militants posing a terrorist threat to many countries that could jeopardize Iran's standing and subject it to direct military conflict.

The Quds Force will regard Hezbollah's military wing as its main militia force in the Levant. It is likely that it will trim its militia forces to around twenty thousand of the most qualified non-Hezbollah militants, to be based in Iran and Iraq. This force could still be a major player in the region for decades to come.

Notes

INTRODUCTION

1. Mohsen Sazegara, interview with the author, Washington, DC, 29 August 2017. Mr. Sazegara returned to Iran from Neauphle-le-Château on Khomeini's plane, as his press officer, and soon became a founding member of the Revolutionary Guards, the IRGC. He served in the original five-member IRGC Command Council, along with Danesh-Monfared, Qarazi, Rafiq-doost, and Afrooz. I conducted six interviews with Mr. Sazegara during the summer and fall of 2017, covering the early days of the formation of the IRGC and the IRGC's extraterritorial branch, which would later become the Quds Force. I am grateful for his descriptions of the early days of the IRGC with details that were simply priceless.

1. IRAN AT WAR

1. General Ahmad Qolampour, "Conversation with General Ahmad Qolampour," Fars News Agency, 5 October 2016.

2. The estimate of 200,000 armed Shia militia men organized by Iran came in a 2016 speech by the commander of the IRGC, General Mohammad Ali "Aziz" Jafari. See Fars News Agency, "The Young Religious Generation Is One of the Miracles of the Islamic Revolution," 12 January 2016 (in Farsi).

3. IRGC general Ali Falaki, who served as a Quds Force adviser in Syria, told *Mashreq News* that a "Shia Liberation Army" had been formed under the command of Quds Force commander Soleimani. See *Orient News*, "Iranian General: Suleimani Is Forming 'Shia Liberation Army,'" 19 August 2016.

4. Carlotta Gall and Ruhullah Khapalwak, "Taliban Leader Feared Pakistan before He Was Killed," *New York Times*, 9 August 2017.

5. Mujib Mashal and Fatima Faizi, "Iran Sent Them to Syria, Now Afghan Fighters Are a Worry at Home," *New York Times*, 11 November 2017.

6. Noga Tarnopolsky, "In Most Serious Military Clash in Decades, Israel Hits Iranian Targets in Syria," *Los Angeles Times*, 10 May 2018.

2. THE SHIA LIBERATION ARMY

1. IRGC General Ali Falaki, who served as a Quds Force advisor in Syria, told *Mashreq News* that a "Shia Liberation Army" had been formed under the command of Quds Force Commander Soleimani. See *Orient News*, "Iranian General: Suleimani Is Forming 'Shia Liberation Army,'" 19 August 2016.

2. Fars News Agency, "The Young Religious Generation Is One of the Miracles of the Islamic Revolution," 12 January 2016 (in Farsi).

3. GlobalSecurity.org, "Anti-Soviet Mujahedeen," 18 August 2012.

4. Ibid.

5. Alfoneh Ali, "Tehran's Shia Foreign Legion," Carnegie Endowment for International Peace, 31 January 2018.

6. For video footage of Hadi al-Amiri during the Iran-Iraq war, see www.youtube.com/watch?v=W251ltDpL5E, 21 September 2015.

7. Joseph Felter and Brian Fishman, "Iranian Strategy in Iraq: Politics and 'Other Means,'" Combating Terrorism Center at West Point, Occasional Paper Series, 13 October 2008.

8. Khamenei.ir, Twitter, 9 March 2017.

9. Matthew Levitt, *Hezbollah: The Global Footprint of Lebanon's Party of God* (Washington, DC: Georgetown University Press).

10. Majid Rafizadeh, "In First, Hezbollah Confirms All Financial Support Comes From Iran." *Al Arabiya English*, 25 June 2016.

11. U.S. Department of State, "Country Report on Terrorism 2016," July 2017.

12. Ibid.

13. Gili Cohen, "Israeli Army Intelligence Chief: Hezbollah Is Setting Up a Weapons Industry in Lebanon with Iranian Know-How," *Haaretz*, 23 June 2017.

14. Musing on Iraq (blog), "Badr Organization: A View into Iraq's Violent Past and Present," 30 January 2015.

15. David Andrew Weinberg, "Bahrain and Iran Expel Each Other's Diplomat," Foundation for Defense of Democracy, 5 October 2015.

16. Michael Eisenstadt and Michael Knights, "Mini-Hizballahs, Revolutionary Guard Knock-Offs, and the Future of Iran's Proxies in Iraq," War on the Rocks, 9 May 2017.

17. Noor Zahid and Mehdi Jedinia, "Iran Sending Afghan Refugees to Fight in Syria," Voice of America, 29 January 2016. Different reports put the number of Afghan militias at 5,000 to 12,000. The figure 10,000 is my estimate based on interviews with experts in the field.

18. Al Jazeera, "Saudi Forces Intercept Riyadh-Bound Houthi Missile," 19 December 2017.

19. Matthew Levitt, "Iran and Bahrain: Crying Wolf, or Wolf at the Door?" PolicyWatch 2255, Washington Institute for Near East Policy, 16 May 2014.

20. Fars News Agency, "Gen. Soleimani's Rare Threat against al-Khalifa Regime," 20 June 2016 (in Farsi).

21. Louis J. Freeh, "Khobar Towers," *Wall Street Journal*, 23 June 2006.

22. David D. Kirkpatrick, "Saudi Arabia Said to Arrest Suspect in 1996 Khobar Towers Bombing," *New York* Times, 6 August 2015.

23. BBC News, "Sheikh Nimr al-Nimr: Saudi Arabia Executes Top Shia Cleric," 2 January 2016.

24. Associated Press, "Azerbaijan: 22 Held as Iranian Agents in a Terror Plot, Officials Say," *New York Times*, 15 March 2012.

25. Liz Fuller, "Azerbaijani Political Movement Said to Have Been Suborned by Iran," Radio Free Europe/Radio Liberty, 31 January 2017.

26. Israel Intelligence Heritage and Commemoration Center, "Iranian Support of Hamas," 12 January 2008.

27. Anna Ahronheim, "Hamas's New Leader Radically Shifts Military Strategy," *Jerusalem Post*, 27 September 2017.

28. For a comprehensive identification of Jihadist groups, including Iraqi Shia militias, see Middle East Forum, "Jihad Identifiers Database," 17 June 2018, http://jihadintel.meforum.org/.

3. THE YEARS OF REVOLUTION AND WAR

1. The term used by Khomeini to describe the new order was *hokumat-e Islami* [Islamic state]. The name *Islamic Republic* was later chosen for the regime to distinguish it from the Islamic caliphates and monarchies.

2. Afshon Ostovar, *Vanguard of the Imam* (New York: Oxford University Press, 2016), 43.

3. Mohammad Ataie, "Revolutionary Iran's 1979 Endeavor in Lebanon," *Middle East Policy* 20, no. 2 (2013): 137–57.

4. National Foreign Assessment Center, "Iran: Exporting the Revolution," 10 March 1980, 6.

5. Mohsen Milani, "Why Tehran Won't Abandon Assad(ism)," *Washington Quarterly* 36, no. 4 (Fall 2013): 80.

6. Mohammad Ghoshani, "Unity of Iranian and Lebanese Shias," *Sharq*, 27 July 2006, quoted in Milani, "Why Tehran Won't Abandon Assad(ism)."

7. See Stanford University, "Badr Organization of Reconstruction and Development," Mapping Militant Organizations, http://web.stanford.edu/group/mappingmilitants/cgi-bin/groups/view/435.

8. Kenneth Katzman, "Iraq: Post-Saddam," in Steven J. Costel, ed., *Surging out of Iraq?* (New York: Nova Science, 2008), 86.

9. Ibid.

10. Stanford University, "Badr Organization."

11. Robert Pear, "Khomeini Accepts 'Poison' of Ending the War with Iraq; U.N. Sending Mission," *New York Times*, 21 July 1988, A8.

12. National Foreign Assessment Center, "The Amal Movement in Lebanon," 20 November 1981, 6.

13. Jalaleddin Farsi was the first candidate of the ruling Islamic Republic Party during the first presidential election in Iran. His candidacy was rejected by Ayatollah Khomeini because of his Afghan nationality. In 1992, Farsi was convicted of murder but was not sentenced to prison.

14. Abbas W. Samii, "A Stable Structure in Shifting Sands: Assessing the Hizbullah-Iran-Syria Relations," *Middle East Journal* (Winter 2008): 35.

15. Author's Skype interview with a former Lebanese militant.

16. C. Jonattan, "PLO Chief, in Iran, Hails Shah's Fall," *Washington Post*, 19 February 1979.

17. Author's Skype interview with a former Lebanese militant.

18. *Near East South Asia Report*, "Foreign Broadcast Information Service Hizbullah Issues 'Open Letter' on Goals, Principles," JRPS-NEA-85-056, 19 April 1985.

19. In 2003, the U.S. District Court in Washington, DC, named *Islamic jihad* as the name used by Hezbollah for some of its operations in Lebanon, the Middle East, and Europe. *Anne Dammarell et al. v. Islamic Republic of Iran*.

20. Con Coughlin, *Hostage* (New York: Time Warner, 1993), 3.

21. Ted Gup, *The Book of Honor* (New York: Doubleday, 2000), 28.

22. Matthew Levitt, Why the CIA Killed Imad Mughniyeh," *Politico*, www.politico.com/magazine/story/2015/02/mughniyeh-assassination-cia-115049, 9 February 2015.

23. In 2003, the U.S. District Court in Washington, DC, determined that the bombing was carried out by Hezbollah with approval of and financing by senior Iranian officials. The decision was upheld by the U.S. Supreme Court in 2016, www.reuters.com/article/us-usa-court-iran-idUSKCN0XH1R.

24. U.S. Secretary of Defense Caspar Weinberger said during a 2001 *Frontline* interview that the U.S. suspected Hezbollah, supported by Iran, to be behind the attacks, www.pbs.org/wgbh/pages/frontline/shows/target/etc/cron.html.

25. James Glanz and Marc Santora, "Iraqi Lawmaker Was Convicted in 1983 Bombings in Kuwait That Killed 5," *New York Times*, 7 February 2007. Also see Michael Weiss and Michael Pregent, "The U.S. Is Providing Air Cover for Ethnic Cleansing in Iraq," *Foreign Policy*, March 2015.

26. C. Dickey, "Kuwaiti Ruler Eludes Attack by Car-Bomber," *Washington Post*, 26 May 1985.

27. Hazarajat is a central Afghan region inhabited by the Hazara people. The region encompasses Bamiyan, Maidan, Ghani, and other nearby provinces.

28. See Stanford University, "Badr Organization."

29. Patrick Cockburn, "Iran 'Supplying Arms to Fuel Kurdish Civil War,'" *Independent*, 21 August 1996.

30. Gordon Bardos, "Iran in the Balkans: A History and a Forecast," *World Affairs* (January/February 2013).

31. Thomas Juneau, "Iran's Policy Towards the Houthis: A Limited Return on a Modest Investment," *International Affairs* 92, no. 3 (2016): 647–63.

32. Gaith Abdul-Ahad, "Diary in Sanaa," *London Review of Books* 37, no. 10 (21 May 2015): 42–43.

33. International Committee in Search of Justice, "Destructive Role of Iran's Islamic Revolutionary Guard Corps (IRGC) in the Middle East," March 2017.

34. *Times of Israel*, "Warrant for AMIA Attack Suspect Not Lifted with Nuke Deal," 3 August 2015.

35. C. Leonning, "Iran Held Liable in Khobar Attack," *Washington Post*, 23 December 2006.

36. D. Kirkpatrick, "Saudi Arabia Said to Arrest Suspect in 1996 Khobar Towers Bombing," *New York Times*, 26 August 2015.

37. Other people assassinated during this period include Abdullah Ghaderi Azar, Ghassemlou's aide, in Vienna in July 1989; Karim Mohammadzadeh, a Kurdish Iranian dissident, in Sweden in April 1990; Efat Ghazi, member of the Democratic Party of Iranian Kurdistan, in Sweden in September 1990; Fattah Abdoli and Homayoun Ardalan of the Democratic Party of Iranian Kurdistan, in the Mykonos Restaurant assassinations in Berlin in September 1992; and Kamran Hedayati, an Iranian Kurdish dissident, in Sweden in July 1996. Also assassinated in this period was Hitoshi Igarashi, Japanese translator of Salman Rushdie's *The Satanic Verses*, in Japan—however, a link to the Quds Force has not been established. It is believed Igarashi's assassination was linked to Intelligence Ministry agents.

38. Fars News Agency, excerpt from a speech delivered on 12 January 2016 by IRGC Commander Major General Mohammad Ali Jafari.

4. GATEWAYS TO AFGHANISTAN AND IRAQ

1. Matthew J. Morgan, ed., *The Impact of 9/11 on Politics and War: The Day That Changed Everything?* (New York: Palgrave Macmillan, 2009), 222.

2. CBC News, "Bin Laden Claims Responsibility for 9/11," 30 October 2004, www.cbc.ca/news/world/bin-laden-claims-responsibility-for-9-11-1.513654.

3. Gary C. Schroen, *First In: An Insider's Account of How the CIA Spearheaded the War on Terror in Afghanistan* (New York: Ballantine Books, 2005).

4. Michael Eisenstadt and Michael Knights, "Iran's Influence in Iraq: Countering Tehran's Whole-of-Government Approach," Washington Institute for Near East Policy, April 2011, 5.

5. Suzanne George, "Breaking Badr," *Foreign Policy*, 14 November 2014.

6. Marcus Weisgerber, "How Many US Troops Were Killed by Iranian IEDs in Iraq?" *Defense One*, 8 September 2015.

7. Eisenstadt and Knights, "Iran's Influence," 7.

8. Stanford University, "Mahdi Army," Mapping Militant Organizations, http://web.stanford.edu/group/mappingmilitants/cgi-bin/groups/view/57.

9. Patrick Cockburn, *Muqtada* (New York: Scribner, 2008).

10. Nicholas Krohley, "Moqtada al-Sadr's Difficult Relationship with Iran," Hurst, 7 August 2014, www.hurstpublishers.com/moqtada-al-sadrs-difficult-relationship-with-iran/.

11. For a look at AAH development, see Stanford University, "Asa'ib Ahl Al-Haq," Mapping Militant Organizations, http://web.stanford.edu/group/mappingmilitants/cgi-bin/groups/view/143.

12. For a narrative on Kata'ib Hezbollah founding and its organization, see Matthew Levitt and Phillip Smyth, "Kata'ib al-Imam Ali: Portrait of an Iraqi Shiite Militant Group Fighting ISIS," Washington Institute for Near East Policy, 5 January 2015; and Stanford University, "Kata'ib Hezbollah," Mapping Militant Organizations, http://web.stanford.edu/group/mapping militants/cgi-bin/groups/view/361?highlight=kataib+hezbollah.

13. Alaa Bayoumi and Leah Harding, "Mapping Iraq's Fighting Groups," Al Jazeera, 27 June 2014.

14. Michael Eisenstadt and Michael Knights, "Mini-Hizbollah, Revolutionary Guard Knock-Offs, and the Future of Iran's Military Proxies in Iraq," *War on the Rocks*, 9 May 2007.

15. Dexter Filkins, "The Shadow Commander," *New Yorker*, 30 September 2013.

16. William Branigin, "Iran's Quds Force Was Blamed for Attacks on U.S. Troops in Iraq," *Washington Post*, 11 October 2011.

17. Sean D. Naylor, "Inside U.S. Commandos' Shadow War against Iran," *Daily Beast*, 1 September 2015.

18. BBC, "US Links Iran to Attack in Iraq," 2 July 2007.

19. BBC, "UK Hostage Peter Moore Released Alive in Iraq," 30 December 2009.

20. Naylor, "Inside U.S. Commandos' Shadow War."

21. Stanford University, "Kata'ib Hezbollah."

22. Filkins, "The Shadow Commander."

23. Jim Loney, "Iran-Backed Force Threatens U.S. Iraq Bases—General," Reuters, 13 July 2010.

24. Tim Craig and Ed O'Keefe, "U.S. Military Says Iran Behind Rising Deaths," *Washington Post*, 30 June 2011.

25. Ibid.

26. Ibid.

27. Ali Nouri Zadeh, "Iranian Officers: Hezbollah Has Commando Naval Unit," *Asharq Al-Awsad*, 29 July 2006.

28. For a discussion of the Quds Force's delivery of weaponry and training to Hezbollah during the period, see Kimberly Kagan, Frederick Kagan, and Danielle Pletka, "Iranian Influence in the Levant, Iraq, and Afghanistan," American Enterprise Institute, 15 February 2008.

29. Jack Khoury, "Report: Nasrallah Admits Iran Supplies Hezbollah with Arms," *Haaretz*, 4 February 2007.

30. *Al-Monitor*, "Hezbollah Brushes Off US Sanctions, Says Money Comes via Iran," www.al-monitor.com/pulse/afp/2016/06/lebanon-hezbollah-banks.html.

5. UPRISINGS, CIVIL WARS, AND INSURGENCIES

1. Morocco, Iraq, Algeria, Lebanon, Jordan, Lebanon, Kuwait, Oman, and Sudan witnessed sustained street demonstrations demanding better living conditions or targeting official corruption and autocratic rule.

2. From an account of the encounter told by Iranian MP Esmail Kowsari, a former IRGC general officer, who acted as an aide to Hezbollah's Nasrallah during his stay in Iran. Kowsari made the remarks in an interview with Iran's Fars News Agency in November 2013, nearly two years after the event. See Ali Hashem, "In Syria, Iran Sees Necessary War," *Al-Monitor*, 16 March 2017.

3. See Ruth Sherlock, "Iran Boosts Support to Syria," *Telegraph*, 21 February 2014.

4. From an interview with a former senior Iranian official.

5. Henry A. Ensher, "Iran-Syria Relations and the Arab Spring," *Critical Threats*, 25 May 2011.

6. Geneive Abdo, "How Iran Keeps Assad in Power in Syria," *Foreign Affairs*, 25 August 2011.

7. Joby Warrick and Liz Sly, "U.S. Officials: Iran Is Stepping Up Lethal Aid to Syria," *Washington Post*, 3 March 2012.

8. Ibid.

9. Con Coughlin, "Iran Sends Elite Troops to Aid Bashar al-Assad Regime in Syria," *Telegraph*, 6 September 2012.

10. Nick Paton Walsh, "Iranian Drones Guiding Syrian Attacks, Rebels Say," CNN, 31 October 2012.

11. People's Mojahedin Organization of Iran, "Iranians Captured in Syria Are IRGC Officers—Iranian Opposition," 14 August 2012.

12. Ian Black and Saeed Kamali Dehghan," Syria and Iran Swap Prisoners after Months of Complex International Talks," *Guardian*, 9 January 2013.

13. Columb Strack, "Syrian Government No Longer Controls 83% of the Country," Jane's 360, 24 August 2015, www.janes.com/article/53771/syrian-government-no-longer-controls-83-of-the-country.

14. Al Jazeera, "Syria's Assad Admits Army Struggling for Manpower," 26 July 2015.

15. From an interview with a former senior Iranian official.

16. Reuters, "Iran Quds Chief Visited Russia Despite U.N. Travel Ban: Iran Official," 7 August 2015.

17. Reuters, "Insight—How Iranian General Plotted Syrian Assault in Moscow," 6 October 2015.

18. Ian Black and Saeed Kamali Dehghan, "Iran Ramps up Troop Deployment in Syria in Run-Up to 'Anti-Rebel Offensive,'" *Guardian*, 14 October 2015.

19. Mona Alami, "Meet One of Hezbollah's Teen Fighters," *Al-Monitor*, 28 January 2016.

20. Noor Zahid and Mehdi Jedinia, "Iran Sending Afghan Refugees to Fight in Syria," Voice of America, 29 January 2016.

21. Nader Uskowi, "Iran Deploys Ground Troops to Syria—Report," www.uskowioniran.com, 15 October 2015.

22. Abbas Qaidaari, "Is Iran Worried About IS on Its Border?" *Al-Monitor*, 5 June 2015.

23. Ibid.

24. Ibid.

25. For reports and discussion of Shia militia sectarian behavior, see Fazel Hawramy and Luke Harding, "Shia Militia Fightback against Isis Sees Tit-for-Tat Sectarian Massacres of Sunnis," *Guardian*, 12 November 2014. Also see Juan Cole, "Iraq: Is the Sunni-Shiite Slaughter at Jurf al-Sakhr Really a US Victory?" Informed Comment, 28 October 2014, www.juancole.com/2014/10/slaughter-really-victory.html.

26. From an interview with a former senior Iranian official.

27. Thomas Juneau, "Iran's Policy towards the Houthis: A Limited Return on a Modest Investment," *International Affairs* 92, no. 3 (2016): 647–63.

28. Yossi Mansharof and E. Kharrazi, "Iran's Support for the Houthi Rebellion in Yemen: 'Without Iran There Would Be No War in Syria and Ansar Allah Would Have Never Emerged,'" MEMRI, 20 April 2015, www.memri.org/reports/irans-support-houthi-rebellion-yemen-without-iran-there-would-be-no-war-syria-and-ansar.

29. Testimony by General Joseph Votel of the U.S. Central Command to the House Committee of Armed Services, 29 March 2017.

30. Alex Lockie, "Photos: Former US Navy Ship Extensively Damaged after Missile Strike by Iranian-Backed Rebels Near Yemen," *Business Insider*, 5 October 2016.

6. LAND CORRIDOR TO SYRIA

1. Columb Strack, "Syrian Government No Longer Controls 83% of the Country," Jane's 360, 24 August 2015, www.janes.com/article/53771/syrian-government-no-longer-controls-83-of-the-country.

2. Reuters, "Iran Quds Chief Visited Russia Despite U.N. Travel Ban: Iran Official," 7 August 2015.

3. Martin Kramer, "Syria's Alawis and Shi'ism," in *Shi'ism, Resistance, and Revolution*, ed. Martin Kramer (Boulder, CO: Westview Press, 1987), 54.

4. Nader Uskowi, "Iran Deploys Ground Troops to Syria—Report," www.uskowioniran.com, 15 October 2015.

5. Mona Alami, "Meet One of Hezbollah's Teen Fighters," *Al-Monitor*, 28 January 2016.

6. Ian Black and Saeed Kamali Dehghan, "Iran Ramps up Troop Deployment in Syria in Run-Up to 'Anti-Rebel Offensive,'" *Guardian*, 14 October 2015.

7. Noor Zahid and Mehdi Jedinia, "Iran Sending Afghan Refugees to Fight in Syria," Voice of America, 29 January 2016. Different reports put the number of Afghan militia members at 5,000–12,000. The figure 10,000 is my estimate based on interviews with experts in the field.

8. Human Rights Watch, "Iran Sending Thousands of Afghans to Fight in Syria," 29 January 2016.

9. Aron Lund, "Stand Together or Fall Apart: The Russian-Iranian Alliance in Syria," Carnegie Middle East Center, 31 May 2016.

10. Mays Al-Shobassi, "Timeline: Syria's 13 'People Evacuation' Deals," Al-Jazeera, 16 May 2017.

11. Tasnim News Agency, "Evacuation of Syria's Kafraya, Foua Underway," 20 December 2016.

12. Lund, "Stand Together or Fall Apart."

13. Notwithstanding Russia's claim that its airstrikes targeted the Islamic State, the strikes were mainly targeting the Syrian opposition. See Bill Chappell, "Syrian Opposition Says Russian Airstrikes Aren't Targeting ISIS," NPR, 1 October 2015.

14. Nader Uskowi, "Russian-Supported Syrian Coalition Advances South of Aleppo," www.uskowioniran.com, 17 October 2015.

15. Al Jazeera, "Syria War: Rebels Capture Strategic Aleppo Village," 6 May 2016.

16. Amir Toumaj, "IRGC, Allies Sustained Significant Losses in Battle for Khan Touman," FDD's Long War Journal, 11 May 2016.

17. Tasnim News Agency, "Funeral Held for 4 Iranian Commandos Killed in Syria," 16 April 2016.

18. Nader Uskowi, "Aleppo Offensive: IRGC Servicemen Killed in Action," www.uskowioniran.com, 27 October 2015.

19. Saeed Kamali Dehghan, "Senior Iranian Commander Killed in Syria," *Guardian*, 9 October 2015.

20. Paul Bucala and Frederick W. Kagan, "Iran's Evolving Way of War: How the IRGC Fights in Syria," Critical Threats, March 2016. The IRGC general officers killed during that battle were Hossein Rezaie, Sattar Varang, Mohsen Ghajarian, Ahmad Majidi, and Ali Ghorbani.

21. Nader Uskowi, "IRGC General, Former Saberin Commander, Killed in Syria," www.uskowioniran.com, 13 October 2015.

22. Colonel Hamid Mokhtarband, former commander of the 1st Hazrat Hojjat Brigade, was killed on 12 October 2015. The brigade is part of the 7th Vali Asr Division based in Khuzestan.

23. The Isfahan-based 8th Najaf Ashraf Division had nine casualties in the first month of the operations. On 8 November 2015, IRGC Major Musa Jamshidian was killed near Aleppo. See Nader Uskowi, "IRGC, Basij Officer Killed in Syria," www.uskowioniran.com, 8 November 2015.

24. IRGC Brigadier General Majid Sanei and Second Lieutenant Moslem Nasr of the IRGC's elite 33rd Mahdi Airborne Brigade were killed near Aleppo on 27 October. Sanei became the third general officer killed in action during the Aleppo offensive. See Nader Uskowi, "IRGC General and Airborne LT Killed in Aleppo," www.uskowioniran.com, 28 October 2015.

25. IRGC Captain Sajjad Hosseini of the 15th Khordad Artillery Group was killed near Aleppo in late October.

26. Basij's Mohsen Fanusi, an engineer with the IRGC's 43rd Imam Ali Engineering Group, was killed near Aleppo on 3 November. See Nader Uskowi, www.uskowioniran.com, 4 November 2015.

27. Nine Basij members were reported killed in the first three weeks of the Aleppo offensive. See Nader Uskowi, www.uskowioniran.com, 26 October 2015.

28. Raz Zimmt, "Spotlight on Iran," Meir Amit Intelligence and Terrorism Information Center, Tel Aviv, 26 November 2017.

29. *Rojava* is an abbreviation of the Kurdish words "Rojava-ye Kurdistan-e," meaning "Western Kurdistan," with northern Kurdistan in Turkey, southern in Iraq, and eastern in Iran.

7. THE IRAQI CAMPAIGN

1. From testimony of the commander of the Iranian Army ground forces, Brigadier General Ahmad-Reza Pourdastan, to the Iranian Majlis on 24 May 2015. Quoted in Abbas Qaidaari, "Is Iran Worried About IS on Its Border?" *Al-Monitor*, 5 June 2015.

2. Ibid.

3. Ibid. General Pourdastan's testimony was the first public account of the role of Artesh in penetrating Iraqi territory to stop the ISIS advance toward Iran in the early days of the war.

4. Shahryar Hedayati SHBA, "Topic: Iranian Phantom Jet Strikes the Islamic State in Iraq—IHS Jane's 360," International Military Forum, 2 December 2014.

5. Al Jazeera, "Iran 'Sent Soldiers to Fight in Iraq,'" 23 August 2014.

6. Shahryar Hedayati SHBA, "Topic: Iranian Phantom Jet Strikes."

7. Michael Knights and Alexander Mello, "Losing Mosul, Regenerating in Diyala: How the Islamic State Could Exploit Iraq's Sectarian Tinderbox," *CTC Sentinel* 9, no. 10 (October 2016).

8. Saif Hameed, "Iraqi Forces Say Retake Two Towns from Islamic State," Reuters, 23 November 2014, www.reuters.com/article/us-mideast-crisis-iraq-towns/iraqi-forces-say-retake-two-towns-from-islamic-state-idUSKCN0J70AX20141123.

9. Stanford University, "Kata'ib Hezbollah," Mapping Militant Organizations, http://web.stanford.edu/group/mappingmilitants/cgi-bin/groups/view/361?highlight=kataib+hezbollah. See also Matthew Levitt and Phillip Smyth, "Kata'ib al-Imam Ali: Portrait of an Iraqi Shiite Militant Group Fighting ISIS," Washington Institute for Near East Policy, 5 January 2015; and Counter Extremism Project, "Kata'ib Hezbollah," www.counterextremism.com/threat/kata%E2%80%99ib-hezbollah.

10. Lucas Tomlinson, "US Officials: Up to 100,000 Iran-Backed Fighters Now in Iraq," Fox News, 16 August 2016.

11. David Daoud, "PMF Deputy Commander Muhandis Details Hezbollah Ops in Iraq," Long War Journal, 9 January 2017.

12. Ahmad Majidyar, "Soleimani Details Iran's Military Role in Iraq, Hails Iraqi Paramilitary Forces and Hezbollah," Middle East Institute, 11 July 2011, www.mei.edu/content/io/soleimani-details-iran-s-military-role-iraq-hails-iraqi-paramilitary-forces-and-hezbollah.

13. See Counter Extremism Project, "Qais al-Khazali," www.counterextremism.com/extremists/qais-al-khazali.

14. See Stanford University, "Asa'ib Ahl Al-Haq," Mapping Militant Organizations, http://web.stanford.edu/group/mappingmilitants/cgi-bin/groups/view/143.

15. See Terrorism Research and Analysis Consortium, "Kata'ib al-Imam Ali."

16. See Stanford University, "Kata'ib Sayyid al-Shuhada," Mapping Militant Organizations, 24 March 2017, http://web.stanford.edu/group/mappingmilitants/cgi-bin/groups/view/629.

17. Columb Strack, "Syrian Government No Longer Controls 83% of the Country," Jane's 360, 24 August 2015, www.janes.com/article/53771/syrian-government-no-longer-controls-83-of-the-country.

18. Lisa Bassam and Tom Perry, "How Iranian General Plotted Out Syria Assault in Moscow," Reuters, 6 October 2015.

19. Sinan Salaheddin, "Iraqi Shiite Militia Grow Brutal in Anti-ISIS Fight," *Daily Star*. See also Juan Cole, "Iraq: Is the Sunni-Shiite Slaughter at Jurf al-Sakhr Really a US Victory?" Informed Comment, 28 October 2014, www.juancole.com/2014/10/slaughter-really-victory .html.

20. Loveday Morris, "Lowering of Kurdish Flag, Raising of Iraqi at Kirkuk's Provincial Council Building: CTS's Asadi, Badr's Amiri and PMU's Mohandes Look On," Twitter, 16 October 2017.

21. Ali Vaez, "Image," Twitter, 21 November 2017.

8. SANAA CALLING

1. Soleimani used the phrase "golden opportunity" (*moqe'iyat-e tala'ee* in Farsi) when the news reached him, according to former Iranian senior officials.

2. Nasim News Agency, "Alireza Zakani: Paris Conference Can Only Succeed If Iran Participates in It," 14 September 2014.

3. Yossi Mansharof and E. Kharrazi, "Iran's Support for the Houthi Rebellion in Yemen," Middle East Media Research Institute, Inquiry & Analysis Series 1155, 20 April 2015.

4. Thomas Juneau, "Iran's Policy Towards the Houthis in Yemen: A Limited Return on a Modest Investment," *International Affairs* 92, no. 3 (2016): 647–63.

5. International Committee in Search of Justice / European Iraqi Freedom Association, "Destructive Role of Iran's Islamic Revolutionary Guard Corps (IRGC) in the Middle East," 6 March 2017.

6. Ghaith Abdul-Ahad, "Diary in Sanaa," *London Review of Books* 37, no. 10 (May 2015): 42–43.

7. Mahjoob Zweiri, "Iran and Political Dynamism in the Arab World: The Case of Yemen," *Digest of Middle East Studies* 25, no. 1 (18 February 2016): 4–24.

8. Juneau, "Iran's Policy Towards the Houthis."

9. Zweiri, "Iran and Political Dynamism."

10. Ibid.

11. Carol Landry, "Iran Arming Yemen's Houthi Rebels since 2009: UN Report," *Middle East Eye*, 1 May 2015.

12. Eric Schmitt and Robert F. Worth, "With Arms for Yemen Rebels, Iran Seeks Wider Middle East Role," *New York Times*, 15 March 2012.

13. Alex Lockie, "Photos: Former US Navy Ship Extensively Damaged after Missile Strike by Iranian-Backed Rebels near Yemen," *Business Insider*, 5 October 2015.

14. Phil Stewart, "U.S. Military Strikes Yemen after Missile Attacks on U.S. Navy Ship," Reuters, 12 October 2016.

15. From the testimony of General Joseph Votel, commander of U.S. forces in the Middle East, to the House Armed Services Committee, 29 March 2017.

16. Mohammad Ghobari, "Yemen's Houthis Respond to Air Strike with Missile Attack," Reuters, 10 October 2016.

17. IHS Markit, "Yemeni Rebels Enhance Ballistic Missile Campaign," IHS Jane's Intelligence Review, www.janes.com/images/assets/330/72330/Yemeni_rebels_enhance_ballistic_ missile_campaign.pdf.

18. Ibid.

19. David D. Kirkpatrick, "Saudi Arabia Charges Iran with 'Act of War,' Raising Threat of Military Clash," *New York Times*, 6 November 2017.

20. *Guardian*, "Saudi Arabia Shoots Down Houthi Missile Aimed at Riyadh Palace," 19 December 2017.

21. Christopher P. Cavas, "New Houthi Weapon Emerges: A Drone Boat," *Defense News*, 19 February 2017.

22. NBC, "Houthi Rebels Use Another Unmanned Boat Bomb Against the Saudis," 26 April 2017.

23. Phil Stewart, "In First, U.S. Presents Its Evidence of Iran Weaponry from Yemen," Reuters, 14 December 2017.

24. Taimur Khan, "Iran Smuggling 'Kamikaze' Drones to Yemen's Houthi Rebels," *National*, 22 March 2017.

25. Nader Uskowi, "Convoy of Iranian Ships Parked in Arabian Sea," www.uskowioniran.com, 22 April 2015.

26. CBS, "U.S. Aircraft Carrier Sent to Yemen in Response to Iran," 20 April 2015.

27. Nader Uskowi, "Iranian Convoy Heading Home—Update," www.uskowioniran.com, 23 April 2015.

28. Mohammed Ghobari and Mohammed Mukhashaf, "Saudi-Led Planes Bomb Sanaa Airport to Stop Iranian Plane Landing," Yahoo! News, 28 April 2015.

29. Ahmed Al Omran and A. S. A. Fitch, "Saudi Coalition Seizes Iranian Boat Carrying Weapons to Yemen," *Wall Street Journal*, 30 September 2015.

30. Michael Knight, "Responding to Iran's Arms Smuggling in Yemen," Policy Watch 2733, Washington Institute for Near East Policy, 2 December 2016.

31. Mohammed Al Qalisi, "Yemeni Forces Secure Mukalla after Al Qaeda Rout," *National*, 26 April 2016.

32. *Arab News*, "UAE–Backed Yemeni Force Captures Al Qaeda Stronghold," 30 October 2017.

33. Muhammed Mukhashaf, "Yemen Separatists Capture Aden, Government Confined to Palace: Residents," Reuters, 30 January 2018.

34. See for example Ulf Leasing, "Women of Southern Yemen Port Remember Better Times," Reuters, 22 January 2010.

35. United Nations Office for the Coordination of Humanitarian Affairs, "2018 Humanitarian Needs Overview: Yemen," December 2017, www.humanitarianresponse.info/sites/www.humanitarianresponse.info/files/documents/files/yemen_humanitarian_needs_overview_hno_2018_20171204.pdf.

36. Ibid.

9. UNFINISHED BUSINESS IN AFGHANISTAN

1. Ali Alfoneh, "Shia Afghan Fighters in Syria," Atlantic Council, 19 April 2017, www.atlanticcouncil.org/blogs/syriasource/shia-afghan-fighters-in-syria.

2. Margherita Stancati, "Iran Backs Taliban with Cash and Arms," *Wall Street Journal*, 11 June 2015.

3. Mohammad Reza Bahrami, "Iran's Contacts with the Taliban Are for Intelligence Purposes," Tasnim News, 12 December 2016 (in Farsi).

4. Carlotta Gall and Ruhullah Khapalwak, "Taliban Leader Feared Pakistan before He Was Killed," *New York Times*, 9 April 2017.

5. Carlotta Gall, "In Afghanistan, U.S. Exists, and Iran Comes In," *New York Times*, 4 August 2017.

6. U.S. Department of the Treasury, "Treasury Designates Iranian Quds Force General Overseeing Heroin Trafficking through Iran," 7 March 2012.

7. Tasnim News Agency, "The Funeral of 'Fatemiyoun' Martyrs in Tehran," 5 November 2016 (in Farsi).

8. General Ali Falaki, "Fatemiyoun Were the Vanguards in Battle for Syria," Quds Online, 18 August 2016 (in Farsi).

9. Arash Azizi, "Iran's Afghan Allies Demand Recognition," Iran Wire, 11 January 2018.

10. Human Rights Watch, "Iran: Afghan Children Recruited to Fight in Syria," 1 October 2017, www.hrw.org/news/2017/10/01/iran-afghan-children-recruited-fight-syria.

11. Bill Gertz, "U.S. Identifies Nine Training Camps in Iran for Afghans," *Washington Free Beacon*, 1 June 2016.

12. Bezhan Frud, "Iran Aims to Boost Prestige of Beleaguered Afghan Proxy Force in Syria," Radio Free Europe / Radio Liberty, 16 July 2017.

13. Middle East Eye, "More Than 2,000 Afghans Killed in Syria Fighting for Bashar al-Assad: Official," 6 January 2018.

14. Tasnim News Agency, "The Fatemiyoun Was at First a Home-Based Organization," 18 June 2016 (in Farsi).

15. Eqtesad News, "Important Declaration of Fatemiyoun Division Addressed to General Soleimani about the End of Daesh," 22 November 2017 (in Farsi).

16. Young Reporters Club, "'Fatemiyoun' Fighters Are Real Manifestations of the Unity of Islamic Umah," 1 March 2018 (in Farsi).

17. Mujib Mashal and Fatima Fais, "Iran Sent Them to Syria, Now Afghan Fighters Are a Worry at Home," *New York Times*, 12 November 2017.

18. Fars News Agency, "Fatemiyoun Brigade Forces Deployed at Syrian-Iraqi Borders," 12 June 2017.

19. Ari Heistein and James West, "Syria's Other Foreign Fighters: Iran's Afghan and Pakistani Mercenaries," *National Interest*, 20 November 2015.

20. Gall, "In Afghanistan, U.S. Exists."

21. James Risen, "U.S. Identifies Vast Mineral Riches in Afghanistan," *New York Times*, 13 June 2010.

22. Erica S. Downs, "China Buys into Afghanistan: Report," Brookings Institution, 21 February 2013.

23. Masood Saifullah, "Why Is Russia So Interested in Afghanistan All of a Sudden?" *Deutsche Welle*, 3 January 2017.

10. RESOURCING THE QUDS FORCE REGIONAL CAMPAIGNS

1. Ahmad Majidyar, "IRGC Says Iran Has Tripled Missile Production in Defiance of Western Demands," Middle East Institute, 7 March 2018.

2. Based on interviews with former senior Iranian officials and experts covering the Iranian ballistic missile program.

3. U.S. Energy Information Agency, "Three Important Oil Trade Chokepoints Are Located Around the Arabian Peninsula," 4 August 2017, www.eia.gov/todayinenergy/detail.php?id =32352.

4. Denise Simon, "EW, Jamming GPS by IRGC vs. U.S. Navy," FoundersCode.com, 14 January 2016, https://founderscode.com/ew-gps-by-iranian-revolutionary-guard-corp-vs-navy/.

5. Farzin Nadimi, "Iran Shows Off Its Bounty of Crashed Drones and New UAVs," Washington Institute for Near East Policy, 4 October 2016, www.washingtoninstitute.org/policy-analysis/view/iran-shows-off-its-bounty-of-crashed-drones-and-new-uavs.

6. Jamie Tarabay and Oren Liberman, "Israel: Iranian Drone We Shot Down Was Based on Captured US Drone," CNN, 12 February 2018.

7. Nader Uskowi, "Stuxnet and Its Aftermath," paper presented at "Cyber Conflict after Stuxnet Symposium," Cyber Conflict Studies Association, 13 November 2013.

8. Al Arabiya, "Iran Spending $6 Billion Annually to Support Assad Regime: Report," 10 June 2015.

9. Iran News Update, "The Facts behind Iran's Involvement in Syria," 24 January 2017.

10. National Council of Resistance of Iran, *Iran: The Rise of the Revolutionary Guards' Financial Empire* (Washington, DC: National Council of Resistance of Iran, 2017).

11. Islamic Republic News Agency. Quoted in National Council of Resistance of Iran, *Iran: The Rise*, 104.

12. Stratfor Worldview, "Special Series: Iranian Intelligence and Regime Preservation," 22 June 2010.

13. Reuters, "Israeli Strike Hits Iranian Arms Supply Depot in Damascus: Source," 26 April 2017.

11. LONG ROAD, UNCERTAIN FUTURE

1. Saeid Golkar, "The Islamic Republic's Art of Survival: Neutralizing Domestic and Foreign Threats," Policy Focus 125, Washington Institute, June 2013, www.washingtoninstitute.org/policy-analysis/view/the-islamic-republics-art-of-survival-neut ralizing-domestic-and-foreign-thr.

2. From interviews with several former senior officials of the Islamic Republic government, including retired senior IRGC and Quds Force personnel.

Selected Bibliography

Abdo, Geneive. "How Iran Keeps Assad in Power in Syria." *Foreign Affairs*. 25 August 2011.

Abdul-Ahad, Gaith. "Dairy in Sanaa." *London Review of Books* 37, no. 10 (21 May 2015), 42–43.

Alfoneh, Ali. "Tehran's Shia Foreign Legion." Carnegie Endowment for International Peace. 31 January 2018.

———. "The Revolutionary Guards' Role in Iranian Politics." *Middle East Quarterly* 15, no. 4 (Fall 2008): 3–14.

———. "Shia Afghan Fighters in Syria." Atlantic Council. 19 April 2017.

Amanat, Abbas. *Iran: A Modern History*. New Haven, CT: Yale University Press, 2017.

Arjomand, Said Amir. *The Shadow of God & the Hidden Imam: Religious, Political Order, and Social Change in Shi'ite Iran from the Beginning to 1890*. Chicago: University of Chicago Press, 1984.

Ataie, Mohammad. "Revolutionary Iran's 1979 Endeavor in Lebanon." *Middle East Policy* 20, no. 2 (2013).

Axworthy, Michael. *Revolutionary Iran: A History of the Islamic Republic*. Oxford: Oxford University Press, 2013.

Bardos, Gordon. "Iran in the Balkans: A History and a Forecast." *World Affairs* (January/ February 2013).

Berman, Ilan, Blaise Misztal, Michael Pregent, and Nader Uskowi. "Targeting Iran's Revolutionary Guards: Priorities for the Trump Administration." Iran Strategy Brief 9. American Foreign Policy Council. 2017.

Boroujerdi, Mehrzad, and Koroush Rahimkhani. *Postrevolutionary Iran: A Political Handbook*. Syracuse, NY: Syracuse University Press, 2018.

Bucala, Paul, and Frederick W. Kagan. "Iran's Evolving Way of War: How the IRGC Fights in Syria." Critical Threats. www.criticalthreats.org/briefs/iran-news-round-up/iran-news-round-up-april-14-2016-1.

Central Intelligence Agency, National Foreign Assessment Center. "The Amal Movement in Lebanon." 20 November 1981. www.cia.gov/library/readingroom/docs/CIA-RDP83M00914R000300020014-6.pdf.

———. "Iran: Exporting the Revolution." 10 March 1980. www.cia.gov/library/readingroom/docs/CIA-RDP81B00401R000500100001-8.pdf.

Chubin, Shahram. "Extended Deterrence and Iran." *Strategic Insights* 8 (December 2009).

Clawson, Patrick, and Michael Eisenstadt, eds. "Deterring the Ayatollahs: Complications in Applying Cold War Strategy in Iran." Policy Focus 72. Washington Institute for Near East Policy. July 2007. www.washingtoninstitute.org/uploads/Documents/pubs/PolicyFocus72.pdf.

Cockburn, Patrick. *Muqtada*. New York: Scribner, 2008.

Cooper, Andrew Scott. *The Fall of Heaven: The Pahlavis and the Final Days of Imperial Iran*. New York: Henry Holt, 2016.

———. *The Oil King: How the U.S., Iran, and Saudi Arabia Changed the Balance of Power in the Middle East*. New York: Simon & Schuster, 2011.

Cordesman, Anthony H. "Iran, Oil, and the Strait of Hormuz." Center for Strategic and International Studies. 26 March 2007.

Costel, Steven J., ed. *Surging Out of Iraq?* New York: Nova Science, 2008.

Coughlin, Con. *The Hostage*. New York: Time Warner, 1993.

Crist, David. *The Twilight War: The Secret History of America's Thirty-Year Conflict with Iran*. New York: Penguin, 2012.

Daoud, David. "PMF Deputy Commander Muhandis Details Hezbollah Operations in Iraq." FDD's Long War Journal. 9 January 2017. www.longwarjournal.org/.

Downs, Erica S. "China Buys into Afghanistan: Report." Brookings Institution. 21 February 2013.

Eisenstadt, Michael, and Michael Knights. "Mini-Hezbollah, Revolutionary Guard Knockoffs, and the Future of Iran's Proxies in Iraq." War on the Rocks. 9 May 2017.

———. "Beyond Worst-Case Analysis: Iran's Likely Responses to an Israeli Preventive Strike." Policy Notes 11. Washington Institute for Near East Policy. June 2012.

———."Iran's Influence in Iraq: Countering Tehran's Whole-of-Government Approach." Washington Institute for Near East Policy. April 2011.

Esher, Henry A. "Iran-Syria Relations and the Arab Spring." Critical Threats. 25 May 2011. www.criticalthreats.org.

Felter, Joseph, and Brian Fisherman. "Iranian Strategy in Iraq: Politics and 'Other Means.'" Occasional Paper Series. Combating Terrorism Center at West Point. 13 October 2008.

George, Suzanne. "Breaking Badr." *Foreign Policy*. 14 November 2014.

Global Security. "Anti-Soviet Mujahedeen." 18 August 2012.

Golkar, Saeid. "The Islamic Republic's Art of Survival: Neutralizing Domestic and Foreign Threats." Policy Forum 125. Washington Institute for Near East Policy. June 2013.

Human Rights Watch. "Iran: Afghan Children Recruited to Fight in Syria." 1 October 2017.

———. "Iranian Phantom Jet Strikes the Islamic State in Iraq." International Military Forums. 2 December 2014.

IHS Markit. "Yemeni Rebels Enhance Ballistic Missile Campaign." IHS Jane's Intelligence Review. www.janes.com/images/assets/330/72330/Yemeni_rebels_enhance_ballistic_mis sile_campaign.pdf.

International Committee in Search of Justice. "The Destructive Role of Iran's Islamic Revolutionary Guard Corps (IRGC) in the Middle East." March 2017.

Israel Intelligence Heritage and Commemoration Center. "Iranian Support of Hamas." 12 January 2008.

Juneau, Thomas. "Iran's Policy towards the Houthis: A Limited Return on a Modest Investment." *International Affairs* 92, no. 3 (2016).

Kagan, Kimberly, Frederick Kagan, and Danielle Pletka. "Iranian Influence in the Levant, Iraq, and Afghanistan." American Enterprise Institute. 15 February 2008.

Katzman, Kenneth. "Iraq: Post-Saddam Governance." In *Surging Out of Iraq?* edited by Steven J. Costel. New York: Nova Science, 2008.

———. *The Warriors of Islam: Iran's Revolutionary Guards*. Boulder, CO: Westview Press, 1993.

Kramer, Martin, ed. *Shi'ism, Resistance, and Revolution*. Boulder, CO: Westview Press, 1987.

Knights, Michael. "Responding to Iran's Arms Smuggling in Yemen." Policy Watch 2733. Washington Institute for Near East Policy. 2 December 2016.

Knights, Michael, and Alexander Mello. "Losing Mosul, Regenerating in Diyala: How the Islamic State Could Exploit Iraq's Sectarian Tinderbox." *CTC Sentinel* 9, no. 10 (October 2016).

Levitt, Matthew. *Hezbollah: The Global Footprint of Lebanon's Party of God*. Washington, DC: Georgetown University Press, 2015.

———. "Iran and Bahrain: Crying Wolf, or Wolf at the Door?" Policy Watch 2255. Washington Institute for Near East Policy. 16 May 2014.

Levitt, Matthew, and Phillip Smyth. "Kata'ib al-Imam Ali: Portrait of an Iraqi Shia Militia Group Fighting ISIS." Washington Institute for Near East Policy. 5 January 2015.

Lund, Aron. "Stand Together or Fall Apart: The Russian-Iranian Alliance in Syria." Carnegie Middle East Center. 31 May 2016.

Majidyar, Ahmad. "IRGC Says Iran Has Tripled Missile Production in Defiance of Western Demand." Middle East Institute. 7 March 2018.

Mansharof, Yossi, and E. Kharrazi. "Iran's Support for the Houthi Rebellion in Yemen." Inquiry and Analysis Series no. 1155. Middle East Media Research Institute. 20 April 2015.

Middle East Forum. "Vital Intelligence on Islamic Terrorist Organizations." 2018. http://jihadintel.meforum.org/.

Milani, Abbas. *The Shah*. New York: Palgrave Macmillan, 2011.

Milani, Mohsen. "Why Iran Won't Abandon Assad(ism)." *Washington Quarterly* 36, no. 4 (Fall 2013): 79–93. https://csis-prod.s3.amazonaws.com/s3fs-public/legacy_files/files/publication/TWQ_13Winter_Milani.pdf.

Mousavian, Seyed Hossein. *Iran and the United States: An Insider's View on the Failed Past and the Road to Peace*. New York: Bloomsbury, 2015.

Nadimi, Farzin. "Iran Shows Off Its Bounty of Crashed Drones and New UAVs." Washington Institute for Near East Policy. 4 October 2016.

National Council of Resistance of Iran. *Iran: The Rise of the Revolutionary Guards' Financial Empire*. Washington, DC: National Council of Resistance of Iran, 2017.

Ostovar, Afshon. *Vanguard of the Imam: Religion, Politics, and Iran's Revolutionary Guards*. New York: Oxford University Press, 2016.

Ottolenghi, Emanuele. *The Pasdaran: Inside Iran's Islamic Revolutionary Guard Corps*. Washington, DC: Foundation for the Defense of Democracies, 2011.

Parsi, Trita. *Treacherous Alliance: The Secret Dealings of Israel, Iran, and the United States*. New Haven, CT: Yale University Press, 2007.

Pollack, Kenneth M. *Unthinkable: Iran, the Bomb, and American Strategy*. New York: Simon & Schuster, 2013.

———. *The Persian Puzzle: The Conflict between Iran and America*. New York: Random House, 2005.

Sadjadpour, Karim. "Reading Khamenei: The World View of Iran's Most Powerful Leader." Carnegie Endowment for International Peace. 2008.

Samii, Abbas W. "A Stable Structure in Shifting Sands: Assessing the Hizbollah-Iran-Syria Relations." *Middle East Journal* 35 (Winter 2008).

Schroen, Gary C. *First In: An Insider's Account of How the CIA Spearheaded the War on Terror in Afghanistan*. New York: Ballantine Books, 2005.

Slavin, Barbara. *Bitter Friends, Bosom Enemies: Iran, the U.S., and the Twisted Path to Confrontation*. New York: St. Martin's Press, 2007.

Solomon, Jay. *The Iran Wars: Spy Games, Bank Battles, and the Secret Deals That Reshaped the Middle East*. New York: Random House, 2016.

Stanford University. "Mapping Militant Organizations." 2018. http://web.stanford.edu/group/mappingmilitants/cgi-bin/.

Strack, Columb. "Syrian Government No Longer Controls 83% of the Country." Jane's 360. 24 August 2015. www.janes.com/article/53771/syrian-government-no-longer-controls-83-of-the-country.

Takeyh, Ray. *Guardians of the Revolution: Iran and the World in the Age of the Ayatollahs*. Oxford: Oxford University Press, 2009.

Talmadge, Caitlin. "Closing Time: Assessing the Iranian Threat to the Strait of Hormuz." *International Security* 33, no.1 (Summer 2008): 82–117.

United Nations Office for the Coordination of Humanitarian Affairs. "2018 Humanitarian Needs Overview: Yemen." December 2017. www.humanitarianresponse.info/sites/www.humanitarianresponse.info/files/documents/files/yemen_humanitarian_needs_overview_hno_2018_20171204.pdf.

U.S. Department of State. "Country Report on Terrorism." July 2017.

U.S. Department of the Treasury. "Treasury Designates Iranian Quds Force General Overseeing Heroin Trafficking through Iran." 7 March 2012.

Uskowi, Nader. "Examining Iran's Global Terrorism Network." Testimony submitted to the House Homeland Security Subcommittee on Counterterrorism and Intelligence. 17 April 2018.

———. "A New Battlespace in Syria: Prospects for U.S. Policy." Policy Watch 2821. Washington Institute for Near East Policy. 20 June 2017.

———. "Iran's Presidential Election: Balancing Diplomacy and Confrontation." Policy Watch 2795. Washington Institute for Near East Policy. 11 May 2017.

———. "Stuxnet and Its Aftermath." Paper presented at the Cyber Conflict Studies Association symposium "Cyber Conflict after Stuxnet." 13 November 2013.

Votel, Joseph General. "Military Assessment of the Security Challenges in the Greater Middle East." Testimony submitted to the House Armed Services Committee, U.S. House of Representatives. 29 March 2017.

Ward, Steven R. *Immortals: A Military History of Iran and Its Armed Forces.* Washington, DC: Georgetown University Press, 2009.

Wehrey, Frederick, Jerrold D. Green, Brian Nichiporul, Alireza Nader, Lydia Hansel, Rassol Nafisi, and S. R. Bohandy. "The Rise of Pasdaran: Assessing the Domestic Roles of Iran's Islamic Revolutionary Guards Corps." RAND Corporation, 2009.

Wehrey, Frederick, David E. Thale, Nora Bensahel, Kim Cragin, Jerrold D. Green, Dallia Dassa Kaye, Nadia Oweidat, and Jennifer Li. *Dangerous but Not Omnipotent: Exploring the Reach and Limitations of Iranian Power in the Middle East.* Santa Monica, CA: RAND Corporation, 2009.

Weisgerber, Marcus. "How Many US Troops Were Killed by Iranian IEDs in Iraq?" Defense One. 8 September 2015. www.defenseone.com/news/2015/09/how-many-us-troops-were-killed-iranian-ieds-iraq/120524/.

Yaldin, Amos, and Anver Golov. "Iran on the Threshold." *Strategic Assessment* 15, no. 1 (April 2012): 7–14.

Zanotti, Jim, Kenneth Katzman, Jeremiah Gertler, and Steven A. Hildreth. "Israel: Possible Military Strike against Iran's Nuclear Facilities." Congressional Service Research R42443. 27 March 2012.

Zweiri, Mahjoob. "Iran and Political Dynamism in the Arab World: The Case of Yemen." *Digest of Middle East Studies* 25, no. 1 (24 February 2016).

Index

AAH (Asa'ib Ahl al-Haq), 25, 26, 54–55, 57–58, 100, 102

AAS (Ahrar al-Sham), 84, 93

Abouzar Brigade, 129

Aden (Yemen), 123, 125, 128

Afghanistan: forces fighting in Syria, 133–136; global and regional powers competing in, 138; Herat operations in, 50; Iran-Iraq War and, 131; Iran's cultural and Islamic ties to, 129, 137–138; Iran's Eastern Front and, 9–10; IRGC and Quds Force in, xv; Islamic interests in, 129; ongoing challenges, 180; Quds Force along Iran-Afghan border, 130; Soviets and, 18–19, 130–131; trading with Iran, 137–138; Vahidi and, 43. *See also* Fatemiyoun Brigade; Hazaras; Taliban

AGMC (Al Ghadir Missile Command), 140

Ahlul Bayt World Assembly, 174

Ahrar al-Sham (AAS), 84, 93

air support, 65, 91, 157–158

Alawi beliefs, 79–80, 80–81

Alawi-Shia community, 5

Aleppo, Battle of: about, 21, 27, 66–67, 82–86, 161–162; Artesh and, 85; casualties, 87, 172–173; Iranian interests after, 87–91; Quds Force-led victory, 14, 86; setbacks, 84–85

Al Ghadir Missile Command (AGMC), 140

Amal Movement, 37–38, 39

Amiri, Hadi al-, 19, 25, 27, 56, 57, 102, 108. *See also* Badr Organization

ANF (al-Nusra Front), 83, 93

Ansar Allah movement, 20, 22, 117. *See also* Houthis

antiship cruise missiles (ASCMs), 13–14, 142

Arab Spring/Arab Awakening: Iraqis and, 6–7; origins of, 63, 79; Quds Force and, 7, 17; Syria and, 79–80

Arabian Peninsula, 7–8

Arafat, Yasser, 38, 39

Artesh, 85, 99, 144

Asa'ib Ahl al-Haq (AAH), 25, 26, 54–55, 57–58, 100, 102

ASCMs (antiship cruise missiles), 13–14, 142

Asgari, Ali Reza, 39

Assad, Bashar al-: Iran supporting regime of, 4–5, 14, 63–64, 79–80; moderates opposing, 92–93; Quds Force and, 10, 64, 133–136; territory of regime shrinking, 105. *See also* Syria

Astan-e Quds Razavi, 153

Azerbaijan, 29

Baathist supporters, 57

Bab el-Mandeb, 8–9, 29, 74, 118, 167–168, 171
Badr Brigade, 25, 35–36, 46
Badr Organization, 25, 52–53, 55–57, 72, 100–102, 103–104. *See also* Amiri, Hadi al-
Bahraini regime, 29
Baiji, Battle of, 106–107
ballistic missiles, 3–4, 12, 13, 119, 179; inter-continental, 140, 141; medium-range, 140–141; short-range, 140–141
Baqeri, Qolamreza, 174
Barzani, Masoud, 110–111
Basij Force, 143
Berry, Nabih, 37–38
Bonyad Taavon Sepah, 149–151
Bush, George W., 51

Chamran, Mostafa, 34–35, 37, 38
China, 138, 168
command and control support, 158
commerce disruption, 171
Cooperative Foundation of the Basij Force, 151
Cooperative Foundation of the State Security Forces (NAJA), 152
corruption, 155
costs. *See* economic issues
cyber warfare, 143

Daesh. *See* Islamic State in Iraq and Syria (ISIS)
Dawa fighters, 36
Dawa party, 100
Dehghan, Hossein, 39, 40
Dehghan, Mehdi, 89
Dodge, David, 41
drones, 142
drug trade, 133, 174

Eastern Front, 9–10
economic issues: commerce disruption, 171; Hezbollah receiving financial assistance, 60; IRGC foundations/business entities and, 147–152; Office of the Supreme Leader foundations and, 152–154; operations costs, 92, 145–146, 155–159; opportunities and restraints, 154–155; Palestinian Islamic

Jihad, 153–154; political constraints and costs, 159–160
EFPs (explosively formed penetrators), 46, 57
Emdad Committee, 154
Erbil-based Kurdish Regional Government, 110–111
explosive boats, 119–120, 143
explosively formed penetrators (EFPs), 46, 57
extremists (jihadists), 93

Fallujah, Battles of, 107
Fatemiyoun Brigade, 21, 27, 66, 80, 83, 90, 133–136, 138
FedPol, 101, 103–104, 106–107, 108–109
Foreign Legion in Syria, 90
Free Syrian Army (FSA), 92

GCC (Gulf Cooperation Council), 96
Ghadir Investment Company, 147–149
Green Revolution, 64
ground forces, 143–144
Gulf Cooperation Council (GCC), 96

Hakim, Abdul Aziz, 57–58
Hakim, Ayatollah Muhammad Baqir al-, 35, 36
Hamas, 30, 153–154
Harakat Hezbollah l-Nujaba group, 26
Hay'at Tahrir al-Sham (HTS), 84, 93
Hazaras, 21, 42, 66, 75
Headquarters for Executing the Order of the Imam (SETAD), 152
Herat, 50, 131–132, 137
Hezbollah: early terrorist attacks, 40–41; founding of, 19–20, 22, 38–40, 76, 77; funding for, 153–154, 157, 175; as future player, 181; *Islamic Jihad* kidnappings, 41; Israeli attacks by, 60–61; military capacity, 13; as nucleus of SLA, 17; organization of, 23–24; PMF supported by, 102; political strategy, 15; Quds Force's support of, xvi, 60; in Syrian Civil War, 63–65, 66–67, 81–82; transformation of, 21. *See also* Precision Project
Highlands/Western Yemen, 124
Homs uprising, 65

Hormuz Strait, 29
Houthi, Abdulmalik al-, 117
Houthi, Housein al-, 117
Houthis: about, 28; Bab el-Mandeb and, 118; founding of, 20; Iran arming, 28; logistical challenges, 28; military capacity, 13; Precision Project, 13, 24, 88–91, 170; Quds Force and, xvi, 9, 44, 115–118, 123, 162; Saudis and, 12, 16, 119–122, 168; as SLA nucleus, 17; UAE and, 16, 118, 120–122, 168; in Yemen, 7–8, 73–74, 115–116, 126, 162, 169
HTS (Hay'at Tahrir al-Sham), 84, 93
Hudaydah (Yemen), 123, 124
humanitarian crisis in Yemen, 127
Hussein, Saddam, 34–35, 51, 97

IA (Iraqi Army), 98, 104
ICBMs (inter-continental ballistic missiles), 140, 141
Idlib groups, 93
improvised explosive devices (IEDs), 57
information operations, 14
intelligence operations, 156
inter-continental ballistic missiles (ICBMs), 140, 141
Iran: Afghanistan trading with, 137–138; Afghanistan's cultural and Islamic ties to, 129, 137–138; attacking U.S. in Iraq, 101; border with Iraq, 98; changing regional role, 175–176; complexity of political system in, 180; Eastern Front, 9–10; goals of, 97, 177; Hezbollah, support for, 24; Hormuz Strait, 29; Iran-Saudi conflict in Yemen, 122; Iraq, battle for, 68–70; map of surrounding areas, 2; military strategy, 3–4, 14–15; Ministry of Intelligence and Security, 174; Saddam's Iraq and, 34–35, 97; sectarianism and, 71; Shia-Sunni divide, 12; Southern Front, 7–9; in Syria, 4–5, 90, 95; Western Front, 4–7. *See also* Iran-Iraq War; Iraqi campaign; Islamic Revolutionary Guard Corps (IRGC); Quds Force; Syria; Yemen
Iran-Iraq War, 19, 21, 34–36, 100–101, 131, 177

Iraq: AAH and, 54–55, 57–58; Badr fighters and, 43, 52–53; collapse of Saddam's regime in, 51; costs of operations, 157; invading Iran, 75; Kata'ib al-Imam Ali, 55–56; Kata'ib Hezbollah, 55–56; KH, 57, 59; Mahdi Army and, 53–54; nationalism in, 172; PMF incorporated into armed forces, 27; post-Daesh, 72; Quds Force accomplishments and challenges in, 51–52, 178–179; risks of Iran's presence in, 11; sectarianism, 12; Shia groups, 25, 30–32, 77, 172; as threat in post-ISIS period, 163; U.S. conflict in, 6. *See also* Hussein, Saddam; Iran-Iraq War; Iraq War; Iraqi campaign; Islamic State in Iraq and Syria (ISIS); Kurds and Kurdistan
Iraq War, 56–59, 97, 163
Iraqi Army (IA), 98, 104
Iraqi campaign: Iran's border and, 98; Kurdistan and, 110–111; Mosul offensive, 108–109; Mosul victory by ISIS, 98–100; PMF's commanders and militia groups, 102–103; PMF's origins, 100–102; Quds Force battles beyond Mosul and Kirkuk, 111–113; Tal Afar offensive, 109
Iraqi security forces (ISF) units, 52–53, 68, 70, 72, 103–104. *See also* Popular Mobilization Forces (PMF)
IRGC. *See* Islamic Revolutionary Guard Corps (IRGC)
ISF (Iraqi security forces) units, 52–53, 68, 70, 72, 103–104. *See also* Popular Mobilization Forces (PMF)
Islamic Amal, 39–40. *See also* Hezbollah
Islamic Jihad, 41
Islamic Republic: financing the revolution, 180; founding of, 75; government of, 164; Middle East as interconnected to, 165–166; Office of the Supreme Leader in, xv; political system of, xv; Quds Force's endurance compared to, 165; U.S. sanctions against, 164. *See also* Iran
Islamic Revolution, 18, 33–34, 38–40, 180. *See also* Khomeini, Ayatollah

Islamic Revolutionary Guard Corps (IRGC): Afghanistan and, 9–10; ballistic missile support, 3–4; Cooperative Foundation, 149–151; cyber warfare and, 143; deterrence *vs.* offensive strategy, 144–145; early years of Shia militias and, 18–20; economic opportunities and restraints, 154–155; foundations and business entities under, 147–152; ground forces, 143–144; Houthis and, 8; in Iran-Iraq War, 100–101; Israel and, 15; military rankings, 42; mission and founding of, xiv, 1–2, 33–34, 42–44, 75; proxy warfare, 161–162; Quds Force created by, 75; Quds Force supported by, 139–145, 180; weaponry, 140–143. *See also* Quds Force

Islamic State (ISIS of Daesh), xiv

Islamic State in Iraq (ISI), 6

Islamic State in Iraq and Syria (ISIS): defeat of, 166; founding of, 6; Iran and, xiv–xv, 6–7; Iraq and, 98–100, 104–107; Mosul cleared of, 108–109; Shias uniting against, 112–113, 172; Tal Afar cleared of, 109; U.S. fighting in Iraqi campaign, 105–109

Israel: Fatemiyoun fighting to annihilate, 135–136; Hezbollah's attacks on, 60–61; Iran's Precision Project and, 88–91; Iran's presence challenging, 179; Quds Force in opposition to, 67, 78, 169–170; regional strategy and, 15; responding to Iran in Syria, 161–162; Russia and, 166–167; as Shias' and Sunnis' common enemy, 30

Israeli Air Force (IAF) in Syria, 5

Jalula, Iraq, xiv, 99

jihadists (extremists), 93

Jordon, 93

Jurf al-Sakhr, Battle of, 106

Kabi, Akram al-, 103

KACHQ (Khatam al-Anbiya Construction Headquarters), 147

Karbala compound, 58

Karzai, Hamid, 50

Kata'ib al-Imam Ali (KIA), 26, 55–56

Kata'ib Hezbollah (KH), 25, 26, 55, 59, 101–102

KH (Kata'ib Hezbollah), 25, 26, 55, 59, 101–102

Khamenei, Ayatollah Ali, 23, 24, 63, 163

Khan, Ismail "Lion of Herat," 131–132

Khan Touman (Syria), 85

Khatam al-Anbiya Construction Headquarters (KACHQ), 147

Khatam al-Osia Construction Headquarters, 151

Khazali, Qais al-, 54, 58, 103

Khobar Towers, 29, 44

Khomeini, Ayatollah: accepting peace, 36, 177; author's meeting with, xiii, 177; focusing on revolution, 77; Houthis and, 7; on Iran-Iraq War, 177; IRGC created by inner circle of, xiv, 75; revolution and, 33–34; sectarianism and, 30; Shia Islam and, 1–2. *See also velayat-e faghih* religious doctrine

KIA (Kata'ib al-Imam Ali), 26, 55–56

Kurdish People's Protection Units (YPG), 67, 88, 94

Kurds and Kurdistan, 71, 94, 96, 100, 110–111, 167

Kuwait City, 55

land-attack missiles (LACMs), 141

land corridor: as bridge to nowhere, 177; Fayemiyoun's role in, 136; as Iran's mission after Aleppo, 88, 161; Khomeini and, 34; PMF focusing on, 25; Quds Force establishing, xvii, 4; Soleimani's goal of, 4, 111–113; as strategy in Lebanon and Iraq, 77–78

Lebanon: assassination of French ambassador in, 40; IRGC organizing Shias, 37–38; land corridor and, 34. *See also* Hezbollah

logistics centers, 157–158

Mahan Air, 115

Mahdi Army, 101

Mahfad (Yemen), 123

Mahre governorate, 125

Mandeb Strait, 8–9, 168

Mansur, Mullah Akhtar Muhammad, 132–133

Marib/Northeast Sanaa/al Jawf region (Yemen), 124
Mashhad (Iran), 137
medium-range ballistic missiles (MRBMs), 140–141
MeK (Mujahedeen Khalq), 174
Middle East interconnectedness, 165–166
military bases, 90–91, 170
Ministry of Intelligence and Security (MOIS), 174
missiles. *See* weaponry
Mohtashemi, Ali Akbar, 38, 40
MOIS (Ministry of Intelligence and Security), 174
Moore, Peter, 58
Mostazafan Foundation, 152–153
Mosul, Battles of, 98–100, 108–109
MRBMs (medium-range ballistic missiles), 140–141
Mughniyah, Imad, 39–40, 41
Muhammadawi, Abdal Aziz al-, 103
Muhandis, Abu Mahdi al-, 19, 25, 27, 41, 55–56, 57, 100–102, 172
Mujahedeen, 9, 130–131
Mujahedeen Khalq (MeK), 174
Mukalla (Yemen), 123, 125

NAJA (Cooperative Foundation of the State Security Forces), 152
Nasrallah, Hassan, 24, 60, 63
North Yemen, 125
Northern Alliance, 49–50, 131
Nusra Front al- (ANF), 83, 93

Obama, Barack, 92
Office of the Supreme Leader: foundations, 152–154; funding Quds Force, 174, 180; Special External Operations and, 173–174
Oman Air, 121
Operation Enduring Freedom, 49, 50
Operation Iraq Freedom, 163
operations: costs of, 92, 145–146, 155–159; information operations, 14; intelligence operations, 156

Pakistan, 27. *See also* Zaynabiyoun division of SLA
Palestinian Islamic Jihad, 153–154

Patriotic Union of Kurdistan (PUK), 100, 110–111
peace comparison, 36, 177
personnel costs, 156
Petraeus, General David, 58–59
Popular Mobilization Forces (PMF): about, 25–27, 100–102; founding of, 53, 56; Iraqi Shia groups, 30–32; leaders of, 72, 102–103; liberating Baiji, 106–107; in Mosul, 108–109; political strategy, 15; Sunnis and, 71; Tal Afar offensive, 109. *See also* Asa'ib Ahl al-Haq (AAH); Kata'ib Hezbollah (KH); Muhandis, Abu Mahdi al-
Precision Project, 13, 24, 88–91, 170
proxy warfare, 161–162, 169, 181. *See also* Aleppo, Battle of
PUK (Patriotic Union of Kurdistan), 100, 110–111
Putin, Vladimir, 65, 79

Qaeda, al-, 6, 49. *See also* Islamic State in Iraq and Syria (ISIS); September 11 terrorist attacks
Quds Force: about, 139; Arab Spring and, 7, 17; battles beyond Mosul and Kirkuk, 111–113; challenges of, 169–175; changing strategy of, 78; companies of, 165; conflicts of, 1, 2; costs of war, 155–159; creating revolutionary movement, 164–165; founding of, 42–44, 75; funding for, xvi, 145–146, 154–155, 174–175; Hezbollah and, xvi, 60; Houthis and, xvi, 9, 44, 115–118, 123, 162; hybrid military support network, xvi; on Iran-Afghan border, 130; IRGC supporting, 139–145, 147–152; in ISF, 103–104; Islamic Republic's endurance compared to, 165; Israel and, 5, 67, 170; Kurdistan and, 110–111; land corridor established by, xvii, 4; military capacity of, 13–14; mission of, 3, 163–166; ongoing challenges, 178–179; overplaying their hand, 76; political constraints, 159–160; political strategy, 15–16; in post-9/11 period, 50–51; in post-Daesh Iraq, 72; regional strategy, 14–15; rise of, 11, 75–76; risks of,

11–12; Shia militia and, 2–4, 6–7; Special External Operations, 173–174; structure of, 158–159; successes of, 169; in Syria, 63–67, 78, 81–82, 179; Taliban and, 132–136; terrorism of, 44; three fronts of, xiv–xv, 178–179; U.S. and, 50, 164. *See also* Afghanistan; Aleppo, Battle of; Asa'ib Ahl al-Haq (AAH); Houthis; Iraq; Popular Mobilization Forces (PMF); proxy warfare; Shia Liberation Army (SLA); Shia militia; Soleimani, General Qasem; Syria; Yemen

Qusayr, al- (Syria), 82

radar systems, 143
Rafiqhdoost, Mohsen, 39
Ramadi, Battle of, 106, 107
Revolutionary Guards, 33. *See also* Islamic Revolutionary Guard Corps (IRGC)
Rojava (Syria), 94
Russia: in Afghanistan, 138; in Aleppo, 84, 86; Assad and, 105; in Syria, 65–66, 79, 95, 166. *See also* Soviet Union

Saberin Force, 143
Sadr, Ayatollah Muhammad Baqir al-, 35, 36
Sadr, Muqtada al-, 53–54, 172
Sadr, Musa, 37
Sadrist Movement, 53–54
Saleh, Ali Abdullah, 117–118
Saraya al-Khorasani group, 26
Saudi Arabia: Houthis and, 12, 16, 119–122, 168; Iran-Saudi conflict in Yemen, 122; not accepting Iranian involvement in Syria, 96; Saudi-Emirati coalition, 74, 121–122; Saudi Hezbollah, 29, 44; as Sunni player, 167–168; in Yemen, 8, 73–74, 116, 121–122, 124, 169–170, 179
Sayyidah Zaynab Mosque, 80
Sazegara, Mohsen, xiv
SCIRI (Supreme Council for Islamic Revolution in Iraq), 19, 35–36, 57–58
sectarianism, 12, 30, 71, 80–81
September 11 terrorist attacks, 46–47, 49, 132–136

SETAD (Headquarters for Executing the Order of the Imam), 152
Shah, Mohammad Reza, xiii
Shahid Foundation, 153–154
Sheibani, Mustafa al-, 54, 103
Shia-Alawi regime, 14, 15
Shia Hazaras, 9, 50
Shia Iraq, 35–36
Shia Liberation Army (SLA): about, xiv, 17; costs of, 156–157; founding of, 76; as key regional project, 23; organization of, 23–28; rise of Quds Force and, 11; risks of, 178; training and arming militia, 17–18, 20, 21–22; transformation to multinational expeditionary army, 21. *See also* Fatemiyoun Brigade; Quds Force; Zaynabiyoun division of SLA
Shia militia: challenges of, 171; defeating Sunni forces in Syria, 4; early years, 18–20; ISIS and, 104–107; opposition parties in Middle East, 29–32; partners with, 3; Quds Force and, 2–4, 6–7; terrorism potential, 173; U.S. and, 6. *See also* Hezbollah; Houthis
Shia-Sunni divide, 12
short-range ballistic missiles (SRBM), 140–141
Soleimani, General Qasem: Aleppo victory, 86; Assad, supporting, 105; Badr Organization and, 52–53; Bahraini regime threatened by, 29; commission of, 42; Daesh, victory over, 7; early years, 35; Hezbollah and, 24; Iraqi politics and, 172; ISIS campaign and, 97–100; land corridor and, 4, 111–113; Petraeus, communicating with, 59; PMF and, 102; in post-9/11 period, 50–51; power of, 112–113; as Quds Force commander, 45–46; Sanaa's fall and, 73–74; Syria Civil War and, 64–67; in Tikrit, 105–106; in Yemen, 115–116. *See also* Aleppo, Battle of; Iraqi campaign; Quds Force
South Yemen, 125
Southern Front, 7–9
Southern Transitional Council (STC), 125
Soviet Union: comparisons, xvi, 2; invading Afghanistan, 9, 75, 130–131

STC (Southern Transitional Council), 125
Strait of Hormuz, 74, 171
suicide bombings, 41, 44
Sunnis: protesting in Iraq, 6–7; as second-class Iraqi citizens, 71; SLA outreach to, 30; Syrian Civil War and, 4, 67; UAE and, 167–168
Supreme Council for Islamic Revolution in Iraq (SCIRI), 19, 35–36, 57–58
Syria: Afghan forces recruited to fight in, 133–136; Arab Awakening in, 6; Assad regime, 10; Civil War in, 63–67, 79, 95, 166; competing goals of international actors in, 95–96; costs of operations in, 92, 145–146, 157; GCC's position on, 96; Hezbollah deployed in, 24; Iran's conflict with, 4–5; Iran's goals in, 95; Iran's presence as risk in, 11; Israel responding to Iran's presence in, 161–162; jihadists' position on, 93; Kurds' position on, 94; land corridor in, 34; in Lebanon, 37–38; military bases in, 90–91; moderate opposition to Assad, 92–93; political landscape after Civil War, 91–96; Putin involvement, 79; Quds Force in, 63–67, 78, 81–82, 179; regional strategy in, 14–15; sectarianism in, 12; Turkey and, 96. *See also* Aleppo, Battle of; Assad, Bashar al-; Islamic State in Iraq and Syria (ISIS)

Tal Afar offensive, 109
Tal el-Eis (Syria), 85
Taliban, 10, 46, 50, 131–133, 136
Task Force 17, 59
terrorist threats, 173, 180, 181
Tikrit, Battle of, 105–106
Tiyas Military Base (T-4 Airbase), 88, 162
Turkey, 96, 167

UAE. *See* United Arab Emirates (UAE)
UAVs (unmanned aerial vehicles), 120
United Arab Emirates (UAE): Houthis and, 16, 118, 120–122, 168; Iran in Syria, not accepting, 96; Quds Force, opposing, 8; Saudi-Emirati coalition, 74, 121–122; as Sunni player, 167–168; in Yemen, 123, 125, 128, 169–170, 179

United Islamic Front. *See* Northern Alliance
United States: Afghanistan and, 10, 138; Asa'ib Ahl al-Haq and, 26; foreign Shia militia attacking, 36; Houthis and, 118; Iran's potential collusion course with, 11–12; Iraq and, 22, 56–59, 68, 163; IRGC and, 33–34; ISIS fighting against, 105–109; Kata'ib Hezbollah and, 26, 55, 101; Kurds abandoned by, 111; Mahdi Army pushing out of Iraq, 53–54; Quds Force joining against Taliban, 50; Quds Force pushing out of Iraq, 51–52; as Shias' and Sunnis' common enemy, 30; in Syria, 92, 167; Taliban and, 132–133
unmanned aerial vehicles (UAVs), 120, 142

Vahidi, Brigadier General Ahmad, 42–59
velayat-e faghih religious doctrine, 24, 33, 36, 37–38, 40, 53, 134

Wahdat (Unity) party, 130
waterways, control over, 8–9
weaponry: Al Ghadir Missile Command, 140; antiship cruise missiles, 13–14, 142; challenges of supplying to Houthis, 120–121; costs of, 156–157; cyber warfare, 143; drones, 142; EFPs, 46, 57; explosive boats, 119–120, 143; of Houthis against Saudis, 119–120; IEDs, 57; inter-continental ballistic missiles, 140, 141; of Iran in Iraqi campaign, 100; Iran providing Syria with, 81–82; Israel's reaction to delivery of, 170; land-attack missiles, 141; missile attacks between Israel and IRGC, 15; missile force of IRGC, 140–142; ongoing challenges of, 181; Quds Force military capability, 13–14; radar systems, 143; of Shia militias, 20; short-range ballistic missiles, 141; Taliban receiving from Quds Force, 132; training provided by SLA, 18; unmanned aerial vehicles, 120. *See also* ballistic missiles; Precision Project
Western Front, 4–7

Yazdi, Ebrahim, xiii
Yemen: battlespaces, 124–125; chaos in national government, 128; cities of, 116; costs of operations, 146, 157; fall of Sanaa, 73–74; fracturing of, 125; Houthis in, 7–8, 73–74, 115–116, 126, 162, 169; humanitarian crisis, 127; Iran-Saudi conflict in, 122; Iran's military capacity and, 13; Iran's presence challenging, 11, 179; Mandeb Strait, 9; political strategy of, 16; possible future, 128; proxy warfare limitations, 169; Quds Force challenges, 126–127; Shia-Sunni divide, 12; UAE and, 123, 125, 128, 169–170, 179. *See also* Houthis
YPG (Kurdish People's Protection Units), 67, 88, 94
Yugoslavia, 43

Zaidi, Shibl Muhsin Faraj al-, 103
Zamani, Abbas "Abu Sharif," 38
Zaydi-Shias, 7, 8, 22, 28. *See also* Houthis
Zaynabiyoun division of SLA, 27, 66, 80, 83, 90

About the Author

Nader Uskowi is a subject matter expert on the Islamic Republic of Iran and its military strategy. He is a senior fellow at the Scowcroft Center for Strategy and Security at the Atlantic Council. He was the senior policy adviser to the United States Central Command, the branch of the U.S. military whose area of responsibility includes Iran and the Middle East, focusing on geopolitical and military developments across the region. Uskowi has recently testified before Congress, published articles, appeared on radio and TV news programs, and presented papers at seminars and symposiums on Iran. He lives with his wife, Patti, in Reston, Virginia.

Printed in Great Britain
by Amazon

49342726R00135